Augsburg
George S
Minneapolis, Minnesota 55404

George Sverdrup Library

A Gift From

The
A. Richard Johnson
Collection

In life the Highest Aim is Truth.

AUGSBURG COLLEGE and THEOLOGICAL SEMINARY

THE CONTEMPORARY SCIENCE SERIES.

Edited by HAVELOCK ELLIS.

THE VILLAGE COMMUNITY.

THE VILLAGE COMMUNITY.

WITH

SPECIAL REFERENCE TO THE ORIGIN
AND FORM OF ITS SURVIVALS IN BRITAIN.

BY

GEORGE LAURENCE GOMME,

Fellow of the Society of Antiquaries, and Director of the Folklore Society.

WITH MAPS AND ILLUSTRATIONS.

THE WALTER SCOTT PUBLISHING CO., LTD.,
PATERNOSTER SQUARE, LONDON, E.C.
CHARLES SCRIBNER'S SONS,
153-157 FIFTH AVENUE, NEW YORK.
1912

CONTENTS.

CHAPTER I.
　　　　　　　　　　　　　　　　　　　　　　　　PAGE
THE VILLAGE COMMUNITY AS A PRIMITIVE INSTITUTION　　1

CHAPTER II.
THE RACE-ELEMENTS OF THE VILLAGE COMMUNITY　...　20

CHAPTER III.
METHODS OF DEALING WITH THE BRITISH EVIDENCE　...　42

CHAPTER IV.
THE NON-ARYAN ELEMENTS IN THE ENGLISH VILLAGE
　　COMMUNITY　...　...　...　...　...　69

CHAPTER V.
THE HOMESTEAD OF THE VILLAGE COMMUNITY　...　116

CHAPTER VI.
TRIBAL COMMUNITIES IN BRITAIN　...　...　...　132

CHAPTER VII.
TRANSITIONAL TYPES OF THE VILLAGE COMMUNITY IN
　　BRITAIN ...　...　...　...　...　...　...　147

CHAPTER VIII.

THE FINAL TYPE OF THE VILLAGE COMMUNITY IN BRITAIN ... 157

CHAPTER IX.

FRAGMENTS OF THE VILLAGE COMMUNITY SURVIVING IN LOCAL CUSTOM ... 232

CHAPTER X.

SUMMARY AND CONCLUSION ... 290

INDEX ... 297

LIST OF MAPS AND ILLUSTRATIONS.

---o---

	PAGE
VILLAGE OF ASHBORNE EARLY SEVENTEENTH CENTURY	44
PRIMITIVE ARYAN HOUSE IN MEDIA	45
MAP OF WILTSHIRE	73
TERRACES AT NEWLANDS KIRK	79
BRYNGLAS CULTIVATION	101
MANOR HOUSE EARLY SEVENTEENTH CENTURY	118
ELIZABETHAN COPYHOLD HOUSE	121
PLANS OF SURREY COTTAGES	122
MAP OF LAUDER IN BERWICKSHIRE	149
PLAN OF CHIPPENHAM, WILTS	173
PLAN OF MALMESBURY CORPORATION LANDS	188
LONDON STONE AS IT IS NOW PROTECTED	219
REAPING MACHINE USED IN ROMAN GAUL	278
THE HIGHLAND SPADE	279
THE CASCHROM	280
ANGLO-SAXON TWO-OXEN PLOUGH	284
ANGLO-SAXON REAPING SCENE	285
PLAN OF DONISTHORPE TOWNSHIP	289

PREFACE.

I HAVE sought in this little book to bring into prominence a view of the place which the village community occupies in English institutions. So far as I know, this has not yet been considered by scholars. The subject has occupied my attention for the past twelve years or so, and I have studied it side by side with other subjects which of late years in increasing force I have conceived to be in intimate relationship with it. To many who take a considerable interest in the early history of institutions, it will appear strange that folklore should be adduced in evidence. But to those of us who have watched, and perhaps aided in some slight way, the development of the science which underlies so much that constitutes what is called folklore, there will be no surprise. If we want to get at the true origin of what is now found on English soil as heirlooms of the past, we must take into our purview not one particular section, not one particular period, or one particular area ; we must consider all the remains of the past and pick out from the whole group the evidence we seek for. Englishmen did not begin their history in the land they named, but their history in older England had much the same original characteristics as those of other Aryan tribes in their early homes. Because we study these characteristics at home, we are too apt to accentuate the forces of political progress and to minimize the forces of peasant crystallization. The latter has had no historian by the very nature of things. The history of the former is contained in thousands of volumes, and attracts the notice of all advanced thought. But the relative proportion of historical record does not measure the relative proportion of influence. What I am most struck with in investigating the facts of local life is the enormous influence of tradition in stamping custom and belief upon a people. For centuries of English history there was little to disturb either primitive economic customs or primitive belief. We have ample evidence of the survival of both, and it is with these survivals in their relationship to each other that I have dealt in the following pages.

I am conscious of much that I should like to improve upon and of much more that I should like to add in the elucidation of this fascinating but intricate subject. But the last word has not yet been said upon it; and I hope that my contribution to it may help towards the desired end. The present series seems peculiarly fitted for such a subject. It has not only a scientific interest, viewed as a chapter in the history of institutions; it has an interest viewed as a contribution to some of the sociological problems of the day. The peasants of to-day are no longer unlettered, and just as we are beginning to study their past and re-read the history of the national past by the light of this new study, they are reading too, and influences which were of old traditional and unconscious are now philosophical and conscious. The future of man with his immense mental activity and mental grasp must take a very different line of development to that of the past, and so far as I may presume to judge, the difference lies largely in the interest awakened and to be awakened in subjects like the present. They tell us of man with communal rights, duties, and privileges, with intimate relationship to his fellows, and an almost unbroken and unbreakable interest in the soil and institutions of his country. I am far from urging that it is wise to return to these old feelings, survivals of the past; I only suggest that these old feelings are re-awakened, and if properly guided may be guided to the good of the nation and of humanity.

I owe many thanks to kind friends for help of various kind.

PREFACE.

Mr. Seebohm has kindly read through all my proofs. It will be seen that I have ventured to differ from his views somewhat. His help, therefore, is all the more generous, and I shall not easily forget the marginal notes of guidance, criticism, and appreciation with which he has favoured me.

To Mr. Hubert Hall of the Record Office I am indebted for kindly help with reference to the illustrations I received from him in that institution; and to the Town Clerk of Malmesbury I owe the copy of the map of that place.

To my friend, Mr. Ralph Nevill, to the Society of Antiquaries of Scotland, the Cambrian Archæological Society, the publishers of Violett le Duc's "Habitations of Man," Mr. Elliot Stock, and others, I am indebted for the loan of blocks or permission to copy.

Mr. Havelock Ellis has throughout helped my revision of the proof sheets by many useful emendations and hints.

Some portions of the work are adapted and altered from papers originally published at various times in *Archæologia*, Transactions of the Glasgow Archæological Society, Middlesex Archæological Society, and in the *Archæological Review*.

G. L. GOMME.

BARNES COMMON, S.W.
 10th March, 1890.

THE VILLAGE COMMUNITY.

CHAPTER I.

THE VILLAGE COMMUNITY AS A PRIMITIVE INSTITUTION.

In order to understand properly what the village communities of Britain really represent in the history of our race, it is necessary we should start with a clear view of what a village community is. The term has become popular, and has lost somewhat of its more precise historical and archæological meaning. The two sources of its popularity in England are the writings of Sir Henry Maine and Mr. Frederic Seebohm. Sir Henry Maine some years since drew attention to the traces of the village community in English local institutions and customs, basing his proofs upon the parallel which exists between some English and Indian phenomena. Mr. Seebohm, more recently, has chronologically traced back the existence of certain economical phenomena in English villages to a period which, speaking roughly, may be identified with the Roman occupation of this island, and he seeks, in the events of this period, the origin of the village community in its English form. And it happens that, in the contrast between the village community as represented by each of these great scholars, the institution which the term connotes has become somewhat indefinite and obscure. A group of men cultivating their lands in common and having rights and duties in common is the typical form; but students are divided as to whether this institution is of historical origin and growth, or of primitive origin and growth.

It is just this question of origin which is of the first importance, and if, as I suggest, the village community can be proved to be a primitive institution, this must have a most important bearing upon its history in Britain. It means that the village community originated at a stage of social development long prior to the political stage, and that hence its appearance among the local institutions of Britain is of the nature of a survival from prehistoric times. If this view is once fully understood and accepted, much of the difficulty arising from a conflict in terminology will vanish, because the whole method of future research must be coloured by the evidence as to origin. If the village community is of primitive origin, and its later existence a survival, we should be able to note its opposition to the political phenomena of civilized history. If it arises out of the advanced political organization of the Roman Empire we should be able to note that it has developed into and forms part of the political and economical phenomena of civilized history, which, indeed, under this hypothesis it must have helped to form; for, with all the spur of Roman civilization, it must have so influenced English institutions as to make English institutions themselves but a continuation of Roman institutions. Thus the evidence as to origin is of great importance; and before we can properly examine the types in Britain, or ascertain what they really represent in English history, we must know something of the more primitive types, which alone can tell us anything of origin.

If the village community is a primitive institution, it must be granted that from the present position of the subject in the hands of those students who have dealt with it, there are some considerable obstacles to be got over in taking up this new position. In the first place, we must sooner or later come to the question of race in the formation of such an institution, because in Britain alone we have certain evidence of an Iberic, a Celtic, and a Teutonic population, all of which lived in communities, and all of which have left their mark upon later British history. With the researches of Professor Boyd Dawkins and Mr. Elton before us, it is idle to attempt an investigation into any

THE SCOPE OF THE INQUIRY.

section of English institutions without taking count of the ethnic influences. Secondly, we have to disentangle ourselves from the notion that the form in which the village community is found in Britain could only have arisen from the influences of civilizing powers, a position forced upon us by Mr. Seebohm; we have to get rid of the idea that as an institution it is a special heritage of the Aryan race, a position forced upon us by Sir Henry Maine. And, finally, we shall have to establish if possible that it is exactly similar in its wide extension to other ascertained phases of human society, and must, therefore, be reckoned with as one of the phases through which practically all mankind who have reached a certain stage of development must have passed. Thus it will be seen that in attempting to investigate the village communities of Britain our study is, in fact, a chapter in the science of comparative custom, not in the chronological history of a nation. What we shall be doing is to trace out the history of an institution, which may be said to be almost universal, during its existence in a special country, namely, Britain, where it has been subject to special influences; it is not the history of a British institution, but the history of a human institution in Britain.

It seems remarkable that the early history of institutions in this country, and in the Western world generally, should have been so infrequently studied side by side with the monumental and other evidence of the existence of different ethnic stocks. Cave dwellers, hill men, lake dwellers, dolmen builders, have all left very important proofs of their lengthened occupation of this country, but their influences are never reckoned with when anything but monumental archæology is being considered. Mr. Elton was the first to point out that certain rude customs among the peasantry could best be accounted for by the theory of their survival from non-Aryan tribes; but, except to explain the prevalence of junior right in a certain well-defined tract of country, he does not suggest that this survival may possibly direct our attention to these race influences for an explanation of much that is obscure in our remarkably diversified local institutions. In the meantime Sir Henry Maine had put a more express limit upon the value of race influences in comparative jurisprudence. The tribes of men with which the student of jurisprudence is concerned, he tells us, are exclusively those belonging to the races now universally classed, on the ground of linguisitic affinities, as Aryan and Semitic: besides these he has at most to take into account that portion of the outlying mass of mankind which has lately been called Uralian, the Turks, Hungarians, and Finns.[1]

Now an appeal to comparative custom to unlock some of the hidden secrets of our own early life means that we must study not only the prehistoric monuments and the barbaric customs of Aryan nations, but the very rude forms of life still existing; for, as Mr. McLennan has well observed, the preface of general history must be compiled from the materials presented by barbarism. Rude stone monuments tell us something of the rude people who built them; philology tells us something of the archaic social conditions of Aryan man; but the knowledge gained from these two sources of scientific observation, however true as to general outline, is not rich in detail. For this we can only go to comparative custom; and it is in detail that an institution like the village community must be examined.

Comparative custom, not seeking for evidences of early man merely in the written records of ancient nations, does not define as old everything that is chronologically early. It has ascertained that man is an unchanging being under certain conditions which have been present over a large part of the globe; it therefore seeks for evidence of early man from the unchanged representatives still living, and it defines as old that which has not advanced and become progressive. If we can find rude types of the village community in India and in Europe, we may conclude that these rude types are probably as old as the Indo-European race; and if we can go one step further and find rude types of the village community in still more backward races of the world, we may conclude that these

[1] "Early History of Institutions," p. 65.

rude types show us what early man was capable of doing in the matter of social and economical organization before there was any chance of his contact with any civilized or civilizing system.

This seems to be the necessary starting-point in our researches. We must first note some of the details available from this source of information, in order to set forth as clearly as may be that the village community belongs essentially to the primitive and archaic stage of social development; and we can then see if there are any traces of continuity between the rudest forms of this institution and the forms found to exist in civilized Britain.

For this purpose I shall first of all turn to some examples of the village community among savage races, and I shall choose the Fijians, the Basutos, and the Dyaks. Low down in the scale of humanity, it will be seen that these people have yet developed a system of village economy remarkably close to that surviving in India and Europe. The effect of such evidence is twofold. It shows that the mental efforts which called forth such a system did not serve to make the race other than savages; and it suggests that in these savage institutions we have types of the early stages of our own history when the village community was first formed. It may seem a far-off cry from the Fijians of to-day to the inhabitants of our own island in prehistoric days; but while we know from the evidence of monumental remains that man in his most primitive condition lived in these islands long enough to impress his barbarism upon the successive waves of civilization, while we can trace evidences of that stage of barbarism in a race of people which must at least have extended from Central Asia to Britain, and while we know that modern savagedom retains habits and beliefs which best explain the silent monuments of ancient savagedom,[1] it is abundantly clear that to understand the

[1] A very good example of this is to be found in Dr. E. B. Tylor's comparison of the Digging Sticks as the earliest agricultural implements, used both among the North American Indians and in Sweden, and the system of shifting-brand tillage among the Basutos and in Sweden. See *Contemporary Review*, vol. xxii. p. 64.

survivals of early institutions in civilized countries, we must examine existing types of these self-same institutions in the rudest form in which they are to be found. And if authority is needed for such a course as I propose to take, I am content to stand by the great name of Dr. E. B. Tylor, who, in one of his most pregnant essays on primitive society, connects the various steps in the history of legal ownership of land by evidence which commences with the low savages of Brazil, and leads up to the old Scandinavian and Teutonic communities. "The case is indeed plain," says Mr. Tylor, "showing us that while we have a land law modified from that of our barbaric ancestors, their law again had its origin in the simplest form of tenure still to be found among savages who have but just come to the agricultural stage."[1]

But there is something more to be said for such a comparison. I have suggested that an examination of the village community among the most backward races will go far to establish the widespread extension of this institution as a phase of development through which mankind must have passed to reach civilization. And let me note how necessary a complement this is to those other researches into the early history of man which are identified with the names of Tylor, McLennan, Morgan, and Lubbock. These scholars have established landmarks in the social, religious, and mental development of man to which every day brings further research, either confirming or varying the conclusions arrived at. But nothing, or very little, has been attempted to set out the landmarks of primitive economics. The totem tribes, with female kinship and exogamous marriages, in their progress towards male kinship and full tribal society, built their stone circles and their burial mounds, their rude habitations, their extensive defences against hostile tribes, and we are beginning more and more to trace out the connection between the monuments and their builders. But there also existed throughout all this period of early culture a system of economics which governed or marked the life of the tribes. Primitive economical conditions are just

[1] *Contemporary Review*, vol. xxii. p. 66.

as important in tracing out the early history of man and the bearings of that early history upon all succeeding periods as other primitive conditions. They may be studied by the same methods, illustrated by the same types of modern barbarism, and traced along the same lines of development, which have been adopted in the corresponding studies of early man ; and thus, when from the evidence of contemporary savagedom we for our present purposes come to select one or two instances to guide us to the earliest stages of primitive economics, we may allow this evidence to stand as typical of what further research would bring forth upon the question of the widespread existence of the village community.

Proof of this widespread existence of a definite primitive economical system cannot now be undertaken, because it is a subject by itself, and needs immense research into some of the byways of the literature of travellers. But I may indicate some of the lines which such a study would proceed upon, and where such lines converge upon the examples I shall more particularly examine. It appears to me that the true way to study primitive economics is to commence with the structural details of primitive residences.

In prehistoric archæology a very considerable section is occupied by the remains—sometimes structural, sometimes consisting of mere deposits of domestic utensils—of early dwelling places. In savage archæology we meet with examples of early dwelling places peopled still by those who built or adapted them. If there is an overlapping of these two departments of archæology at any given point, they must illustrate and elucidate each other, because they both deal with the same phenomenon—the swarming of human groups into their shells during a vast period of time. It is important, therefore, to ascertain, if possible, whether such an overlapping does take place, and if so, at what point.

But to accomplish this task with anything like success it would be necessary to gather together the evidence, now almost hopelessly scattered, as to the dwelling places and home economy of the savage races. Only one authority, so far as I know, has paid close attention to this subject, namely, the late Mr. Lewis Morgan, but his book relates entirely to the evidence derived from the American Indians. His researches, however, into this branch of the human race are so true that it is not unimportant to note that they are confirmed in all essential particulars when we extend the area of research to other uncivilized peoples. For the rest, it would be necessary to pick our way among the recorded observances of travellers who have seldom noted the essentials of savage economics.

Mr. Tylor has remarked that "thinking of the nests of birds, the dams of beavers, the tree platforms of apes, it can scarcely be supposed that man at any time was unable to build himself a shelter."[1] That he does not do so is due to causes which are inseparably connected, though how we cannot exactly say, with the form of the society in which he is living. In such types of society which may perhaps best be identified with the primitive human horde to which Mr. McLennan worked back,[2] there is no room for artificially-built dwellings. Such, for instance, are the wild Bushmen of South Africa. "A cave with its opening protected by a few branches, or the centre of a small circle of thorn trees, round which skins of wild animals were stretched, was the best dwelling place that they aspired to possess; if neither of these were within their reach they scooped out a hole in the ground, placed a few sticks or stones round it, and spread a skin above to serve as a roof, or sometimes nothing more than a reed mat on the side from which the wind was blowing: a little grass at the bottom of the hole formed a bed, and though it was not much larger than the nest of an ostrich, a whole family would manage to lie down in it."[3] This is the indiscriminate squatting of a human horde, the atoms of which are kept together by forces which operate from outside, instead of by forces originating from the recognition and use of the ties of blood relationship, as among more advanced peoples. The use of constructed dwellings

[1] "Anthropology," p. 229.
[2] Cf. my paper in *Journ. Anthrop. Inst.*, vol. xvii. pp. 118-133.
[3] Theal's "Compendium of South African History," p. 55.

would not fit in with the mental attitude or with the unregulated individualism of this stage of human life, and accordingly it seems possible to date the rise of a permanent form of dwelling from the time when blood kinship began to be utilized in the building-up of society. Much profitless discussion has taken place upon Mr. McLennan's theory as to a period in human history when blood relationship was not recognized. That blood relationship has always *de facto* existed of course needs no proof; that it has always to some extent been one of the means of calling forth the springs of natural affection in the human race, may be accepted also as a general fact; that it has not always been utilized as the foundation of political societies, that it has not always been made the cement which bound large groups of men and women together, are the points to which Mr. McLennan has directed attention.

The stage when permanent forms of artificial dwellings were constructed seems to mark a definite point in the line of development; and we may proceed from it to fix upon such races as the Fijians, Basutos, and Dyaks as sufficiently indicative of the rudest forms of the village community. When we have examined the details presented by these examples we shall be able to affirm that the formation of the village community as a human institution arose in the period of primitive economics, and that a reasonable conclusion may be drawn from this, namely, that its existence among economical conditions which were not primitive is not due to such conditions, but to a resistance which all primitive institutions actively exert when they are brought into antagonism with a system which must in the end overthrow them.

(*a*) Villages in Fiji are sometimes inhabited by land-owning tribes, and sometimes by people who have no land of their own. Our business is with the former of these two classes, but it is worth while pointing out that the existence of this distinction shows some advance in social development. The village inhabited by landowners is surrounded by moat and mound and war-fence. It is divided into two sections separated by a ditch, which sections are subdivided into quarters. Apparently in some cases the sections do not appear, but the quarters generally do.

The houses are thus arranged. Each family group has its own town lot. It is subdivided into smaller lots until each family or household has its own. This is the precinct, and may be surrounded by a fence at the will of its owners. Each family lot must be built upon so as to leave a pathway between it and the adjoining lot. It is sacred against all encroachments of any kind.

Each of the quarters belongs to a section of the community called a *mataqali*, a word which means literally a number of men who are twisted together, *i.e.*, of common descent. It is composed of the descendants of a band of brothers, from each of which is descended a minor division called a *yavusa*, and each *yavusa* may be again subdivided into a number of *vuvale*, consisting of brothers with their families who inhabit either the same house or adjoining houses. The people of a village are theoretically of common descent, though they are not actually so.

The village has its own lands distinct from those of other villages. They are of three kinds : (1) the Yavu or town lot ; (2) The Qele, or arable land ; (3) the Veikau, or forest. The town lot, as we have noted, is that which is occupied by the house and the garden, and there seems to be a close connection between this town lot and the arable land, the ownership of one appearing to go far towards establishing that of the other. The arable land lies beyond the village. In some places it is divided into lots, and subdivided into smaller lots, each having its owner or owners. Elsewhere it is not so divided, and all the joint owners appear to use any piece that may be convenient. Beyond the arable is the forest. It is not subdivided like the arable, but is common to all the *mataqali* of the village. Its members have the joint right of felling timber for building and other purposes, but one community may not trespass upon the forest of another.[1]

(*b*) The villages of the Dyaks of Borneo are mostly built along

[1] *Journ. Anthrop. Inst.*, vol. x. p. 332 *et seq.*

the banks of the rivers, though here and there are solitary houses hidden from view among the forests at a short distance from a stream or creek. The houses are from 80 to 100 feet in length, 20 to 30 feet in width, and with walls about 10 feet high, the ridge of the roof rising another 5 or 6 feet. The house proper has only one floor, raised about 15 to 20 feet from the ground on posts of hard timber. Under the actual habitation is a raised floor or platform of boards and bamboo poles, about 4 or 6 feet from the level of the ground and open on all sides. Here the women pound their rice, the men hold *bitcharas* or councils, the infants are nursed, and the rising generation play or practise war-dances. The ground under and around these platforms is occupied by the pigs, cats, dogs, and fowls. The floor of the house proper is reached by a ladder consisting of a block of timber or thick board, in which deep notches are cut to form steps. The floor is composed of bamboo and the walls of mixed bamboo and timber boards. The roof is covered with wood or with the split leaves of the nipa palm. Internally the house is divided longitudinally by a bamboo partition. One of the long compartments so formed serves as a sleeping place for the unmarried youths and men, and as a general living room for all the occupants; the other compartment is subdivided into a series of smaller rooms for the married members of the family and the women.

Every Dyak has his rice-field, on which he grows sufficient rice for his own consumption. He selects a piece of forest land and begins, with the assistance of his family, to clear the ground. The large trees are cut down and the undergrowth fired, the ashes of which act as manure. Having sown their rice, they build small huts in the rice-fields, remaining there till the miniature plants are transplanted out into the newly-cleared field, on which the women have all the time been busily engaged.

Near the houses are plantations of maize, bananas, pisangs, a sort of turnip, sugar-cane, penang, and a few cocoa-nut palms.

Their agricultural implements are the mandau and a peculiar

axe or adze, the iron of which is fastened with cords made from the sinews of deer plaited in chequer fashion to a shaft made of a piece of hard wood. This again is stuck into a large handle, to which it is firmly fastened by means of gutta-percha.[1]

(*c*) The tribes of the Basutos are subdivided into groups, which form a number of little villages, *motsis*, placed under influential men. The village settlement is nearly always in the form of a vast circle, the centre being occupied by the flocks, while the huts form the circumference. The site being chosen, the chief drives into the ground a peg covered with charms, in order that the village may be firmly nailed to the soil. The highest spot is reserved for the habitation of the chief. Near this is a large court, formed by a circle of rushes or boughs, which is the general place of resort for the men, but women are not allowed to enter. Here public affairs are discussed, lawsuits decided, and criminal causes adjudged. In the centre of the village are large enclosures, perfectly round, formed of branches of the mimosa, in which the cattle are shut in the evening; the ground is so holy that it serves as a burial-place for the chiefs and their families.

In the country of the Batlapsis, the Barolongs, and the Baharutsis, where the heat is excessive and wood abundant, the hut is high and well ventilated. It is in the form of a conical dome, round which is a little verandah which serves to support the roof. The Basutos, who inhabit a mountainous country, endeavour to shut out the cold and wet, and their huts are in the form of a large oval oven, and are entered by creeping along a very narrow passage, which serves to prevent the wind from reaching the interior. The walls are perfectly well plastered, and often decorated with ingenious designs. The sleeping place is on the ground. The most remote part of the hut generally serves as a receptacle for the enormous vases of coarse earthenware, containing the provision of wheat, and

---

[1] Bock's "Head Hunters of Borneo," pp. 195-202; *Journal Ethnological Society* (New Series), vol. ii. p. 28.

other articles of food. The door by which they go in and out of the hut leads into a circular court surrounded by rushes or branches; in which place is the fire and where the family generally assemble. Each hut is occupied by a married couple and their children. A polygamist has the same number of huts as he has wives.

The land is understood to belong to the whole community, and no one has a right to dispose of the soil from which he derives his support. The sovereign chiefs assign to their vassals the parts they are to occupy, and these latter grant to every father of a family a portion of arable land proportionate to his wants. The land thus granted is insured to the cultivator so long as he does not change his locality. If he goes to settle elsewhere he must restore the fields to the chief under whom he holds them, in order that the latter may dispose of them to some other person. The bounds of each field are marked with precision. The possession of pasture land is also subject to rules. It is understood that the inhabitants of one village should prevent their flocks from grazing on ground which belongs to another. Among the Basutos it is the duty of every petty village chief to see that a part of the adjacent territory is reserved for winter pasture.

The cultivated fields are generally situated at some distance from the village. When a piece of land is exhausted, another piece is cleared by its side.

The Basutos, Bechuanas, and Caffres use oval hoes. The blade is thick in the middle, and gets thinner towards the two sides and the lower part, which renders it at the same time solid and sharp. It is furnished at the top with a kind of elongated tail, which is inserted into a hole bored in the end of the handle. The hoe is raised perpendicularly over the head, and allowed to descend almost by its own weight. The Tembukis and Amakosas dig the ground with a little wooden spade.

The Basutos assemble every year to dig up and sow the fields appropriated for the personal maintenance of their chief and his first wife. Hundreds of men, in a straight line, raise and lower their mattocks simultaneously, and with perfect regularity.

The Basutos preserve their *sorgho* (a grain) in large straw baskets in the shape of a dome. The Caffres have recourse to pits. They make deep excavations in the enclosures where their cattle are penned. The walls of these pits are carefully plastered. The opening, which is only large enough to admit a man, is even with the ground. When the subterranean granary is filled the opening is hermetically sealed, and the whole is covered with a thick coating of dung and earth.

Most of the flocks and herds captured in war become the property of the chief, and the subjects regard it as a favour to become the depositaries and guardians of these new acquisitions. The milk belongs to them; they use the oxen as beasts of burden, and from time to time obtain permission to kill an animal which is already old.[1]

It seems not difficult to trace in these three types of the primitive mode and condition of life, represented by modern savagery, the roots of the tribal and village communities which have been hitherto identified with Aryan races only. We have representatives of lake-dwellers in the Dyaks; of totem tribes in the Basutos; of the early crystallization of a village system in the Fijis. That lake-dwellers, totem-formed tribes, and settled villagers are represented in the archæological remains of early Britain is well known, and there is no scientific reason why we should not pursue the parallel in order to find out what we can of the economical system of the early inhabitants of our land. I have stated the details somewhat fully in order to show how frequently they conform to the evidence of archæology in Europe, but an analysis of the economical details presented by these examples will show at once where the real interest of this suggested parallel begins. We may tabulate such an analysis as follows:

1. The chief, actually present in the Basuto village, has been pushed upward into a caste, and hence disappears from the Fiji village to form the Fiji state.

---

[1] Casalis, "The Basutos," pp. 123-178.

2. Common living is the basis of the Dyak unit; the possession of a wife that of the Basuto; common descent that of the Fiji unit.

3. Common descent brings with it the conception of the sacredness of the homestead among the Fijians.

4. The grouping of houses into a village among the Fijians.

5. The homestead determines the right of user in the village lands among the Basutos and Fijians.

6. The division of the tribal territory into homestead, arable and pasture among the Basutos and Fijians.

7. The houselands being carved out of the unoccupied forest lands by the Dyaks, and the shifting of the arable lands by the Basutos.

8. The village council as the source of village rights.

If we strike out of this analysis the names of the savage tribes which have been the subject of our examination, we might use very nearly the same terms to describe the features of the village system of Britain as it survives in different parts of the country.

Such evidence enables us to say that the village community is of primitive origin; and that it is not stamped with the marks of advanced political progress. And it is significant that when we come to consider its position among the institutions of the Western world, we never see it as the dominant factor in the constitution of nations. In all the countries of Europe, including those occupied by the great classical centres of civilization, it is found to have existed during times which are well within the ken of history. But it is always subordinated to a more or less strong central governing power, and, according as it is interfered with by the central authority for purposes of government, so is the proportion of its completeness as a primitive institution. While almost every local institution of Great Britain—the parish, the manor, the borough—bears upon it the impress of its origin in the primitive village community, no local institution of any importance is an exact representation of what might be expected to have resulted from a normal development of the primitive village community. There is always a twist somewhere. Most generally this may be discovered from the growing commercialism of post-Norman times when the customary law of England was being incorporated into the king's law. Where we can succeed in subtracting the commercial elements in English manorial and village history we come upon the remnants of the primitive village community. These are represented by practices and customs whose startling antagonism to anything appertaining to commercial economy or political progress is the one remarkable phenomenon in English economical history which quadrates with those old faiths, beliefs, and usages, which, under the generic title of folklore, students have now shown to have existed side by side, but subordinated to, the established religion of the nation. This subordinate position of the village community in the Western world, contrasted with its prominent position elsewhere, is a feature in its history which has escaped notice, and which, when examined, helps us to understand many elements in its composition hitherto explained by an appeal to events of political history which do not seem to come into the question at all. It places it among the institutions of the land whose origin is lost in the unrecorded history of the past; it answers the question of those who suggest that, because the village community is never mentioned in the charters and diplomatic documents of advancing political times, therefore it is of modern origin; and, above all, it forces upon the student the recognition of a most important factor in its history, namely, the cause of its long continuance, after the era to which it essentially belongs had wholly passed away. The consideration of this point, indeed, forms a most material section of the history of the village community as a primitive institution.

The village community is thus presented to us as a primitive institution, having a prominent position among the backward races and a subordinate position among the advanced races of the world, and it is suggested that the latter of these two phases is a survival from the former. It should, therefore, be marked by all the characteristics of a survival. One of these characteristics will be found in the traditional sanction given to local practices by long ages of ancestral usage. The evidence of folklore is very important at this stage. If there is any value in the contention of folklorists that the elements of folklore are survivals from primitive belief and custom, they must have belonged to some form of social organism. They were not always waifs and strays, but once helped to consolidate the social structure of which they formed a part. As Professor Sayce well says, the religion of the primitive villager "in its outward form was made up of rites and ceremonies which could only be performed collectively."[1] It seems, therefore, that we may fairly classify the survivals of folklore and the survivals of the village community as belonging to the selfsame stage of primitive social development. This conclusion is considerably strengthened by the fact that the causes of the survival of folklore and of the survival of the village community are identical, namely, the persistence of traditional usage. Proof of this in the case of folklore is hardly needed, and this is not the place to set it forth. Proof of the traditional sanction for the customs belonging to the village community has never been set forth, and has never been sufficiently insisted upon as an important element in the question of origin. But it is overwhelming. Fortunately for science, the backward condition of agriculture in this country, during the last years of the eighteenth century and the first decade of the present, was so alarming as to arrest the serious attention of the government. Under the able and indefatigable guidance of Arthur Young and Sir John Sinclair, the Board of Agriculture set to work to collect information, county by county, about the actual state of agricultural industry, the obstacles to improvement, and the best means of introducing something like scientific principles. The one answer which seems to have almost overwhelmed the inquirers was that the then existing system was carried on simply because it had always been so from time immemorial—an answer which was backed up by deep-rooted aversion to change of any sort, especially when change meant an enclosure of lands and the allotment of several parcels, held in common by a group, to individual owners. Over and over again in the reports presented to the

[1] "Introduction to Science of Language," vol. ii. p. 290.

Board of Agriculture, and in contemporary literature dealing with the same subject, was this view of the case brought prominently before the economical reformers, and over and over again do they complain of the unreasoning folly of the peasant farmers, who loved to do only what their fathers had done, and who looked upon the improvements at last gradually introduced as so extraordinary that they must have been the result of a disordered intellect.[1]

A fact of the highest importance has thus been obtained from the lips of the villagers themselves, namely, that the agricultural practices observed at the beginning of the century were not the result of known economical forces; but were, on the contrary, derived from immemorial usage, were therefore traditional methods of agriculture. Now, traditional methods of agriculture, like traditional methods of belief, are valuable to the scientific inquirer just because they are traditional, and this brings prominently before us an historical fact of some importance, namely, that the attitude of civilization towards primitive institutions, in tolerating them and keeping them alive even long after their meaning and usefulness have been lost, cannot be determined without taking count of primitive economics. The sanction of traditional reverence for habits and ways that have come down with men from that far-off time which memory and fancy hold so dear, transcends and keeps in check even the forces of political economy which we have been taught to look upon as so irresistible, and it is worth bearing in mind that some of the traditional features of the village community are not very far removed from the socialism of to-day. In the history of human thought it will be found that the influences of traditional ideas far outweigh the influences of philosophy.

Thus our preliminary examination of the village community by the light of comparative custom has led us first to see that it is a product of the backward races of the world, not of the foremost; secondly, that its existence amidst the more advanced institutions of civilization is due to survival, not to creation; and,

[1] See Stewart's "Highlanders of Scotland," vol. i. pp. 147, 228.

finally, that from its widespread existence, absolute proof of which has not however been undertaken, it represents a phase of economic development through which all progressive races must have passed.

CHAPTER II.

THE RACE-ELEMENTS OF THE VILLAGE COMMUNITY.

It has been generally assumed that the various types of the village community originate with the particular race among which they are found in full working order, and that hence both the Hindu and European types are purely Aryan in origin. But the examples of the village system of the Fiji and Basuto tribes no longer make it possible for comparative custom to ignore non-Aryan evidence, and it becomes an important question as to whether we cannot trace out the point of contact between the Aryan and non-Aryan village system. Now fortunately in India civilization has not crushed out race distinctions, and we are still able to examine the village communities as they exist among the aboriginal non-Aryan races, and as they exist in districts occupied by the Aryan races. Two distinct types of the institution are hereby revealed. If there are some points where these two types converge and synchronize, and if there are some points where they altogether differ, the evidence will be of importance; but if we may go somewhat further than this, and prove that the points of difference between the two systems are also the points which mark the Aryan overlordship of an original non-Aryan settlement, if the so-called Aryan village communities can be proved by the Indian evidence to be a composite system so far as race is concerned, consisting both of Aryan and non-Aryan elements, the evidence introduces an entirely new feature into the history of the village community, and one which must be reckoned with wherever that institution becomes the subject of scientific examination.

The subject is one of some difficulty, but it is worth while attempting an examination of its main features here, because in comparative custom as in other branches of comparative science, India affords a remarkable key to the facts that present themselves, without explanation, in Europe. Civilization in Europe has not succeeded in altogether stamping out archaic types of society; but it has succeeded in stamping out nearly all direct evidence of the origin of such types. We shall have occasion later on to point out the value of Indian parallels to European custom; it is well therefore to bring out clearly all the initial stages of Indian village life, so that the parallels from time to time brought forward in explanation of some of the details in the village life of Britain may not appear to be the chance results of a haphazard comparison.

If we were to examine the economical system of some of the numerous non-Aryan hill tribes of India, we should find that their continued existence amidst the greater civilization of the plains affords some key to the phenomena presented by the villages inhabiting these plains. And, moreover, it would be found that in these examples of non-Aryan settlements in India we meet with many facts which reappear in the history of the village community as it is known in India and Europe. The shifting of the cultivation site season after season, the establishment of a central house for the unmarried of the tribe and the sacred connection of the fire place therein with the meeting place of the council, the influence of the widow in matters of succession compared with the husband dwelling with the wife's parents, the natural succession of the youngest son to the house from which all but he have departed, the assistance of the community towards building a house for its newly-married members, are among the most interesting features of these non-Aryan village customs. And it seems impossible to get away from the fact that they represent on the outlying lands of India, the home of the Aryan, that system of primitive economics which, as we have seen from the evidence examined in the first chapter, early man must have been almost universally acquainted with.

What, then, is the relationship of this non-Aryan village to the Hindu system? In the pure hill examples there is no appearance of any mixture of race, and the features common to each are not sufficiently overlapping to suggest anything like a settled political government as the source of their origin. But in other examples we may plainly see written on the face of the facts presented to our observation the influence of race admixture, and in these we invariably discover the non-Aryan village in complete organization under an Aryan overlordship at the apex of the village system. I will give one significant example of this before passing on to more general evidence.

Among the Khonds the village generally consists of two streets,[1] each with a double row of huts, one of which is occupied by themselves and the other by the tribe named *Pardi*, of low caste, and who are weavers by trade. Their huts are built of wattle and daub, and the roof thatched with grass. Most of the villages are surrounded by a stout plaiting of bamboo fence, and in some few places they are well stockaded. In one part of the enclosure their cattle are folded, and the other portion is converted into a vegetable garden. In the jungles trees are rudely felled, and oil-nut, dholl, cotton, &c., cultivated. After the lapse of a few years, when the soil shows symptoms of exhaustion, a fresh site is selected, and jungle once more covers the first. Each family raises a sufficiency to supply its immediate wants.[2] There is no system of tenure, the right of possession being simply founded in the case of the tribe upon priority of appropriation, and in the case of individuals upon priority of culture. Landed property descends exclusively in the male line by equal division among all the sons, or in case of failure of issue among all the brothers. The elder sons, as they are married, have a house of their own, the youngest always remaining in the house of his father. On the failure of heirs male, land becomes the property of the village, and is divided among its members.[3]

[1] Campbell, "Wild Tribes of Khondistan," says "one street," p. 49.

[2] Shortt's "Hill Ranges of S. India," vol. iii. p. 13; Carmichael's "Manual of the Vizagapatam District," p. 90.

[3] Carmichael, *op. cit.*, pp. 95, 96.

Now to these interesting details we can add a very important fact from the observations of Colonel Campbell. Each village, he says, has its own chief, or mulleko, and with him is joined an officer called Digaloo, or interpreter, of the Panoo caste, who transacts all business for the Khonds, who consider it beneath their dignity to barter or traffic. Districts again are governed by chiefs of Ooryah extraction, named the Bissoi, who are Hindus by race, and the Khonds regard them as much more capable of ruling over them and leading them to battle than any of their own tribe.[1]

Our next task is to point out how this evidence of race admixture is confirmed from the general conditions of Indian village settlement. Three distinct races in India took a part in forming Hindu society as we now find it. First, the Mongoloid tribes of Malayan affinities, speaking languages belonging to the Kolarian family; secondly, the Australioids, speaking Dravidian languages; and lastly, the Aryans, speaking dialects connected with Sanscrit. Of these races the first are now best known through the so-called Kol tribes of Western Bengal and Central India, who still hold their own several districts, and keep quite separate from the Hindus. The second are represented by the forty-six million people in Madras, who speak Tamul, Teloogoo, and other cognate dialects, and the Gonds, Khonds, Ooraons, Bhuyas, and other tribes in Bengal and Central India, who, where they still retain their native speech, speak languages belonging to that family; while almost all the upper classes throughout the length and breadth of India, and the great mass of the population in the Punjab, North-West Provinces, Bengal, and Bombay, claim to belong to the third.[2]

From this point we may follow the able guidance of Mr. J. F. Hewitt, a settlement officer, whose opinion is guided by actual observation. Mr. Hewitt shows that "not only Aryan

---

[1] Campbell, "Wild Tribes of Khondistan," p. 50.

[2] *Journal Society of Arts*, vol. xxv. p. 615. Mr. Hewitt's classification is not essentially different from that of Mr. Justice Campbell in his article on "The Ethnology of India," in *Journal Asiatic Society of Bengal*, vol. xxxv. part ii.

and semi-Aryan tribes divided the country into townships, peopled and cultivated by associated villagers, but that such townships exist also among those like the Kols and Ooraons of Chota Nagpore, in Western Bengal, who have always hated the Aryans, and have never been conquered by them, or subjected to their influence;" and that "from the examples of others, in which Dravidians and Aryans confessedly live together, the Aryan village is formed on the lines laid down by Kolarians and Dravidians, and it is only altered in certain details to make it suit with the Aryan ideas of the sanctity and continuity of the family, and of the equal rights of all holding land in the village."

These conclusions invert the old ideas of the village community by proving that the village settlement and modes of cultivation are non-Aryan, while only the government and administration are Aryan;[1] but because they are derived from actual types of race distinction it is no longer possible to think of the Indian village community as due to only Aryan influences. A result so important to the study of comparative institutions wants careful analysis, and Mr. Hewitt has reduced the characteristics of the non-Aryan tribes into a systematic grouping, which enables him to detect the exact race influences.

Examining the characteristics of the social organization and tribal economy of these races we will deal first with the Kolarians. Mr. Campbell says the more civilized and numerous tribes of this race occupy an extensive country about 150 miles west from Calcutta, and are known as Moondahs, Bhoomiz, Hos, and Santals,[2] to which Colonel Dalton has added the Kheriahs, Korewahs, and the Juangas.[3] Beyond their original settlements in the district of Chota Nagpore, Mr. Hewitt says they can still be traced westwards, occupying parts

---

[1] Sir Alfred Lyall, in his "Asiatic Studies," p. 154, comes to much the same conclusion as Mr. Hewitt; cf. also J. B. Lyall's "Settlement Report of Kangra District," p. 25.

[2] *Journal Asiatic Society of Bengal*, vol. xxxv. part ii. p. 34.

[3] Ibid., pp. 153–157.

of their former settlements. In the Central Provinces we find tribes like the Kurkoos of Hoshungabad, who speak the language and retain the customs of their forefathers, and others are found in every stage of transition from nearly pure Kols to low-caste Hindus. Even in the cultivated parts of Bombay traces of them appear, and if the Kolis of Maha Kanta belong to this race, they still retain a separate organization of their own, even in this far west region.[1] Thus they are to be studied in their primitive state, and also when they form part of an Aryan village community. Of their primitive characteristics Mr. Hewitt enumerates the following as bearing upon the history of the village community.

1. They are a totemistic people. Each clan of the tribe has, as its distinguishing totem, some natural object, which is reverenced by its members, and marks distinction of lineage. When the totem is an article of food none of the clan may eat it, and as no one can marry in his own clan, every man seeking a wife must make his choice out of the girls of families with different totems.

2. They are partly wanderers in the forests, occupying temporary clearings, and partly a fairly settled people, living in fairly permanent villages, under hereditary chiefs.

3. Their settlements are generally founded by families having the same totem, who live as they used to do, near together, and the villages occupied by the several clans of the united section of the tribe, find their centre of union in the Byga, or tribal priest, who, besides offering common sacrifices to the sylvan deities for all the confederated clans, is generally arrow-maker to the community. The heads of the clans are chosen from those who gain the greatest influence over their fellows, but neither these offices, nor that of tribal priest, is hereditary or necessarily permanent, all are dependent on popular opinion, which may any day reduce the holders to the level of the ordinary tribesman.

4. The territorial divisions are first the parha, or tribal territory, under a hereditary chief called manki; then each

[1] *Journal Society of Arts*, vol. xxxv. p. 620.

parha is divided, in the more cultivated parts of the country, into twelve or more villages.[1]

5. The houses occupy some space and are somewhat isolated. They have verandas, well-raised plinths, and separate apartments for the married and single members of the family. Sometimes as many as twenty houses will be formed together round a square interior space.[2]

6. Each village has its local deity or deities, called Desauli, to which common sacrifices are offered by the villagers. The Desauli is the local spirit, or spirits, of that part of the forest where the village clearing was made, for whose residence a few trees of the old forest are always left. The priest is paid by dues from the villagers.

7. The government is by a council of the mankis and the mundas and chief tenants of the villages. There is no trace in the Kol system of government of the existence of a king, or any power above the mankis, and the united assembly of mankis, mundas, and chief tenants. They regulated all matters within the tribal territory, but it was only by negotiation, or war, that questions between adjoining tribes could be settled.

8. They always hoed the land, as they were ignorant of ploughs, and the use of plough-cattle. When they keep cattle, they only keep enough for purely agricultural purposes, as they never drink milk, and oxen are too valuable to be used as food.

Thus we have the distinctive features of the Kolarian race —(1) organization by the totem; (2) occupation of forest clearings; (3) settlement under a non-hereditary chief, elected clan chiefs, tribal and clan priests; (4) territorial division of the tribe and clans; (5) independent houses; (6) clan deities of the forest; (7) government by a council; (8) ignorance of the plough and objection to cattle as food.

We next pass to the Dravidian race. We may take their general characteristics from the description given by Mr. Hewitt.

[1] Dalton in *Journal Asiatic Society Bengal*, vol. xxxv. part ii. p. 159.
[2] Ibid., p. 176.

They entered India from the west, and are celebrated as the principal opponents of the Aryans. They are apparently allied to the race described in the early Persian writings as worshippers of the demon and great snake Azidahaka. They were essentially a ruling and thoroughly practical race, who believed firmly in the necessity of a strong central government to maintain order and unity. What they sought in their slow and steady advance through India was fertile lands, where they could live in peace, and they moved in large masses like an army. Hence they preferred to settle in lands which had been already cleared. They were accompanied by their wives, children, and property.

Enumerating the characteristics which bear upon the history of the village community we have the following:

1. They are totemistic.[1]

2. Their settlement was on the model of their camps, placing the central provinces under the king as general-in-chief, and assigning the outlying districts to the subordinate chiefs who, with their respective forces, were appointed to guard the frontiers.

3. The territorial divisions are the old parhas as the provincial divisions of the kingdom, only massing several parhas together where a large province was required, and they retained the villages.

4. The family lives very promiscuously in a small, indifferently-constructed, untidy looking hut, and the village consists of a street or court of such huts. They have no gardens or orchards attached to individual houses, but in and about the villages are some fine trees which are common property. In every village young men and girls were separated from their parents when they were little more than children, and obliged to live in separate lodgings, the young men in what is called in Chota Nagpore the *dhumkuria*, or bachelor's hall, under the care of one of the elders of the village; and the girls in another similar building superintended by one of the matrons.

[1] Colonel Dalton in *Journal Asiatic Society Bengal*, vol. xxxv. part ii. p. 192.

5. The pahan had still to perform the sacrifices necessary to satisfy the forest spirits called Desauli and the distinctive village god; but their chief function was to make offerings to the great earth-god worshipped by the Naga races.

6. The central government received contributions from the villages, and was represented in each village. Hence a certain proportion of the best land, called manjhus land, varying in area according to the size of village, was set apart for the service of the raja or king. The produce of this land was either stored in the royal granaries or, when the village was assigned by the raja to a subordinate, made over to the assignee. The rest of the land was divided into allotments, called koonts: three of these were assigned to the families who received the right to fill the village offices. All these offices were made hereditary. They were called bhunhiars, and were chosen from the original settlers. One of these allotments was set apart for the munda, or headman, but he was no longer supreme in the village. He divided his authority with the pahan, and with a new officer appointed by the Dravidians, the mahto, or accountant, who held the two other allotments.

7. The descendants of the men who formed the village are a privileged class, the head of whom is called the moondah, and is generally the representative of the old moondah chief of the village. They had a right to a certain area of cultivated land, proportionate to their ability to till it. On the admission of a new tenant, the cultivated land was redistributed, so as to give each cultivator a portion of each kind of soil in the village, calculated according to the number of plough bullocks he had. In large villages the heads of the families, who were the oldest settlers, had a great deal of power, and formed part of the village council. They were always consulted before a redistribution of land was made, or a new tenant was admitted. The privileged families paid no taxes in grain, or afterwards no money, but gave general suit and service to the ruling authorities, carried their baggage on a journey, supplied them, as well as travellers, with wood and grass when

they visited the village, thatched and repaired the houses and granaries of their chief, looked after the village boundaries, and kept order in the village. The subordinate village officers were generally paid in grain, though sometimes in land; the water-carrier, who was also the pahan's assistant, is found in every village, and beside him were others, viz., the blacksmith, the potter, the cowherd, the barber, the washerman, and the watchman. There was also in every parha the ojha, or sorcerer and witchfinder.

Thus the distinctive features of the Dravidian villages show us a strong central government, great advance towards territorial settlement and boundaries, the redistribution of village lands at the time of admission of a new villager, and the imposition of dues or payments for the purposes of government. From an ethnological point of view there is not much difference between the two races Kolarian and Dravidian: both based upon a tribal organization, their chief characteristic in the history of the village community in India is their power of amalgamation within the bounds of the village system. The amalgamation produced no alteration in the principle of social organization. The village, before the advent of the Dravidians, was the same unit as the village after its absorption of the new-comers. The internal structure had to be knit closer together; the external shell was still the village.

The question, then, becomes: What did the Aryans do towards the construction of the village community, the essential factors of which had already been constructed by non-Aryan races? If we consider for one moment the characteristics of the Aryan race we must allow that they do not suggest any assimilation with an institution which was based upon an agricultural economy. Bearing in mind what Cæsar and Tacitus have said of the German social organization, I will once more quote Mr. Hewitt for the Indian side of the question.

The Aryans, when they entered India, were almost entirely a pastoral people, whose wealth consisted in their cattle, and who looked on agriculture and trade as degrading. Their earliest laws forbade these occupations to the two highest classes—the Brahmins, or priests, and the kshattryas, or warriors—and the latest recension of the laws of Manu, the most elaborate of the early codes, declares that "for a Brahmin or kshattryas, agriculture is blamed by the virtuous as the plough with the iron point injures the earth and the beings in it."[1] With these views, their object in making a new home was not to settle down, till the land round their homesteads, and enrich themselves by labour and trade, but to find a country which, in the words of the "Institutes of Vishnu,"[2] consisted of open plains, fit for cattle, abounding in grain, and containing many *vaisyas*, or herdsmen and Sudras, of cultivators of alien race. Such a country they found in the plains of the Punjab, where they first settled during the early period when the Vedic hymns were composed. But this comparatively populous and rich district brought with its advantages dangers, which caused serious anxiety to a people who were both deeply religious and intensely proud of the purity of blood which made them, in their own eyes, the first of the natives of the earth. Among such a people the preservation of their families from intermixture with the despised natives of the country, and the correct performance of the sacrifices due to the heavenly powers they worshipped, were objects of the first importance. Hence their early codes are chiefly composed of rules regulating, in each household—(1) the ritual of the daily sacrifices offered by the head of the house to the gods and his ancestors; (2) for the maintenance of the sacred fire kindled at the wedding of the father and mother of each family; (3) the conduct of students and priests of the sacred law; (4) for the preservation of personal purity; and (5) the avoidance of marriages with strange races.

This was not the race to settle down at once into village communities such as we now know them. They introduced the idea of sacred rights residing in each family; they superimposed upon a strongly organized economic system, a strongly

[1] "Laws of Manu," cap. x. p. 84.
[2] "Institutes of Vishnu," vol. iii. pp. 4, 5.

organized kinship system. Not only are these Aryan villagers bands of cultivators; they are common descendants of one ancestor, common worshippers of one family god. Within the framework of the original Dravidian villages the Aryan race governed the cultivating body, and one of the most significant facts of the race history of the village community in India is that the boundaries of the townships are preserved with the greatest care, and are always under the charge of the aboriginal races of the lowest castes, whose forefathers fixed them.

This evidence appears to be conclusive as to the large part that the non-Ayran races of India have played in building up that form of the village community which is to be found in India, and which, on the faith of its existence there, has been hitherto considered a perfectly homogeneous institution belonging essentially to the Aryans.

It seems to me that if we thus get a clue to some of the race distinctions in India, we may, by following the lines of comparative custom, get a clue to some of the race distinctions in Europe. The details which I have set forth may be somewhat wearisome, but their importance will be seen later on. In the meantime, our next step is to produce such a typical example of the village community in India as will illustrate first the race distinctions which we now know to exist; and, secondly, the close parallel between the village community in India and that in Britain.

We find such an example ready to our hands, described by Mr. Hodgson in the second volume of the Transactions of the Royal Asiatic Society, 1830. It is situated about thirty miles north-west of Madras, in the Carnatic, a southeastern province of India, and is known by the name of Pudu-vayal. Mr. Hodgson prefaces his observations by the statement that "it contains little that is new on the rights of the peasantry of the south-eastern part of the peninsula of India;" and asserts that his object in giving the paper is merely "to render the subject intelligible to those who have not been in India, by divesting the description of all technical terms." We may conclude, therefore, even if no other evidence were forthcoming, that in this example we have a typical case only, one that has close parallels all round it. And indeed Mr. Hodgson goes on to observe that it "has never been under the direct control of any European officer of the East India Company," and thus "exhibits a fair specimen of the ancient usages of Southern India."

There are two classes of villagers, the original settlers or their descendants, and strangers not descended from original settlers. Thus at the outset we have the stamp of race distinction brought out prominently.

The privileges of the original settlers are held by custom in four principal shares, and each principal share is subdivided into sixteen parts, making in all sixty-four shares. By the custom of the village a principal share cannot be sold, because it contains the property of many; but custom admits of the sale of a subdivision of a principal share under certain limitations also defined by custom. The four principal shares are, or are supposed to have been, the shares fixed when the village was first settled. They have remained unaltered as long as tradition or history reaches. The subdivisions of these principal shares are the portions held by the descendants of the first settlers or by the purchasers of their rights.

When the season for cultivation arrives the arable land of the village is allotted to the several shareholders in the following manner. The names of each lot and each shareholder are written on pieces of the leaf of the palm tree, such as is used for village records, and the names of each division of land to be allotted are placed in a row. A child, selected for the purpose, draws by lot a leaf with the name of the principal shareholder, and places it under a number, thus—

1.	2.	3.	4.
Tannappa.	Nina.	Narrappa.	Malliyan.

It is thus settled by lottery that Tannappa and his undershareholders are entitled to cultivate the land of the principal share lotted under No. 1. Tannappa next proceeds to settle in the same way each under-shareholder's portion included in his principal share; and so on until the 64 shareholders receive each his allotment.

The lots are not drawn for all the lands at once, but in sub-divisions according to quality; for instance, for the division nearest the reservoir as being less liable to the effects of drought, first; then for the next division as being further removed from the reservoir; and then for the third, which perhaps receives an adequate supply of water once in two or three years only. Each of these subdivisions of land has an appropriate name in the village register.

The total amount of the arable land thus held is $368\frac{3}{16}$ cánis, or nearly 487 acres. Thus each ancestral share would contain a little more than 120 acres. Beyond this land, however, held by the villagers in common for their own cultivation, was certain so-called "alienated land," that is, devoted to special purposes by custom or by grant. The lands held by grant from the village amounted to $11\frac{5}{16}$ cánis, or 15 acres, and were in possession of a priest and ten other Brahmins. The lands appropriated by custom amounted to $26\frac{6}{16}$ cánis, or 35 acres. They were held as follows:—

> By the temples, *i.e.*, Church lands ... = 3 acres (about).
> For the benefit of the villagers generally = $1\frac{1}{4}$,,
> For the village officers—
> The accountant ... ... = $14\frac{1}{2}$,,
> The village watchman ... ... = $13\frac{3}{4}$,,
> The village carpenter ... ... = $1\frac{1}{4}$,,
> The village blacksmith ... ... = $1\frac{1}{4}$,,
>
> ———
> 35 acres.

Beside the arable allotments the villagers have an exclusive right to pasture over all the uncultivated lands within the boundaries.

The villagers were assisted in their agricultural operations by three classes of servants. First, slaves who were transferred with the other privileges of the village occupants when those privileges were sold or mortgaged. Second, bondsmen, who may be said to have mortgaged themselves, and who can redeem or work out their bondage. Third, hired labourers. All these classes are remunerated or supported by allowances of grain and donations of cloth for clothing and the benefit of gleanings and the sweepings of the treading-floor.[1] They have small plots of ground for gardens, and have presents on marriages or births in their families, and on the new year.

The stranger settlers who are not descendants of the original settlers, and who do not, therefore, possess any portion of the four ancestral shares, cultivate a portion of land set apart for them. They have no claim to a permanent possession of the land, they take no share in the produce of the village corporation lands, and do not obtain the services of the village officials. They are a community, as it were, by themselves, and they pay "a fee of superiority to the original settlers in the village."

The component parts of this Hindu village community may therefore be thus classed:—

The hereditary villagers holding 4 ancestral shares, subdivided into 16 parts each;
The priests;
The village officers;
The servi, bondsmen, and hired labourers;
The stranger settlers.

This group of persons is held together by ties which are not imposed by the State, but which have arisen from its own history. At the top is the Aryan clan, whose bond of union is descent from a common ancestor. Under this are the non-Aryan cultivators, whose bond of union is simply that of a tenantry under a superior proprietary body. But the whole community—Aryan clans founded on common kinship and non-Aryan cultivators affixed to the soil—is now known to the State only by the amount of its revenue paid over to the sovereign. The custom is that $48\frac{1}{2}$ per cent. of the produce is

[1] All the grain is trodden out of the straw by driving cattle over it, tied together by the neck.

retained by the villagers, and 51½ is paid over to the State. Though so large a proportion is paid away, considerable advantages remain to the community. They divide among themselves the produce of the land exempted from revenue granted when (to use their own emphatic expression) the village was born; they levy a fee of superiority from all cultivators not descendants of the original settlers; they have the labour of the village officers—the carpenter, blacksmith, potter, washerman, watcher, barber, herdsman, distributor of water—free of any personal charge. And they themselves stand forth before the world and in their own eyes as free-villagers, independent alike of national laws and national economy, self-governing and self-supporting.

To this I must add an important description of the system of the Pathán tribes of the Peshawar district, who are believed by the best authorities to be of Indian origin. Their language is called Pashto or Pakhto and is an Aryan speech. Dr. Bellew and Major James identify them with the Pactiyans of Herodotus, and seem half inclined to connect them with the Picts of Britain. The settlements on the unoccupied lands, as among the Yusafzai, were in families at one spot, or in villages adjacent to each other. The remainder of the *tappa* or tribal land was held in common, and used chiefly as pastruage. Each family cultivated its bakhra or any portion of it at pleasure, paying no tribute or share of the produce to any one, its duty to the tribe being to join in all offensive or defensive operations. Very little land in the immediate vicinity of the villages was at first brought under cultivation. In the conquered districts aboriginal cultivators were allowed to settle amongst them. These were styled *fakirs*, and the system usually adopted with them was to require service only in lieu of the land which they were allowed to cultivate on their own account. The claims of a settled government introduced a more complicated system. When fiscal demands were enforced it became the object of the Pathán proprietors to cast the burden upon the cultivators, and this gave rise to the large exemptions which exist in all villages in respect of the estate cultivated by the proprietors themselves, the maliks or heads of families. Owing to the peculiar jealousy amongst Pathâns of the assumption of authority by individuals, the number of this class was very large, and a village was a cluster, not merely of several branches of a tribe, but of small families, the members of which, bound together by the closest ties of kindred, yielded obedience only to their respective *maliks*, which office was in its nature hereditary. In one village, therefore, there might be thirty or forty maliks.[1]

The natural result of this fiscal arrangement has been to increase the rights of the *fakir* class. They have all the rights of proprietorship, except that of sale or transfer, and they hold their shares upon hereditary right.

The division and distribution of the lands forming the village site is effected in the same manner as in the case of the cultivated fields, a separate quarter being apportioned to every clan, and in every clan to every section or sub-section. Each quarter is a collection of separate tenements of the individual families forming a clan section. Each tenement consists of the house and the court-yard; these shelter the family as well as their dependants and cattle. The court-yards are large, with a patch of vegetables or a clump of mulberries in the enclosure. The house is within a walled enclosure, one side of which is taken up by the dwelling-house. Each quarter has its own chief, whose authority is confined to it. His duties are to maintain order, settle disputes amongst the householders of his quarter, to collect the revenue, and see to the fair distribution of the crops, &c. Each quarter has its own mosque, its own assembly-room, both of which are situated on the outskirts; and in villages beyond the border its own power of defence or *burj*. The mosque is under the care of an establishment of priests who are subordinate to a leader. They are supported by rent-free lands attached to the mosque, and receive, besides, daily supplies of food from the residents

---

[1] "Report on Census of Punjàb," vol. i. p. 201; "Gazetteer of Peshawar District," pp. 124-127.

of their quarter. The assembly-room is a public room, with court-yard and stables attached. In most instances it is the property of the chief of the quarter, who is expected to feed and shelter all visitors and travellers; beds, bedding, and forage, are provided by the *fakirs*, or aboriginal class, in rotation. In the assembly-room the chief meets the residents of the quarter for the discussion and settlement of their public business. It is also the sleeping place of all the bachelors of the quarter. The *burj*, or watch tower, in the villages beyond the border, is always attached to the house of the chief, and is in constant use as a place of refuge and observation in case of feuds between the different clans of a village community as well as against enemies outside. One ward was often pitted against another in deadly feud.

The habitations of the villagers are mostly constructed of mud, one storeyed, and not higher than ten feet. In the Khattak hills, stone, of which there is plenty, cemented with mud and unplastered is used. Inside the house will usually be found a corn bin made of clay, which contains the corn supply for immediate use; some beds, stools, swing-cots for the children, clothes-chest or safe made of wood, some spindles and earthen dishes. In the enclosures there is a shed for cattle and a large corn bin; this is raised from the ground, in shape like a bathing-machine, and contains the year's supply of grain, and it is from this the bin inside is replenished.

The tribal territory is parcelled out into blocks, of which each is held separately, by a clan or section of a clan. Periodical redistributions were provided at fixed periods. These were made by casting lots. At a redistribution a re-enumeration of the tribes was made, and if it happened that the division of land which had fallen to a certain tribe contained more than the number of shares to which they were entitled by the new enumeration, a part of another tribe, whose shareholders were in excess of the land which had fallen to them, or colonists who had accompanied the main tribe, were associated for the shares with the tribe who had land in excess of shareholders. The mode of apportionment is thus described by Dr. Bellew. The land to be divided is first marked off into compact blocks, each of which is subdivided into the required number of allotments. After the measurement and primary division of a block its distribution is regularly by lot. It is thus managed. The representative of each of the clans to share in the distribution selects a private mark (a piece of wood or a rag, a grain of maize, or pellet of sheep's dung, or a stone, or any substance near at hand), which, in the presence of all, he hands over to the "greybeard" appointed to cast the lot, declaring it to be his token. The greybeard, having collected all the tokens and seen them severally recognized, gathers them together in the skirt of his frock, and then walks round the block of land, followed by the assembly; and as he passes them throws on each of the plots marked off the first token that comes into his hand. The several plots then become the possession of the clans severally represented by the token thrown out on them. Each plot is then successively divided and allotted in a similar manner to the divisions of the clans and their several respective families. In the ultimate divisions the portions of land are often of very small extent, and are frequently styled *pucha*, after the process thus described. In thus dividing the lands for cultivation the clan blocks are in detached plots all around the village roads, watercourses and wastes intervening. Each block is known by a separate name expressing some quality of the soil. The division gives each section or tribe or clan a fixed possession in the soil. Each individual's share is scattered according to lot in the different blocks. Very often it is customary to exchange places at fixed periods of five, ten, or more years. The land always remains the share of the original owners, but is mapped out afresh for distribution amongst the new owners, who all share equally with their own tribal divisions without reference to rank. In these exchanges between the tribes only the houses are left standing, and often these are deprived of their timbers. The title of the individual is never allowed to become extinct, though the actual extent of that title was never definitely assigned beyond his right to work one, two, or more ploughs in the *daftar*, as the fractional portion of a share. A man might leave his home and return after the lapse of years to find his claim uncontested.

The elders and the chiefs compose the village council; they are referred to on all matters of custom and matters affecting the village society. The village servants usually receive small grants of land free of charge in consideration of their service. They only intermarry among themselves, weaver with weaver, and so on.[1]

I do not think we could get much better evidence than these two examples of the position I have been striving to establish for the village community in comparative custom.

Before, however, passing away from them there is a fact to bring into prominence which is of considerable importance to the study of the question in Britain. It is the relationship of the tribe to the village—the tribe as an unstable human swarm, the village as the material shell within which the swarm has settled. Before the village community came under scientific observation, the chief factor in human organization, as it appeared to the student, was the tribe; now that attention has centred upon the village community, the tribe has been lost sight of, and the family has taken its place. Within the village community was discovered the joint family, and it has been assumed rather than proved that the grouping of these primitive families together was the origin of the village community. Our evidence takes us to the exactly opposite view of the case. It suggests that the village community arose from the breaking up of the tribes into families, and that the break up of the families led on to the individualism of modern civilization. The question is one of general interest in inquiries of this kind, but it is of special importance to us now, because the relationship of the tribe to the village community will go a long way to explain the history of the village community in Britain. The Indian example we have just examined exhibits very clearly the tribe separating into ancestral units, and again

[1] "Gazetteer of the Peshawar District, Punjab," pp. 52, 120, 126; "Report on the Census of the Panjáb," vol. i. p. 192.

breaking up into family units, and this is the phenomenon produced from other parts of India, where "the tribe may be watched breaking up into villages, and the village disseminating the germ of fresh village colonization."[1] Thus, as Mr. Tupper has remarked upon evidence from the Punjab, "it is usual for the tribe first to hold its mark jointly, and tribes thus at first enjoying land in common do, as a matter of fact, afterwards crystallize into villages of the familiar description."[2] And it is worth while going on to point out another feature in the history of the village community in India, namely, that "its roots strike their firmest grasp and its stock grows with its greatest vigour in the soil of anarchy and private war; ... any exceptional strength of the corporation and unusual degree of union amongst its members may often be directly due, like the endurance of the Arab character, to the dangers of its environments."[3]

We shall presently examine the parallels to these Indian examples, which are to be found in Britain. As we proceed with this examination, more details of the Indian village community will be brought into relief, but it must be borne in mind that these details will not be merely abstract observations, drawn up by the student from some general field of study, but actual living details belonging to some such definite examples of the village community in India, as the two we have just had before us. If these details of the Indian village community illustrate and explain a rural custom or a phase of village economy in Britain, they likewise take back that custom or economical feature to the village community which once enshrined it within its borders, but which has now nearly everywhere been broken up into congeries of local observances, rural practices, peasant thoughts which lie loosely scattered up and down the country like the tesseræ of some shattered mosaic pavements revealed only by the rude disturbance of the plough. In some cases we may piece these fragments together. Only the light shed by comparative custom will

[1] "Punjab Customary Law," vol. ii. p. 28.   [2] Ibid., p. 22.
[3] Ibid., p. 24.

enable us satisfactorily to accomplish this, and we shall frequently have occasion to refer back to the Indian examples just examined. If we find by this means that much of the village life of Britain may be restored to its place as fragments of village communities, there will remain the further question as to the origin of these institutions, and here again we shall find it necessary to refer back to the Indian evidence.

We have ascertained, therefore, as general results from our examination of the Indian evidence, first, that the village community originated in the tribe; secondly, that it owes its most permanent features to the unrest of warlike times. As particular results we have to note that the village community does not belong to one ethnic stock, but is sufficiently elastic to embrace within its system contributions from successive waves of people, where these people have followed up conquest by settlement. If we can find in the British evidence stages in the history of the village community parallel to those in India; if we can see the village community commencing in the tribe, and the tribe breaking up into the village; if we can discover traces of ethnic influences and the results of fierce contests waged over the heads of the villages, we may at least fairly conclude that the village community in Britain has had much the same sort of history as it has in India, and that therefore all the forces which have helped to build it up must have been derived from such primitive tribes as we know to have lived and settled in the land.

CHAPTER III.

METHODS OF DEALING WITH THE BRITISH EVIDENCE.

Now that the evidence of comparative custom as to the primitive origin and characteristics of the village community is placed fairly before us, it becomes an important question as to the right method of dealing with the British evidence. Clearly it must be re-arranged; for until now no notice has been taken of the race elements, while very great prominence has been given to the dominating force of Roman influence. Rome was a highly centralized and highly civilized power, and long before the appearance of its forces in Britain it had passed through the stage of the village community. According to our evidence it cannot have entered into the English village system at all, and the striking out of such an important factor necessitates a re-examination of the methods of dealing with the British evidence.

It is singular how persistent the practice has been to trace back everything in English institutions to Roman influences. It was the invarying object of most of our earlier antiquaries, and in this age the learning and research of a great scholar have revived in double force the old theories. While, however, the judgment which Mr. Freeman passed upon the conclusions of Mr. Coote—a judgment endorsed by Sir Henry Maine—seemed to be confirmed by the absolute silence with which Mr. Coote passed over the evidence as to the survival of the primitive village community in Britain, this institution, in the masterful hands of Mr. Seebohm, has itself been brought within the area of Roman influences. What Jacob Grimm has said of the old attempts to trace the gods, mythic fancies, and pagan rituals of our ancestors to the intrusion of Roman ideas, I am inclined to repeat with reference to these attempts to trace back English institutions to the Roman chronological era, and there to leave off the inquiry as if there was nothing more to be said, or as if no races prior to the Romans had occupied the country. "At that rate," says the great German scholar, "Wuotan might without more ado be traced back to Jupiter, Holda to Diana, the Alp to the genius, all German mythology to Roman, and nothing be left us of our own but the bare soil that drank in the foreign doctrine." But even the soil is not our own if Mr. Seebohm is correct in his opinions that the English village community was reared on the undestroyed and living Romanized land system. And the wonder of it is that with this excessive saturation of Roman influences we have still left to us an English language which presents us unhesitatingly with English words for all these Roman institutions, and yet *ex hypothesi* tells us nothing of the English institutions which had thus become replaced. The difficulties of such a position, however, are too numerous to be stated succinctly. Let the word *folkmoot* translate whatever Roman word for council it may be supposed to best represent, and still the English institution rears itself up quite independently of the Roman, and tells us of a bit of the old Aryan world. The plain fact is, that just as in mythology, according to the overwhelming proofs of Jacob Grimm, so in institutions there is very little room for Roman elements on English soil; and the more so when it seems certain that we must find room for an intrusion of the more primitive elements of earlier and ruder races. Undoubtedly there is much which is not Teutonic or Celtic in the village community as it is found in Britain. But before we can turn to Roman institutions as the source of this extraneous influence we must be quite sure that the natural course of events following upon the successive waves of an Aryan conquest of an extensive Iberic population does not adequately account for the phenomena.

Let us pass on from the question of race to some of the

other results brought out by authorities up to this time. At the most the theory of a Roman origin for the English village community only seeks to account for the economical phenomena. The village community in serfdom, under a manor and its lord, is the formula which is presented to us, the dual constitution of village and manor appearing as two distinct institutions which meet together on the Romanized soil of England, but always remaining distinct. Unquestionably we have here a phase of economical development which needs some kind of explanation to bridge over the period from its origin to the point where the history of commercial economics begins, and we will endeavour to see how the Roman theory accounts for it.

If we get behind the formula, presented to us for convenience of argument, we may first consider its application to the homestead. The Roman villa is clearly not the parent of such a state of things as Mr. Thorold Rogers has pictured from the records of old manorial accounts. He finds that the houses of the villagers were built of wattles smeared inside and out with mud or clay, and were crowded near the church in the street of the settlement. In all cases the church was the common hall of the parish and a fortress in time of danger, occupying the site of the stockade which had been built when the first settlers occupied the ground. In the body of the church were frequently stored products, corn and wool. Here, too, the common feasts of the parish were held. The only houses of any pretension in the village were the lord's, the parson's, and the miller's.[1] What these latter were may be gathered by some of the remains which have lasted down to modern days. Some eighty or ninety years ago there was in Shropshire an old building called Gatacre Hall. It was nearly an exact square. At each corner and in the middle of each side and in the centre was an immense oak, hewed nearly square and without branches, set with its head on large stones laid about a foot deep in the ground, and with its

[1] Rogers' "Economical Interpretation of History," p. 14. The sketch is taken from an Elizabethan MS. in the Record Office. Compare the stockaded Pathān village with its burj, *ante*, p. 37.

PRIMITIVE CHARACTERISTICS OF ENGLISH VILLAGES. 45

roots uppermost, which roots with a few rafters formed a complete arched roof.[1] Here we have, with most singular exactness, a description in miniature of the primitive Aryan house which is to be met with in Media.[2] These being the hives which held the human swarm it is impossible not to perceive that they

THE ARYAN HOUSE IN MEDIA.

belonged to a primitive stage of society. There is no indication here of commercial intercourse, no connection with the world outside the village community, which was to the villagers

[1] "Archæologia," vol. iii. p. 112; Guest's "Origines Celticæ," vol. ii. p. 65. Compare Clarke's "Survey of the Lakes," p. xx.
[2] *Cf.* Viollet le Duc's "Habitations of Man," p. 126.

a world of foreigners.[1] And how completely the theory of a Roman origin of such homesteads breaks down is emphasized by the fact that though contiguity with Roman civilization may here and there be shown in the English villages,[2] continuity of Roman systems of building is disproven by the absolute disappearance in England, between the Roman era and the fifteenth century of such a great manufacturing industry as brickmaking.[3]

The villager in his wattle and daub, the lord in his oak-rooted hall, surely carry us back to primitive economics within which there is no room for the great commercialism of the Roman world, stretching by means of its magnificent system of road inter-communication from one end of Europe to the other. This cannot by any theory be compressed into a sufficiently small compass to stand inside the world of the English villager, which was bounded only by his village lands. It would have to be deprived of all its centralizing forces, and among these of one of its principal economical features, namely, its system of taxation. The vast empire of Rome was necessarily supported by a complete method of taxation by which the various peoples brought under its sway were compelled to contribute to the expenses of government. Thus taxes appear to have formed one of the causes of the revolt of the Iceni, and are mentioned as oppressive in the harangue of Boadicea to her forces before the battle with Suetonius. But the economical system of Rome, which thus includes a system of regular taxation, does not find a place in the primitive economics of Teutonic England, where no such system existed.[4] On every side in England we see Rome and its

---

[1] The instances of villagers considering all outside their own boundaries as foreigners are curious survivals of the primitive conditions of things, and the fact has been recorded in the present century.

[2] Seebohm's "English Village Community," pp. 424-436; *American Journ. Arch.*, June, 1888, p. 219; *Antiquary*, Nov., 1885, p. 224.

[3] Rogers' "Economical Interpretation of History," p. 279; *cf.* Baring Gould's "Lives of the Saints," vol. i. p. 169.

[4] "Essays in Anglo-Saxon Laws," 60; Dowell's "History of Taxation and Taxes," vol. i. p. 7.

civilization destroyed or pushed on one side. Not only are cities and villas and roads trampled underfoot or under the plough, but commerce and its economical system are pushed out of the way by village communities and their self-contained, self-supporting exclusiveness. Stone and bricks lie in heaps as at Caerleon, Wroxeter, Silchester, and Verulam, to be replaced by wattle and daub and uncarpentered oaks.[1] Manufactured luxuries of all kinds ceased to exist, and the villager was clothed from the products of his own village, woven by the females of his own family. We shall find, as we proceed, that commercial economy made very slow progress in Britain until quite late down in its history; one village, it may be, exchanged raw produce with another village, villagers performing common duties and paying common dues; but all of it—exchanges and payments alike—was based not upon any possible theory of economics, but upon what was *customary*. As Mr. Maitland puts it of the thirteenth century, "when men spoke of a manor they thought primarily of the single group of tenants who worked in common at their ploughings and their reapings."[2] But then these agricultural communities, though decked with the title of manor, were not created by any definite act of State or sovereign—they were the product of deep-rooted custom and dependent upon custom for all their doings and all their rights. On the outskirts of our land we find such facts as the following: Coarse flax sown in the ground was manufactured into shirts and other linens by the farmer's wife and daughters during the long winter evenings, and the farmer himself was clothed from the fleece of his little flock. They ground their corn by means of the quern, *i.e.*, a couple of light millstones set in motion with the hand by

[1] Too little attention has been given to the structural details of old houses. On the use of rudely carpentered timber in early times there is very useful evidence yet to be made known. A high room in Castle Grant, Abernethy, appears to have been floored with deals which were never planed, but were first split with wedges and then dressed with axe and adze. The marks of the adze across the boards are still visible. Sinclair's "Stat. Acc. of Scotland," vol. xiii. p. 132.

[2] "Select Pleas of Manor Rolls," p. xl.

means of a staff fixed to the upper stone. All the bread thus made was generally consumed by the month of June, and they then chiefly subsisted on their own sheep and the milk of their cows, with what fish they chanced to catch. And that this picture from the Scottish islands was parallelled in England is proven by the tenacity with which, even in villages which had won their place among municipal towns, the old industrial economy was made the basis of the new municipal rights, and for centuries kept the conception of rent away from the facts of municipal organization. I shall have occasion later on to give examples of the village community in municipal institutions; but, in the meantime, I must point out here that an absolute wrench from the old commercial economy of the Roman world to the primitive economy of the village system is the only means which adequately accounts for some of the facts connected with the early English history of many of our chief towns. No better example could be given than that of London, and I will briefly point out some of the main features of this evidence.

London originated in the Roman hill-fort, for I take it that whether we agree with Dr. Guest or not as to Plautius in A.D. 43 having first occupied the site of the future capital of England,[1] there can be no doubt that any Celtic existence which the place may have had was not of a nature to influence its later history. But from Roman times the remarkable fact remains that commercial greatness began to dispute for preeminence with military greatness. London took her place in the Roman Empire. Roadways converged to her. The two great roads, Ermyn Street and Watling Street, entered Roman London at our now-called Bishopsgate and Newgate points of the city boundary proper, and connected the city with all parts of Britain. In Mr. Green's words, " the route which crossed the downs of Kent from Richborough to the Thames linked the roads that radiated from London over the surface of the island with the general network of communication along

---

[1] "Origines Celticæ," vol. ii. p. 405.

THE FALL OF ROMAN LONDON.

which flowed the social and political life of the Roman world."[1]

Such roadways were among the first undertakings of the Romans in a conquered country,[2] and by their means the towns grew up to an importance quite out of proportion to their native capacity. London became a great centre of Roman commerce. Her life was connected with all outer life by the great causeways which the Roman soldier had built; her wall girt her round securely from the immediate outer world, and when her citizens looked for the means of gaining the necessaries of life and wealth they took their stand at the city gates and looked up the roadways which led to Verulamium, Etocetum, and Uriconium; to Duromagus and Eboracum, to Portus Magnus, and to Continental Rome.[3]

This is one of the most important and distinctive facts to notice in connection with Roman London. The native capacity of British cities for greatness depended on causes perfectly local in character; but as soon as Rome brought them, by means of her great system of roadways, into the imperial system, development moved at a pace measurable, not by British skill but by Roman necessities. This important factor in the history of Roman towns in Britain has not been sufficiently dwelt upon. It accounts for a great deal that is otherwise unaccountable. It bridges over years of rapid progress with a history that belongs not to Britain but to Rome; it accounts for the rapid uprising of London into Augusta, and it accounts for her wonderful progress and wealth during the Roman rule. During all this time London is the London connected by roadways with the commerce and progress of the Roman world; her British history, if she had any, is past and gone, and one has to think of her, not as situated in Britain, but as situated on the Ermyn and Watling Streets, which were connected with all other parts of Britain,

[1] "The Making of England," p. 3.
[2] Arnold's "Roman Provincial System," p. 16.
[3] See Arnold's "Roman Provincial System," p. 208, for the relation ship of a town to the surrounding district.

and which brought London more closely into connection with other cities situated on the roadways than with the natives who still occupied the open country. She dominated the country round her, no doubt, just as all Roman cities did; but she was independent of it, and used it for her own purposes, as contributory to her wealth and luxury, not to her necessities. Thus, then, the distinction which we see Roman London occupying, and one which is very important to our present subject, is its connection with the Roman world, its place on the Roman roadways; and not its connection with the Celtic Britons, who lived near it, nor its place on the map of Britain.

Now let us turn to the significant story of her fall. It is a story for the most part told from the silence of history rather than from the monuments of history. London was nothing, and meant nothing, to the barbaric conquerors who gradually closed upon her. The Saxon conquerors did not march, as the Roman conquerors had done, straight to this stronghold, and pounce upon it as a point of vantage; or as the Danes did later on, and William still later. The fight between Roman London and the Teutons was of a different character altogether. Sharp sword-and-shield conflicts there were, no doubt, but these did not decide the battle. It was the breaking-up of her connection with the outer world that broke the power of Roman London.

Mr. Green has depicted the events with incisive force. "The conquest of Kent," he says, "had broken its communications with the Continent; and whatever trade might struggle from the southern coast through the Weald had been cut off by the conquest of Sussex. That of the Gwent, about Winchester, closed the road to the south-west; while the capture of Cunetio interrupted all communication with the valley of the Severn. And now the occupation of Hertfordshire cut off the city from Northern and Central Britain."[1] It was thus that Roman London passed into another stage of her history—the work of two hundred long years of almost

[1] "The Making of England," p. 110.

unbroken silence so far as history is concerned, but a work as effectual and a silence as eloquent as if the clash and din of arms had dictated the most stirring epic poetry.

What we have now got to do is to ascertain what this silence of history really means. It can be explained if the Saxon conquerors came into the land organized upon the tribal system, and therefore unacquainted with the system that made commerce one of the chief agents of social and political progress. Their treatment of the towns shows that they did not understand their value, and, barbarian-like, they trod them under foot. A conspicuous example of this is to be found in the well-known account which Roger of Wendover gives of the fall of Andredesceaster. The citizens "were all put to the sword and their town totally destroyed. The desolate site is still pointed out by the traveller. Ella and his three sons remained in that district, which they proceeded to cultivate; it is called, to this day, in English, 'Sussex,' or the country of the South Saxons."[1] It is not the recorded destruction which is the important point here, as most historians have seemed to think, but that after the destruction the destroyers settled and began to cultivate. They commenced, in short, at the very bottom of the ladder of political life. They did not occupy the palaces, or the temples, or the senate-house, or the dwelling-places of the conquered Roman citizens. They nestled down on the open lands by the side of the old city, and began to cultivate in their own fashion.

The cultivation and improvement of the country, says Adam Smith, must be prior to the increase of the town.[2] The facts connected with the post-Roman history of London exactly fit in with this rule of political economy. We see the Saxon cultivator approaching near. Mr. Green tells us by what route and how;[3] and, though I cannot agree with the

[1] "Roger of Wendover," anno 492; "Anglo Saxon Chronicle," anno 491.

[2] "Wealth of Nations," book iii. cap. i.

[3] "Making of England," p. 110.

opinion of Dr. Guest that good reasons may be given for the belief that even London itself for awhile lay desolate and uninhabited, we must recognize the settlement of the little village of Charing within bow-shot of its ruins. Kensington and Fulham occupy clearings to the west, while Hampstead and Islington on the north almost complete the chain.

If we pause to consider what these settlements were like, we cannot doubt that they were based upon the village community system. Mr. Seebohm has been enabled to trace out evidence of the open-field system in the lands at Westminster which made up the scenery for the dying eyes of Edward the Confessor;[1] and when we come to consider that Lammas lands, and all the historical significance of these curious relics of the early village system, existed on the site now occupied by Leicester Square, there can be no difficulty, I think, in concluding that the settlement at Charing and elsewhere near London was an agricultural settlement. This, then, is where the Saxon destroyers of London were busying themselves during that long period of history of which we know nothing; and the reason that we know nothing is that the business was the business of settlement and "making"—that ordinary routine of life which is never chronicled by indigenous historians—but which nevertheless was fatal to the London of Roman origin.

Without going into the history of commerce in Anglo-Saxon Britain, there are sufficient broad facts to indicate the wide difference of the London built upon the old Roman ways and the London hemmed in by Saxon communities.

The evidence of early Anglo-Saxon commerce is meagre enough, so meagre indeed as to suggest the probability of its not being very extensive.[2] The first important notice which we have of the subject is not of earlier date than the close of the eighth century;[3] and the chief articles of commerce were

---

[1] Seebohm's "Village Community," p. 100.

[2] See Macpherson's "Annals of Commerce," vol. 1.

[3] Craik's "History of British Commerce," p. 62; *cf.* also for this later period Spence's "Equitable Jurisdiction of the Court of Chancery," vol. i. p. 53.

objects of gold and silver, slaves, horses, and the metals. The tolls imposed at the landing-place of Billingsgate by Ethelred all relate to wine, fish, and other produce of this nature. What I am anxious to arrive at is that the Saxon commerce of London was not a food commerce, showing the city to be simply an emporium for the surrounding agricultural communities. Mr. Craik says there is no evidence or reason for believing that a single cargo of corn was ever exported from England during the whole of the Anglo-Saxon period;[1] and, looking at the nature of the settlement in England by self-supporting communities, we can well understand this to be so. We can get a step further from another standpoint. Mill observes that the things most liable to fluctuations in value, those directly influenced by the seasons, and especially food, were seldom carried to any distance in Europe during the Middle Ages. Each locality depended as a general rule on its own produce and that of its immediate neighbourhood. In most years accordingly there was in some part or other of any large country a real dearth;[2] and in this fact we get a clue to the chief causes of the famines that occurred in England during the early ages. Not only was there not a single cargo of corn exported from England, but it was not exported from one locality to another.[3]

[1] "History of British Commerce," vol. i. p. 69.
[2] "Political Economy," book iv. cap. ii. sec. 4.
[3] So late as 1257 the importation of corn from Germany to meet a famine is looked upon as a special and unusual circumstance, and as such is recorded in the "Chronicles of the Mayors and Sheriffs of London." In this year, it says, there was a failure of the crops; upon which a famine ensued to such a degree that people from the villages resorted to the city for food, and then upon the famine waxing still greater many thousand persons perished; many thousands more, too, would have died of hunger had not corn just then arrived from Almaine (p. 40).

At the latter part of the last century most of the villages in England, and almost all of them in Scotland, were independent of the world, so far as food was concerned. The corn they grew and the cattle they fed was sufficient, and more than sufficient, for their support. Carry this fact up the stream of time, and we arrive at a general rule applicable to early Saxon times and their commercial supineness. A curious glimpse of this

The importance of these facts is brought out more clearly when we know that the relics of London municipal history show that the Teutonic conquerors of the city reared up a system of government which is stamped with the mark of its primitive origin. This we shall deal with later on, but we may leave the significant history of the fall of London with the remark that it comes right athwart the continuity of Roman influences and brings into startling prominence the chasm which separated the economical system of Rome from that of Anglo-Saxon Britain. We may accentuate this position by noting the definitions which apply to the two systems—the commercial economy of Rome is the exact opposite of the village economy of early England.

We will now consider the one remaining factor in the famous formula, namely, serfdom. In post-Domesday times this serfdom is stamped with one great mark of an artificial origin, namely, its singular uniformity. Now this can only be explained it appears to me, as the uniformity which belongs essentially to official documents. Commissioners set to find out "Quot villani, quot cotarii, quot servi," existed in the conquered lands of the Norman legal-minded sovereign, would fit in the results to suit the questions; they would see uniformity in spite of innumerable local differences, and they would only note such radical differences as occurred in the Danish districts; and the importance of Domesday as a judicial record would gradually stamp its language upon the land history of the country.[1] Thus both the origin and authority of Domesday

is given by Giraldus Cambrensis, in speaking of the district of Wye, so late as the eleventh century. The country, he says, sufficiently abounds in grain, and if there is any deficiency it is amply supplied from the neighbouring part of England (p. 350).

[1] It is curious to note, however, that Mr. Maitland, in his able introduction to "Select Pleas of Manorial Courts," draws attention to the extreme diversity of the jurisdiction exercised in manorial courts. The English courts, he says, never came to a classification of those franchises similar to that which obtained in France. See p. xxv, *et ante ;* and on page 3 of his text he points out that the custom of stewards carrying about their rolls from manor to manor "must have tended to produce a great uniformity in manorial custom."

have tended to produce uniformity in the details of English land tenure. But even this does not hide its true origin.

The serfdom of the English *villani* when brought down to the uniformity of statistical information tells us of (*a*) three days' work for the lord every week; (*b*) special work at request; (*c*) payments in money or kind; (*d*) the requirement of the lord's licence for the marriage of a daughter. And comparative custom may answer for all these, and prove that not being exclusively Saxon, they were not necessarily produced by facts which belong exclusively to English history. In the Ditmarsh free community " every one was free to employ himself on his own account for three days in the week—from Saturday at sunrise to Tuesday at sunrise "[1]—a service which fits exactly into the facts of the English villein service, but departs most significantly from the mere words of the English formula. Again suit and service, both of money and kind, meet us everywhere in the Indian village communities, and there is a very remarkable development of it in the Fiji communities.[2] So, too, with the fine for the marriage of a daughter, the exact parallel is the Indian custom in Kachahrî : " whenever a cultivator marries off one of his daughters he pays a fee, called bau, to the landed proprietor of his village."[3] These signs of serfdom in Saxon England then *need* not have originated from the Roman villa because they can be shown not to have so originated in other places.

" No doubt," says Mr. Seebohm, " the Teutonic notion of a subjugated people was that of a people reduced to serfdom or villeinage. *They*—the conquerors—were the nation, the freemen. The conquered race were the aliens, subjected to gafol and servitude."[4] But who were the conquered race, these aliens ? Mr. Seebohm carries up the evidence of their existence and position to the earliest Saxon times, and then they become

---

[1] *Archæologia*, vol. xxxvii., p. 378.

[2] *Archæological Review*, vol. ii. pp. 367–376.

[3] Carnegy's " Kachahrî Technicalities," quoted *Folklore Record*, v. 36. Mr. Ashley in his " English Economic History," vol. i. p. 21, illustrates how this became stamped in English law as a mark of serfdom.

[4] " English Village Community," p. 145.

merged in Roman history; but my suggestion will be that they have a history of their own yet unwritten, and which reveals some remarkable lost chapters in early British history. In the meantime, let me emphasize here the vast importance of Mr. Seebohm's results. To those who cannot bridge over years of silent history by appealing to comparative custom, his results are simply invaluable. He proves most conclusively and succinctly that the main features of the village community, though not set down with precise terminology in the chronicles, charters, and other documentary sources of evidence, existed through all the years of Saxon, Norman, and later English history, and did not need explanation because they were so well understood without it. In the face of such an authority as Fustel de Coulanges, the importance of this evidence cannot be over-rated. Because Cæsar and Tacitus and the *leges barbarorum* do not mention the village community and its complex system of social organization, it is no longer open to any one to say that, therefore, the village community arose in later times. Mr. Seebohm's researches stand as a protest against such a conclusion, and a protest which has the force of almost mathematical demonstration. But I desire to emphasize the results of Mr. Seebohm's chronological investigation on other grounds than these. They make perfectly clear the whole period from Saxon to modern times. The village communities wherever they may be found to exist in Great Britain are to all intents and purposes one and the same institution. A nineteenth-century village community is only an unchanged sixth-century institution. Back to the sixth century all is clear, and the evidence I shall bring forward, surviving in records or practices, can at once be labelled as belonging to the sixth century. From this point, however, chronology leaves us and comparative custom only can be our guide. And by this method of research we shall go back into the unknown periods of British history, showing that Teuton, Celt, and Iberian all had a share in the building up of the village communities of Britain, because it is only thus that we can explain the parallel between the villages of Britain and of India, both lands being the battle-ground of races, where the results of the conflict show the non-Aryan agriculturist subordinated to an Aryan overlordship.

What, then, was the relationship between the Roman economical system and the primitive economics of early English villagers? This is a question which must be answered, because in our progress backwards, from the sixth century to the unknown periods beyond, the solid history of Roman Britain has, undoubtedly, to be reckoned with. I have attempted to show that it does not account for some of the more prominent facts of the Anglo-Saxon village system; but it is important to turn from the negative side of the question and ascertain, if possible, what relationship the imperial power in Britain bore to the tribal settlements beneath it.

Let us get at the answer to this question by first noting two interesting facts which bring out the parallel between the Roman of the old civilization and the English of the modern civilization. Mr. Seebohm and, following him, Professor Earle are desirous of establishing the identity of Anglo-Saxon charter boundaries of land with the Roman agrimensorial system. "The boundaries of the land," says the latter, "are described starting from such a point or such an object and passing through a series of stations until the starting-point is reached again—as a general rule this part of the deed is in English; sometimes, however, in Latin or a mixture of Latin and English. It must not, however, be imagined from the use of the vernacular in this part that this member is more native than the rest of the deed. It is just the continuation of an old Roman usage, the formula of which may be seen in the book of Hyginus, the land surveyor. It is the formula that was used by the agrimensores of the Empire when they had to describe the irregular ground which did not well admit of their rectangular system of mensuration and allotment."[1] But it is also a very natural method of describing boundaries and is practised in many places which have never been in the slightest degree affected by Roman

[1] "Land Charters and other Saxonic Documents," p. xxvi.

agrimensorial formulæ. When one considers the valuable information supplied by Mr. Coote as to the existence of very distinct traces of nearly all the forms of Roman terminal marks, including the singular *botontini*, it is a little difficult to believe that the natural boundaries described in the charters are agrimensorial boundaries. And when put to the test of examination by a practical surveyor, we find this difficulty re-stated and accompanied by the only possible solution. Mr. R. Woolley, whose intimate knowledge of the open-field system must be presumed from his business association with his father, who gave such valuable evidence before the Enclosure Commission, in explaining the agrimensorial system says : "It is interesting to compare the powers and duties of a valuer in an enclosure of open-field lands and commons of our day, with those of an Agrimensor, in the foundation of a Roman colony; the Parliamentary Provisional order, the survey, road-making, and setting out allotments, the security of title to the land given by the award, the usages and the award confirmed by the commissioners and deposited in duplicate both in the parish and at the Land Office, publicly denoting the completion of the business and the termination of the valuer's powers—all these come to mind in describing an assignment."[1]

This suggestive comparison shows that the Roman surveying system had passed forward from the contemplation of village communities to the contemplation of landed estates, and had therefore approached the professional English surveyor of to-day, whose education does not include a study of primitive economics. And so it was with the Roman lawyer. "The impression left on my mind," says Sir Henry Maine, "by a variety of passages in the Roman legal records, is that, if a Roman lawyer had been asked to take into his mental view a number of persons having rights together over the same property, he would have contemplated them not as enjoying it in turn, but as dividing it at once between them."[2] The remark holds good of English lawyers, at least from the times of the Tudors. In Elizabeth's reign

[1] "Proceedings of Surveyors Institute," xvi. p. 212.
[2] "Early Law and Custom," p. 344.

they saw what was going on in Ireland, and later, under the East India Company, they saw what was going on in India; and yet could only translate the facts of the village land holding thus coming under their notice by terms applicable to the modern legal conception of estates in absolute possession of individual owners. But English lawyers did not learn this idea of absolute possession from English custom,[1] and the source of their knowledge is an interesting commentary upon this point of our inquiry. The villeins always had security of tenure (*adscripti glebæ*), and it was only the influence of Roman law from the time of Glanvill to that of Edward IV. which introduced the legal doctrine that the villeins could have absolutely no property at all—a doctrine so opposed to English sentiment and English custom that, however glad the Norman lords might have been to lay claim to the ownership of the land under its specious terminology, they did not for whole centuries do violence to public opinion, which, after all, was an inheritance from their fathers which they themselves shared.[2]

It thus appears that the Roman surveyor and the Roman lawyer meet with their true parallel in English history, not in the early days of Anglo-Saxon settlement, but in the modern English surveyor and the modern English lawyer, and we are now enabled to suggest an answer to the question of the relationship between the Roman system of economics and the primitive system of early English villagers. The suggestion I am anxious to make takes us back to India once more. In the "Gazetteer of the Rohtak District," 1883-4 (p. 17), occurs the following important passage: "We know that the hosts of many a conqueror must have carried fire and sword through the land before the southern plunderers and northern fanatics contended for the possession of it; that many a royal state progress must have taken place through the district to the hunting grounds of Hánsi and Hissár; that ever since Delhi became the capital of India, a tract lying so close to it must

---

[1] "The law of real property was really nothing but a collection of customs" ("Essays in Anglo-Saxon Law," p. 56).
[2] Ashley's "Economic History," p. 38.

have been profoundly affected by the events of the dynastic annals; but not a trace of all this remains. Only the villages themselves, unbroken and unchanged, exist as they existed eight hundred years ago. To no tract in North India do the words of Lord Metcalfe, quoted below, more aptly apply than to the Rohtak district—'Village communities seem to last where nothing else lasts. Dynasty after dynasty changes; revolution succeeds revolution; Hindú, Pathán, Múghal, Mahrattá, Sikh, English, are all masters in turn, but the village community remains the same.'" This passage supplies us with the only explanation possible to account for the facts of the Roman occupation of this island. If we took away all the military strength of Britain from India there would remain the village communities to be administered, not conquered, by the next military empire who desired to acquire the wealth of India. When the Romans took away their military strength from Britain there remained the Celtic communities — the clans and the tribes — just as intact as they were before the conquest.[1] Where the Roman influence was most felt was in the tightening up of the loosely-knit communal bonds, resulting in a stronger and more lasting crystallization of existing forms whose natural development had been arrested by the iron hand of a military master. It is the line of arrestment which is so marked in the history of the village community in Britain—a line, on one side of which is all the primitive life of Britain, on the other side of which is the force which kept that primitive life back so long and so unchanged that it lost its elasticity and its capacity for change, and has in consequence survived into later ages. Roman influence never entered inside the village community; it was strong enough as an outside power, forcing loosely-knit tribes into concentrated villages, but it never became, and never could become a part of the village system.

[1] I have explained my reasons for this view in the preface to the volume of "Gentleman's Magazine Library; Roman Remains," to which I may perhaps venture to refer readers interested on the point which is really an important one.

THE WELSH TRIBAL COMMUNITIES.

A most interesting proof of this is derived from the communities of Wales. Mr. Wright has proved on very good evidence that Wales was more thoroughly Romanized than other parts of Britain. And yet in Wales we have that remarkable body of evidence in the laws and in the land customs of later times, which first introduces us to the tribal community, a more primitive institution than the village community. This primitive tribal community must have survived the Roman conquest. If the evidence of Roman influences is to be taken into account, it should be traced more completely in the tribal communities of Wales; and it is exactly here that Mr. Seebohm traces no such influences. "The Welsh system," he says, "was not manorial, its unit was not a village community on a lord's estate; ... the point to be noted is the scattering of the tyddyns [households] all over the country side, and the clustering of them by fours and sixteens or twelves into the group which was the unit paying the food rents." It is very clear that this distinction between the village community and the tribal community is a marked one —so marked, indeed, as to have suggested that differing degrees of Roman influence are the primary cause of it, the village communities, under this view, having been strongly influenced by Rome, and the tribal communities having escaped. But first of all we have seen that this Roman influence does not account for much of the economical phenomena of the village community in England; then we have noted that history proves that Roman influences were as pronounced in Wales, the home of the tribal community, as in England. It would seem, therefore, that we must, *prima facie*, shift our view of Roman influences altogether and see in the artificial clustering of tribal households for the purposes of taxation some relics of that influence which is not so discoverable in the more closely bound system of the village community. Again let us turn to India, and see if the evidence of comparative custom does not help us to discover some clue to the relationship between these two classes of early communities which have been so conveniently termed the village and the tribal system.

One of the most valuable of the settlement reports is that of Mr. J. B. Lyall on the Kangra District of the Panjab. In this district Mr. Lyall found two classes of communities, which he has designated by the not very happy term of hamlet and freehold communities.[1] But in reality these two communities are exact equivalents to the tribal and village communities of Britain. The freehold communities, situated on the plains, hold their arable lands in intermixed allotments; the hamlet communities, situated on the hills, hold their lands in scattered household groups carved out of the waste. And then we have this remarkable statement. The hamlet communities are grouped into mauzahs or circuits, which "seem to have grown out of one man during a length of time, collecting the land rents either as a government agent or government assignee. The circuit as regards its waste lands was a mere arbitrary and loosely defined division of the principality, as regards its cultivated lands it was a chance collection of independent family holdings, which were sometimes one household, but oftener a group of kinsmen, the descendants of a common ancestor holding shares of an ancestral estate and living on it in several houses." And a little later on Mr. Lyall says: "It may be worth while to make a guess as to the original cause of the difference between the tenure of land in these hills and that existing in the plains of the Panjab. It may, perhaps, have to do with the ethnology of the country; there is an idea current in the hills that of the landholding castes the Thakars, Ráthís, Kanets, and Girths, are either indigenous to the hills or of mixed race and indigenous by the half-blood, and that the Rájpúts, Brahmans, Khatris, Jats, and others, are the descendants of invaders and settlers from the plains. . . . The hills remained to a much later date than the plains, inhabited only by aboriginal tribes, and eventually they were invaded, not by tribes of settlers driving back the old inhabitants, but by military adventurers subduing them."[2] Taking into account too the influence of the physical features

[1] Lyall's "Settlement Report of Kangra District," p. 12.
[2] Ibid., p. 26.

of the country, the flat, defenceless plains allowing, if not inviting, a congregation of men into villages, the hills broken and irregular, preventing the formation of villages, I believe we have in these facts of Indian village life a key to the lost facts of English village life. The Roman tax-collector, like the government agent in India, formed the singular system found in Wales—a system arranged according to strict arithmetical rules for the purpose of paying the stipulated tax, and probably, as Mr. Seebohm remarks, for the discharge of other public duties, and not a system founded on a natural territorial arrangement, such as we find in the village communities. It thus appears that the marked artificiality of the Welsh tribal system may have been produced by the taxing system of Roman imperial government, which meeting the tribal community in a more or less developed state, formed it into artificial groups, and so stereotyped this arithmetical artificiality upon the history of Welsh communities.

We have seen that there was no room for Roman life and Roman economics within the villages of Britain. We have seen that keeping outside of this and stretching all along the wide and diversified lands of Britain the Romans produced a line of arrestment which marked the boundary between primitive and civilized life. We may now take into account the different state of things at the Teutonic conquest. Room *had* to be found in the villages or in the village system for these rude conquerors. Organized upon a primitive tribal system, they did not tower over and keep above the village system. They swarmed into the villages, pushing their way in and establishing their lordship to the land. They swarmed thus, quite irrespective of existing towns, pushing on one side all that stood in their path, carving out for themselves new villages where the old ones were not sufficient. Necessarily for such a process the settlements on the plains, not those on the inaccessible hills, were attacked and utilized; and hence the village system in the plains and valleys of Britain, just as the village system in the plains and valleys of India, became more complex and more diversified than the tribal system of the hills, because the settlements in the plains were broken into by an incoming race of villagers who, in taking their place inside the existing village communities, diverted the normal line of progress into that which has allowed us to trace out serfdom and over-lordship. So late as the time of Queen Elizabeth the main features of village life in Britain were traceable in exactly these two lines of hill and valley communities. "The mansion houses of our countrie townes and villages," says Harrison, "in champaine ground stand altogether by streets and joining one to an other, but in woodland soiles dispersed here and there each one upon the severall grounds of their owners."[1] This is only what Mr. Lyall asserts of India and attributes partly to natural causes, partly to the effects of conquest. And we may now assert the like causes for the like results in Britain.

We now pass on to another point in the necessary rearrangement of the British evidence. It is to be observed that the economical features of the village community are neither the most important nor the most ancient of the relics which have survived. The basis of the original settlement in villages was no doubt, as the rude types of savages have shown us, the common interest in procuring a food supply; but the cement which bound together the individual atoms of the Aryan clans which form the upper strata of the village communities of India and Europe was that of kinship. Wherever we find the village community has long been settled, no doubt the cement binding the whole group together has practically changed from kinship to land, but theoretically kinship still forms the basis. In old settlements there is always the danger of bringing into undue prominence the economical features which have imprinted themselves very deeply on the land, and of sinking into the background the social and religious features which, having had to meet the continuous and deadly opposition of such a magnificent religion as Christianity, have become lost to close observation among the local superstitions and customs of the people.

[1] Harrison's "Description of England" (N. Shakspere Soc.), pp. 237, 259.

These lost features of the village community—kinship and religion—have in their earliest forms affected the economical development to a considerable degree. We can in these find the answer to much that is not yet wholly understood in the history of the village community. The homestead was the basis of all rights in the village. The undivided family was the unit, and the individual was unrecognized. Fenced in by the sacredness of the ancient family worship at the hearth; kept together by the sanctity of a common ancestry; sending its superfluous sons to form daughter-communities in the unoccupied territories around; ruled and represented by the oldest male member—the homestead was occupied by its members of one blood and possessed a code of unwritten legal rules and an unwritten religious ritual, which have succeeded in stamping themselves upon the laws, customs, and traditional superstitions of succeeding ages after the old constitution of the primitive homestead had been broken up and distributed among the local institutions and the family rites of civilized times. When we noted in the first chapter how the evidence of folklore assisted us to understand the primitive nature of the village community and its sanction of traditional usage, it implied that there was something more than mere analogy in the aid which folklore renders in tracing out the relics of early village life. The traditional practices of agriculture provide us with the survivals of primitive economics; the traditional practices enshrined in folklore provide us with the survivals of primitive law and religion. And it is only when studying these two sections of the village community together that we can hope to deal adequately with its history on English soil. It would be singular, indeed, if the agricultural survivals led us up to one period of history for their origin, while the survivals of the house-religion led us up to another period. There can be no provable causes for such a twist in social development, and the more we study the types which will come before us, the more we shall find that the lessons of comparative custom point unfailingly to the English village community as a survival from prehistoric times, possessing within its shell evidence of old race conflicts and old race amalgamations, which in no other way are to be restored to historic observation.

Let it be clearly understood what is meant by race in these researches. In ancient times conquest and settlement were performed by races, not by nations. Independent evidence proves that in India, as in Britain and the Western world generally, three great races have exercised the principal influence upon the formation of institutions. In India there are two non-Aryan races preceding the Aryans; in Britain there is one non-Aryan race preceding two Aryan. The elements are the same, though the degrees of amalgamation are different; but the point to note is that successive settlements of distinct tribes over the same area produce certain economic results, the main feature of which is the tighter drawing together of the bonds which fasten the community—the fusion of the influences of kinship with the influences of power. The fusion happens to retain the marks of the original race elements, and hence the most convenient method of tracing out the results of this fusion is by the test of race.

The rearrangement of the British evidence which, from these, among other considerations, seems to be necessary, must primarily be based upon an examination of all existing survivals of the village community. I shall not in these pages attempt such a gigantic task, but I shall proceed upon this principle. No one example can be admitted as the normal type. The greater the accumulation of examples, the more likely are we to come to just and comprehensive conclusions as to origin. Scarcely any two examples are exactly alike, and these very differences afford us splendid material for the elucidation of origins.

For our present purposes we must strike out the word "manor" altogether. It meant different things at different times. At Hitchin, in the nineteenth century, it stands for a far more modern institution than at Aston and Cote in the seventeenth century, but the two centuries separating the two manors do not measure with anything approaching to accuracy the distance between one manor and the other, when considered purely as a matter of social development. From whatever source the term manor is derived, it indicates in historical times an institution of definite import in the country, and this is exactly what the different types of so-called manors do not indicate. Moreover, it is exclusive, and passes by institutions having many of the same features as manors but not the name.

The Wiltshire manors at the end of the eighteenth century were far older in form than those of almost any other county. All over the country it will be found that in some manors there is an advance to meet modern legal requirements, and archaic rights of succession are there translated into modern rights of borough-English, dower and other rules engrossed in the history of real property. There is, in other manors, an advance to meet agricultural improvements, and lands which once lay fallow are there sown with potatoes, peas, and other vegetables; cottagers who once laboured for their small holdings are there surplanted by ploughs and implements which root up old traditional practices. There is, in other manors, an advance to meet new political ideas, and there villagers become tenant farmers and pay rent instead of doing suit and service. On all sides, fortunately for the inquirer, these and other modes of advance, when they take place, are not regular all along the line. There is constant overlapping—a going forward of some, a keeping back of others; and hence it is possible to pick our way amidst this splendidly irregular progress to the line from whence all such progress started.

Getting rid of the limits implied by the use of the term manor and by the strict adherence to chronology, we shall be dealing with survivals of the village community which have preserved their economical features more or less intact while other features have disappeared. Christianity has routed out the old hearth religion from its place in the organization of the village, and has set it floating amidst the popular superstitions and customs which the people have preserved wherever Christianity has not deeply penetrated. Thus we shall not be able to produce a perfect type of the primitive village community in Britain. But our process of research will enable us to note the stages of destruction which have marked its history on British soil.

First, I shall examine the evidence of non-Aryan influences upon the village communities of Britain just as I noted this evidence in India; secondly, I shall examine the remnants of the old hearth cult and trace out its influences upon the history of the village homestead; thirdly, I shall examine some of the surviving types of the village community, and take note of the various phenomena exhibited by them; and I shall seek to explain these various phenomena by the facts already examined as to non-Aryan influences and as to the survival of the house-religion of the early Aryan race. Finally, I shall suggest that the survival of such types, down to quite modern times, with their calm ignorance of all phases of commercial economy, their strong adherence to practices which are customary, is the one great fact which needs to be accentuated in our study. It supplies evidence of an archaic social organization which, in the midst of a higher political organization, is that element in institutions corresponding to the irrational element in folklore, and like it representing primitive times.

CHAPTER IV.

THE NON-ARYAN ELEMENTS IN THE ENGLISH VILLAGE COMMUNITY.

WE have seen that the evidence of comparative custom goes to prove that race elements enter largely into the history of the village community in the East, and that the parallel between the Eastern and English types suggests also parallel lines of development due to race elements. We know that our thousand years of progress have obliterated for all practical purposes all questions of race distinction in these islands, and that while the Celtic and Teutonic stocks have some kind of division in the pages of history and in the geographical aspect of the country, there is nothing in history to divide off from these the races of pre-Aryan origin. We know further that archæology has indicated, though with more or less of uncertainty, some of the monumental remains of this pre-Aryan people. When we come to consider, as we must do now, the influences of the pre-Aryan races upon the history of the village community in Britain, it seems almost as if we should have to begin far back in the records of archæology before we could arrive at anything definite upon this point, and even then to be content with deductions from a great number of isolated fragments of evidence. But the task is, in truth, not so severe as this. It is, for the most part, a re-reading of already known facts, the placing of a fairly perfect group of evidence in its proper ethnological division of the British populations, instead of being content to classify it as prehistoric or Celtic, without seeking to ascertain what these terms connote when they are called on to explain the institutions of Great Britain.

The pre-Aryan races of India, and those which have influenced the formation of the Indian village communities, were, as we have already seen, the hill men; and following up the parallel which is known to exist between India and Britain, we will endeavour to find out whether there are any hill folk who have left marks of their influence upon the development of the village community in Britain. It is abundantly clear that there were hill folk who left their remains in the earthworks and other monuments which, to this day, are the most perfect relics of prehistoric archæology; but the point that is not so clear, or rather the point which has never been made clear, is the relationship which these hill folk bear to the valley folk and those of the plains. In dealing with the neolithic civilization, Professor Boyd Dawkins makes one or two important deductions, from the evidence of its monuments, which it is necessary we should bear in mind. In Britain, he says, the population was probably large. Traces of neolithic civilization have been discovered in almost every part of Europe, under conditions which prove that the manners and customs of the people were tolerably uniform. Their implements and domestic animals and plants have been discovered over the whole of Europe, with the exception of Northern Russia and Northern Scandinavia; and they imply that the civilization was long established, and that it underwent so little change, if any, in the lapse of ages, that no traces of change have been preserved to our times. Finally, Professor Boyd Dawkins points out that to the neolithic peoples we owe the rudiments of the culture which we ourselves enjoy. The arts which they introduced have never been forgotten, and all subsequent progress has been built upon their foundation. Their cereals are still cultivated by the farmer, their domestic animals still minister to us, and the arts, of which they only possessed the rudiments, have developed into the industries: spinning, weaving, pottery-making, mining, without which we can scarcely realize what our lives would be.[1] This being so, it seems scarcely possible to suppose otherwise than that the first wave

[1] Boyd Dawkins, "Early Man in Britain," pp. 290, 306, 307.

of Aryan conquerors and colonists in Britain, like the first wave of Aryan conquerors and colonists in India, met a people who, so far from being wiped out of existence, stood their ground and entered into the new conditions which the contact of Aryan with non-Aryan must have brought about. The haughty Aryan hunting tribes, disdaining agriculture and manual industry, accepted from the defeated occupiers of the land all the advantages of their advancement in culture, and took for their own share in the progress of human history that overlordship which the older races had never tolerated as a development from their own institutions. We have seen how this dual operation worked itself out in the history of the village communities of India, and in the facts of neolithic culture we have the first elements necessary to prove how it worked itself out in the history of the village communities of Britain. What we must do to carry on the proof through all the subsequent stages, is to set out the details which will enable us to understand that the agricultural system of British hill tribes became incorporated with the agricultural system of the village community. The permanence of their industries prepares us to meet with permanence of other tribal influences; and thus by the aid of comparative custom we may trace out the forgotten and lost signs of the overlapping of races in the formation of the village community in Britain.

I can here most conveniently allude to a somewhat lengthy, but most important passage in Mr. Hearn's valuable and suggestive researches, because it gives us, very succinctly, the main lines of evidence upon which we must proceed. " Distinct from the comitatus or military retainers, and yet essential to the existence of that body was the despised and non-combatant class which performed the humble duty of cultivating the warriors' fields. It may be stated, generally, that this class was composed of men outside of the kin, although dependent upon it or upon some of its members, and that it was derived from a conquered and alien race. In most of the countries whither the Aryan nations wandered, they appear to have found hostile populations of a race different from their own. Similar troubles awaited them when they journeyed east and west. So far as their history is known they always conquered, and either absorbed or enslaved their opponents."[1] Mr. Hearn then goes on to enumerate the countries in which the Aryans met and conquered non-Aryan tribes, and there does not appear to be any country where the village community has existed, in the form hitherto supposed to be Aryan, which has not witnessed the meeting of the Aryans with non-Aryans.

We will first test the evidence of race distinctions in Britain by an examination of the modes of settlement; and we are struck by the strong and sharp contrast which is represented by certainly two distinct methods—the one method revealing a people who constructed their residences on the hill tops, and sent their cultivation down the hill sides; the other method showing a race who constructed their residences in the valleys, and sent their cultivation up the hill sides for a short distance only.

We may identify the latter system of settlement as peculiarly indicative of Aryan origin, and we will therefore proceed with this first, because the proof of it, by its contrast with the other system, will lay the foundation of our conclusions with regard to this other system. The record of the Aryan occupation of India is the record of the occupation of the plains and valleys, the aboriginal hill men very frequently retaining their hold of their own homes in the midst of their Aryan conquerors. The record of the Aryan occupation of Britain has been long ago lost, and can only be reclaimed bit by bit, and by the aid of evidence which has to be built up by inquiries which extend into so many branches of archæological knowledge, that it seems almost hopeless to expect any results which will tell us once for all the whole story. Still there are here and there indications of what may be done by local observation, and I will, for my purpose, now turn to the settlement effected in two important districts in England where particularly good examples of the Aryan method of settlement have survived— namely, Wilts and Sussex.

[1] "The Aryan Household."

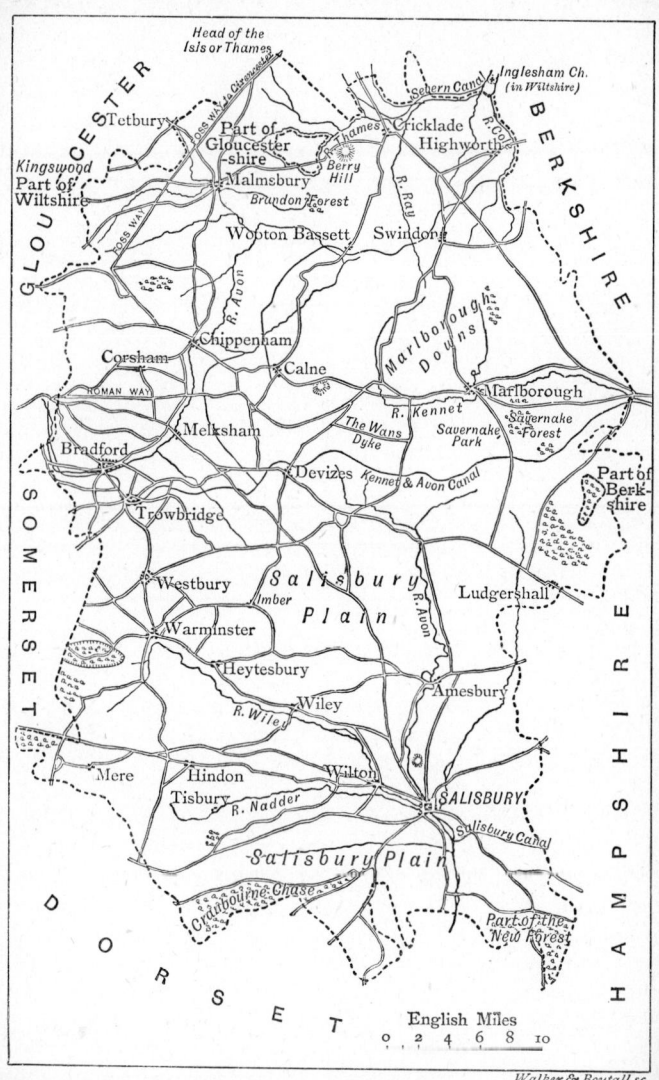

MAP OF WILTSHIRE.

THE ARYAN METHOD OF SETTLEMENT.

The nature of the Teutonic settlement of Wiltshire is reflected in the undisturbed characteristics of the ancient agricultural system of village communities which were observed by the economical reformers of the eighteenth century. We are told that the "valleys of the district are almost, without exception, intersected longitudinally by rivulets. The sides of these rivulets, being the most eligible situation for buildings, were of course crowded with houses. These valleys, with their accompanying rivulets, are frequently from three to five miles apart, hills intervening between them. The shape of the manors, therefore, became a narrow oblong; each manor acquired water and meadow ground, and also wood for fuel. The manors, therefore, were naturally divided into long narrow strips from river to wood, with a right to the use of both."[1] The farm-houses were crowded together in villages situated on the banks of the streams. Forming the centre point of all the village rights, we find, in true archaic fashion, that the application of the "land is most uniform. The common meadows immediately adjoin the river; the houses and small enclosures are as near it as possible. Next follows the arable, *until the land becomes too steep or too thin to plough,* and then the sheep and cow downs; and frequently the woods at the extremity of the manor, and adjoining the downs or woods of the manors in the opposite bourn."[2] Here there is no room for hill cultivation, and it is not provided for in the laying out of the village system of cultivation, it being distinctly observed that the hills are not cultivated.

Let us now turn to the south-east of England. The chalk escarpment is one of the best-marked physical features in England. It is a steep-sided range of hills having its summits remarkably level. From the crest of the escarpment the ground falls gradually away with a slope: at the foot of the escarpment the upper Greensand makes a broad band, beyond which

---

[1] Davis, "Agriculture of Wilts," pp. 5-6.
[2] Ibid., p. 18; *cf.* Marshall, "Rural Economy of Southern Counties," vol. ii. pp. 307-308.

comes the Gault. Now, Mr. Topley,[1] in examining this geological feature, was struck with the fact that the boundaries of the ancient parishes followed exactly one plan so regularly as to afford undoubted evidence of "absolute facts which our forefathers have stamped on the great land divisions of the country." I am not now concerned with the geological facts but with the question of the land settlement. "Everywhere," says Mr. Topley, summarizing his elaborate evidence, "along the foot of the chalk escarpment there is a line of villages. In nearly every case the parishes ascend the escarpment, generally taking in a good deal of the tableland above, but occasionally ending off at or near to the crest. In the other direction they extend over the Gault, and more or less over the underlying beds. As the villages are often quite close together the parishes are narrow, and thus we find a long line of parishes along the chalk escarpment, many of which are remarkably narrow in proportion to their length. The points to be specially noted are: that villages at the foot of the chalk escarpment send their parishes up the escarpment." Mr. Topley has examined these facts, and finds that the face of the chalk escarpment around the Weald is divided amongst 125 parishes, 119 of which belong to villages situated at the foot of the escarpment, the six exceptions being due to perfectly explainable causes which do not really make them exceptions. All along the foot of the chalk escarpment names, in which *-ing* is the final syllable, abound, and Mr. Topley rightly concludes that these facts show that "the earliest settlements in the south of England would take place along the wider chalk valleys in which water could be found, and along the foot of the escarpment, where the settlers found good water, productive soil, and a sheltered situation. In the division of land, consequent upon these settlements, each knot of settlers would take the down land behind them on which to pasture their sheep, the good land around their dwellings would be taken under the plough, and the forest land in the other direction, whether wood or open glade, would afford mast for swine and pasture for cattle."

[1] *Journal Anthropological Institution*, iii. 34, 39, 43, 44, 45, 49.

If we compare this with the Wiltshire system of settlement we find them practically identical, and together they afford very good evidence of the Aryan system of settlement in Britain. That they do not provide for hill cultivation seems absolutely clear. The hill sides were furthest away from the villages, near to which at the foot of the hills, the arable land, cultivated by the villagers, was situated; and I think this glimpse at the mode of the Aryan cultivation enables us to mark off a strong differentiation between it and the hill-folk cultivation.

We will now turn to the hill folk, and endeavour to ascertain something of their method of cultivation and of their mode of settlement. Our examination of this must necessarily be somewhat more minute and in more detail, and we shall find that the method of settlement leads us directly to the method of cultivation, both of which are distinct from the village life of the Aryan races. I think it may be shown, with some degree of precision, that the system of cultivation adopted by the hillmen of Britain was primarily that known as terrace cultivation. In order to investigate the history of this system from the evidence available, it is necessary to consider—(1) the local distribution of the examples; (2) the theories which have been advanced as to their origin; (3) the evidence as to their origin from their position and structural formation; (4) their connection with prehistoric hill forts. Then summarizing these results of the British evidence I shall endeavour to show (5) how the system of terrace cultivation entirely differs from the Aryan system of land settlement in Britain; and that (6) it does, in point of fact, find its true parallel among the non-Aryan hill-tribes of India. And, finally, I shall seek to establish the fact that in this system of terrace cultivation we have remnants of the Iberic or non-Aryan races of Britain.

1. Commencing in the south of England, our first example is from a writer in *The Gentleman's Magazine* (1796, p. 821), who observes that "on the declivities of the elevated and chalky tracts of Wiltshire, Dorsetshire, and other counties, there very frequently occurs a beautiful assemblage of *terraces*, mostly horizontal, and rising in a continued series like the steps of

Egyptian pyramids, or the seats of an amphitheatre. These, which are commonly arable, with their almost perpendicular sides of green turf, are popularly called *lynchets*. The slopes of the downs between Devizes and Calne afford many examples of them, about Beacon Hill, Hedington Hill, and between the junction of Wansdike with the Roman road and the intrenchments of Oldbury." Mr. Marshall, noticing the chalk hills from Devizes to Ludgershall, says, "much cultivation appears on their sides and towards their feet in flat artificial stages, with steep linshets between them."[1]

The south face of the hill, near Bellenton, takes the form of a spacious amphitheatre.[2] "Banks and small terraces" are to be seen in the neighbourhood of Rushmore,[3] on the borders of Dorsetshire and Wilts. In the latter county Mr. Scrope has noted numerous terraces, locally known as balks or lynchets, which contour round the projecting headlands and far up into the intervening combs, being most conspicuous between Mere and Hindon, and near to Warminster and Market Lavington, but are indeed to be met with almost wherever the chalk downs slope into the valleys or low plains.[4]

Among the best examples in Hampshire are those on the down, about three miles south of Winchester, and close to Shawford Station, on the London and South-Western Railway. They may be seen on the west in passing the place in a train. Similar terraces may be observed on the hill sides at Easton, Michelmersh, Houghton, Vernham's Dean, St. Mary Bourne, Woodcot, Wallop, Sombourn, and other places.[5]

Examples may be seen on the steep sides of the Sussex downs and the Chiltern Hills.[6] At Seaford is an ancient

---

[1] "Rural Economy of the Southern Counties," vol. ii. p. 300; at p. 302, he adds, "this sort of artificial terrace is common in different parts of the island."

[2] *Journal of Archæological Association*, vol. xiii. p. 109.

[3] Pitt-Rivers, "Excavations in Cranborne Chase, near Rushmore," p. 2.

[4] "Wilts Archæological Society," vol. xii. pp. 185-192, vol. xvii. pp. 295-297.

[5] *Antiquary*, vol. xvii. p. 51.

[6] Seebohm's, "English Village Community," p. 6.

TERRACE CULTIVATION IN ENGLAND AND WALES.

cultivated terrace extending from the cliff inland for a distance of about a quarter of a mile on the slope.[1]

At Luton in Bedfordshire, at Clothall in Herts, and between Cambridge and Hitchin, are striking examples.[2]

Coming next to the Welsh district we find that the hills which form the watershed on the south side of the Clun rivulet were on the slopes leading to the brook, in many places distinctly marked with ridges or butts curved according to the formation of the ground. The butts were of various sizes, some narrow, some wide.[3]

On several hills in North Carmarthenshire there are also clear evidence of this cultivation. The ridges, or butts, are never more than 6 or 8 feet wide.[4] Near Llangollen there are some fine examples to be seen from the Llantysilio railway station.[5]

We next go to the northern districts of England, and thence into Scotland. In Wharfedale, Coverdale, Wensleydale, and on the slopes of the hills to the east of Nidderdale, the country is covered with little step-like terraces called "reins." "The sides of the limestone slopes of Wharfedale are covered with them—each being twenty or thirty or more yards long, and two or three yards wide, and though they almost always there run horizontally, yet occasionally they lie up and down."[6]

The eastern side of Humbledon, the outermost span of the Cheviots, consists of a series of wide terraces. There is first a level plateau; then a steep ascent; then a similar plateau, and so on, to a fifth or sixth, &c.[7]

Many of the hills on the north of the Cheviot Range have been formed into terraces for cultivation. In speaking upon

---

[1] *Journal Anthropological Institution*, vol. vi. p. 297.
[2] Seebohm, *loc. cit.*, p. 6.
[3] "Bygones relating to Wales," vol. v. p. 211.
[4] Ibid., vol. v. p. 195.
[5] Mackintosh, "On the Origin of the Scenery of England and Wales."
[6] Lucas, "Studies in Nidderdale," p. 61; *cf.* Seebohm's "English Village Community," p. 381.
[7] *Land*, May 5, 1883, p. 192; Pennant's "Tour in Scotland," vol. iii. 284; "Berwickshire Nat. Hist. Field Club," vol. iv. p. 160.

this subject, Mr. Tate said that upon Heethpool he had counted sixteen terraces, rising in succession one above the other, having a platform of from 10 feet to 42 feet, though usually it is about 20 feet in width, and that this mode of cultivation was in some instances resorted to on hills that rose about 1,000 feet above the level of the sea. White Hill, near to the farm-house, is terraced to its summit. These terraces are generally flat, but some are slightly convex, not quite horizontal, nor are they parallel; some run into each other, and in such cases one or two other terraces are intercalated for a short distance. They rise above each other by nearly perpendicular steps, which vary in height from 2 feet to 15 feet, generally it is about 4 feet or 5 feet.[1]

Between Coldstream and Palinsburne, in Northumberland, Pennant observed "several very regular terraces cut on the face of a hill. They are most exactly formed, a little raised in the middle, like a fine walk, and about 20 feet broad, and of very considerable length. In some places were three, in others five flights, placed one above the other, terminating exactly in a line at each end, and most precisely finished. Such tiers of terraces are not uncommon in these parts, where they are called baulks."[2] Near Chollerton is a flight of terraces called Hanging Shaws.[3] At Greaves Ash, near Linhope, are some horizontal ridges, high up on the hill side, which appear to be remains of ancient terrace culture.[4]

At Yetholm, Linhope, and Ingram, in Northumberland, there are many cases of terraced hills.[5]

In Scotland these terraces are to be found in the vale of the Tweed and the neighbouring districts, where they are called Daisses, *i.e.*, bench seats. At Purves Hill, about eight miles below Peebles, the steep hill face is marked all the way down

---

[1] *Gentleman's Magazine*, 1862, part ii. p. 455; "Berwickshire Nat. Hist. Field Club," vol. iv. pp. 245, 448.

[2] Pennant's "Tour in Scotland," vol. iii. p. 281; "Berwickshire Nat. Hist. Field Club," vol. iv. p. 236.

[3] Wallis, "History of Northumberland," vol. ii. p. 70.

[4] "Berwickshire Nat. Hist. Field Club," vol. iv. p. 314.

[5] Ibid., vol. iv. p. 244.

to the haugh by the river side with terraces extending over the space of a quarter of a mile. Another equally marked series of terraces is found on a hill face close to Newlands Kirk, in the west of Peeblesshire. They occupy a piece of the hill face commencing about 40 feet above the immediate banks of the Lyne, and extending upwards about 110 feet. The length of the entire space occupied is now about the fifth part of a mile, but early in the last century it was terraced for about a mile. Similar terraces exist at Kilbucho, in Peeblesshire; and at Dunsyre, in Lanarkshire; at North Middleton, in Edinburghshire; on the south-east slopes of Arthur's Seat, above Duddingston; all around Dunsapie, towards Musselburgh, on the hill behind Markinch.[1]

TERRACES AT NEWLANDS KIRK, PEEBLESSHIRE.

Gordon says, "all along from the village of Romana, about seventeen miles from Edinburgh, for a mile and a half upon the side of a considerable hill, are to be seen seventeen or eighteen distinct rows of artificial terraces raised one above another in a most regular manner, each of them 15 or 18 or 20 feet broad, and as much in height, and may be seen at four or five miles distance; and for a whole mile it appears not unlike a large amphitheatre. About three miles south of Romana, at a place called Kirkurde, upon the water of Terth, are to be seen other rows of terraces like those of Romana. At Skerling are other terraces, near all which places upon the

[1] "Proceedings Society of Antiquaries of Scotland," vol. i. pp. 127-133 with illustration of the terraces at Newlands Kirk, Peeblesshire.

tops of many other hills are to be seen these kind of forts strongly entrenched with double and single ditches."[1]

The hill sides above Swineside Hall, Oxnam, in Roxburghshire, are distinctly terraced.[2]

There are also similar terraces at Castle Sempel, in Argyleshire.[3] It is observable, says a writer on the Grampians, in many parts of the highest inhabited places in the Scottish Highlands, that ridges can be distinctly traced near the summit of our most elevated mountains.[4]

I have not succeeded in identifying any examples in Ireland, but the following passage from Boate's "Ireland's Natural History," 1652, must, I think, allude to terrace cultivation. "It hath been observed in many parts of Ireland, but chieflie in the county of Meath, and further northward, that upon the top of the great hills and mountains, not onely at the side and foot of them, to this day the ground is uneven as if it had been plowed in former times."[5]

It will be admitted, I think, that this is very striking evidence of the wide prevalence of terrace cultivation in Britain. In Wales and Scotland the hill folk have almost a natural home arising from the physical peculiarities of the country; and in those parts of England where hill ranges exist, there also exist traces of this peculiar system of agriculture. I am far from suggesting that all the examples I have adduced are representative of the most primitive form of terrace cultivation, about which we shall have much to say presently. What I am anxious to put into clear prominence first is the fact of terrace cultivation as a distinct feature of the agricultural practices of Britain according to the signs of it which remain upon the hills. It will appear, presently, that these examples really fall into two distinct classes, one of comparatively recent origin,

---

[1] Gordon's "Itin. Septentrionale," pp. 114, 115.
[2] "Proceedings Berwickshire Nat. Hist. Field Club," 1885, p. 26.
[3] "Proceedings Society of Antiquaries of Scotland," vol. i. p. 129.
[4] Campbell's "Grampians Desolate," p. 167.
[5] Boate's "Ireland's Natural History," 1652, p. 83; cf. Wood's "Primitive Inhabitants of Ireland," 1821, p. 220.

THE ORIGIN OF TERRACE CULTIVATION. 81

possessing no very remarkable features, nor extending over a very wide area; the other of unknown origin, possessing features which strike us at once as indicative of a very extensive hill population, and extending over an area which is the centre of archæological interest.

2. We now pass on to consider the theories which have been advanced concerning the origin of these singular terraces. They have excited the curiosity of travellers for many years; and in 1790 Mr. Marshall, one of the most thorough investigators of our agricultural system, observed that "the antiquary might be less profitably employed than in tracing their origin."[1] But the antiquary has not done much during the hundred years since this observation was made to solve the problem, and certainly he has not demonstrated their great significance in the history of our race. An examination of the several theories advanced will, however, assist us in some important particulars. It will show that many of the later suggestions are wide of the mark because they are made with no attention to the complete circumstances of the case, and it will bring once more into prominence the value of local tradition as a factor in the search for historical origins.

The most important theory, because the most far-reaching in its consequences, is that which attributes to these terrace formations a natural origin. Dr. Mackintosh in *The Geological Magazine*, and later in a separate work, considered them to have been formed by the erosive power of sea waves, or marine currents, "at different levels, with or without floating ice." And he specially notes the Llangollen terraces as the finest series of undoubted old coast-lines or raised sea-beaches that he ever met with.[2] The geological origin of the famous parallel roads of Glen Roy has been discussed and accepted by many distinguished geologists;[3] but the true answer to this view seems to be that advanced by Mr. Poulett Scrope,

[1] "Rural Economy of the Southern Counties," vol. ii. p. 302.
[2] "On the Origin of the Scenery of England and Wales."
[3] *Cf.* Macfadzean's "Parallel Roads of Glen Roy," pp. xx, xxi, for a table of the various theories held.

namely, that the cultivation terraces are of a different kind to anything that may have been formed by such vast geological changes as it is necessary to postulate before accepting nature as the author.[1] Thus when Mr. Tate, speaking of the Humbleton Heugh Terraces, says: "they are formed on gravel which lies at the base of the porphyry hills, and which had been accumulated when the whole valley of the Till had been filled with water; and as the land emerged from the water, especially along its shores, places more or less level would appear,"[2]—we can meet this by the objection raised by Dr. Milne Home, who satisfied himself "that they were not terraces formed by water, inasmuch as though some of them were horizontal, others ran obliquely round the hills, and in several instances they coincided with the slope, forming in this last case wide ridges with deep trenches between."[3]

Of the suggestions which declare for the artificial origin of these terraces, the most wild is one advanced by Pennant, who considered them to be places for the militia to arrange themselves on that they might show themselves to advantage, thus placing rank above rank, as nothing could more highly gratify the pride of a chieftain's heart.[4] Similar to this is the theory advanced by Mr. Baird, the minister of Yetholm, who regards the terraces to have been made for the purpose of enabling the inhabitants of the district to come together and witness the ceremonies performed by the Druid priests on the hills.[5] Gordon, in his archæological tour in Scotland in 1726-32, was of opinion that "most of these terraces, especially those so extraordinarily large, are Roman works, and may probably have been thrown up by their armies for itinerary encampments."[6] These theories are, of course, worthless; but let me point out that they postulate the formation of the terraces by manual labour, and while we

[1] "Wilts Archæological Society," vol. xii. p. 189.
[2] "Berwickshire Nat. Hist. Soc.," vol. iv. p. 160.   [3] Ibid., p. 244.
[4] "Tour in Scotland," vol. iii. p. 281.
[5] "Berwickshire Nat. Hist. Field Club," vol. iv. p. 244.
[6] Gordon, "Itin. Septentrionale," p. 115.

THE AGRICULTURAL ORIGIN OF TERRACE CULTIVATION.

must unhesitatingly reject the cause assumed for all this labour, we may note that at the time of Pennant and Gordon, a century and more ago, there was nothing either in popular tradition or in actual practice which gave the clue to their origin, and therefore these two authorities fell back upon the supposition that they were constructed by labour devised for the express purpose.

The only remaining theory is that which considers them to have been formed for the purpose of cultivation. Even Mr. Tate, who argued for their geological formation, suggested that they had been used for agriculture. Such places, he says, "have been further levelled and trimmed by art, and used by the early inhabitants of the district for the purpose of cultivation. Some broad and irregular ridges and furrows running along these terraces I consider evidences of this ancient cultivation."[1] The point we have to note here is that the formation of the ridges and the use of them, just as in the theories advanced by Pennant and Gordon, are deemed to be two different operations, a view which is in direct opposition to the opinions of Mr. Poulett Scrope and Mr. Seebohm. In point of date, Mr. Scrope was the first to suggest that the action of agriculturists was the cause of the terraces. But the theory is intimately connected with the system of cultivation now known to have been adopted by the village community, and it appears to me that the facts ascertained of the latter have coloured the theories about the formation of these terraces. Thus at the very outset Mr. Scrope makes an assumption which does not seem to apply to the most important types of terrace cultivation at all, namely, that the strips lying one above the other were held by distinct occupiers.[2] He then proceeds more cautiously, and I will quote his exact words: "The boundary line between two of these neighbouring strips may have been originally only a mathematical one, and yet a bank would soon have been formed along it, for each upper cultivator will naturally take

---

[1] "Berwickshire Naturalists Field Club," vol. iv. p. 160.
[2] "Wilts Archæological Society," vol. xii. p. 187.

care not to allow the soil of his strip to descend to fertilize that of his neighbour. He would draw the lower limit of his strip by a reversed furrow, throwing the last ridge of soil up hill, thus leaving a slight trench, sufficient, however, to stop the silt washed down from above, which consequently would accumulate there in a bed perhaps only an inch or two in depth. But the next year the process is repeated, and thus by degrees a slight bank of earth is formed, which, in the progress of years, increases into lynchets or balks, *i.e.*, a steep grass-grown bank several feet in height, with a somewhat flattened terrace above, separating the parallel strips on a hill-side in the hands of distinct cultivators."[1] This theory is adopted also by Mr. Seebohm, who says "the custom for ages was always to turn the sod of the furrow down hill, the plough consequently always returning one way idle. If the whole hill-side were ploughed in one field, this would result in a gradual travelling of the soil from the top to the bottom of the field, and it might not be noticed. But as in the open-field system, the hill-side was ploughed in strips, with un-ploughed balks between them, no sod could pass in the ploughing from one strip to the next; but the process of moving the sod downwards would go on age after age just the same within each individual strip. In other words, every year's ploughing took a sod from the higher edge of the strip and put it on the lower edge; and the result was that the strips became in time long level terraces one above the other, and the balks between them grew into steep rough banks of long grass, covered often with natural self-sown brambles and bushes."[2]

It seems to me that such an elaborate process describes perhaps one form of terrace cultivation, namely, that which belongs to the villages which began their settlement at the bottom of the hill, and which gradually extended the area of cultivation up the sides of the hill, leaving off as soon as the hill-side becomes precipitous, and always long before it reaches

[1] "Wilts Archæological Society," vol. xii. pp. 187–188.
[2] "The English Village Community," pp. 5–6.

the top. In the meantime Mr. Scrope himself suggests, though not purposely, some of the objections to the purely agricultural origin of these terraces, objections derived from the actual practice of hill cultivation. In Wiltshire where the hills are under arable cultivation, "the ridge of the soil raised by the mould board of the plough has everywhere a tendency, through the action of gravity upon it, to fall down hill. This down-hill tendency of the disturbed soil is greatly assisted by the wash of heavy rains upon the loosened materials of the sloping surface, and the result is that year by year the whole surface soil of the slope, when under continuous arable culture, is slowly, indeed, but surely, travelling downwards, until it is stopped by some hedge or wall or bank. . . . In the meantime the upper parts of the slope, losing their vegetable mould, get poorer and poorer; . . . and the thrifty farmers of Devonshire therefore often employ their idle hands and teams in winter in digging out the soil which has descended to the bottom of their steep fields, and carting it up to the top again."[1] But, then, such practices, rude as they are, are not illustrative of, and do not produce, terrace cultivation; and until the necessity of such practices are proved to be needless, in consequence of the balks which Mr. Seebohm establishes between each terrace, the formation of these terraces by the sole action of the plough must, on the whole, be considered as unproven.[2] The Rev. Canon Jackson has also challenged this theory, and concludes that while it is intelligible that banks should be formed in this way in certain places and under certain circumstances, these cases would be comparatively few, namely, where the ground slopes very gradually, and where the strips are of considerable breadth.

[1] "Wilts Archæological Society," vol. xii. p. 186-187. See Clarke's "Survey of the Lakes" (1789), p. 64, for a farmer's mode of cultivating the hills.

[2] Mr. Seebohm tells me he knows of actual cases near Hitchin formed by the plough. But these are by no means of the same class as those alluded to and described above; they fall rather under Canon Jackson's exceptions.

In other cases, where the hill falls precipitously, and the terraces are narrow and come close and quick upon the other like a steep staircase, that they could ever be formed according to Mr. Poulett Scrope's idea seems to Canon Jackson a simple impossibility.[1]

Dr. Daniel Wilson introduces us to a new idea concerning these terraces, for the first time suggesting that their formation turns upon the question of an extensive occupation of the hill sites, and noting the popular tradition of their connection with elves. The passage is as follows:—

"In various districts of the neighbourhood of the road from Port Ellen towards the shooting lodge of Islay, the curious traveller may decry amid 'desolate heath' indications on the hill-sides of a degree of cultivation having existed at some former period far beyond what is exhibited in that locality at the present day. These singular terraces occur frequently at such altitudes as must convey a remarkably vivid idea of the extent and industry of an ancient population, where now the grazing of a few black cattle alone tempts to the claim of property in the soil. In other districts the half-obliterated furrows are still traceable on heights which have been abandoned for ages to the wild fox or the eagle. Such evidences of ancient population and industry are by no means confined to the remote districts of ancient Dalriada. They occur in many parts of Scotland, startling the believer in the unmitigated barbarism of Scotland prior to the medieval era with evidence of a state of prosperity and civilization at some remote epoch, the date of which has yet to be ascertained; though there are not wanting periods within the era of authentic Scottish history to which some of these may with considerable probability be assigned. The very simple explanation of such ancient plough marks which has satisfied the popular mind is apparent in the appellation of elf-furrows, by which they are commonly known."[2]

This clearly leads us to that other system of terrace cultiva-

[1] "Wilts Archæological Society," vol. xvii. p. 294.
[2] Wilson's "Prehistoric Annals of Scotland," p. 123.

tion which is far more conspicuous and far more general than any system which could have been formed by the plough. This system begins at the top of the hill, and creeps down the side, leaving off, however, long before it reaches the more gentle slopes near the valley, and is thus in direct contrast to that system which begins towards the bottom of the hill, through the exigencies of modern farming, and does not extend to where the precipitous sides commence. And this is really the only system which is of importance to us to examine, and we shall find that there are no traces of its modern use. As Mr. Seebohm himself puts it, the only right of survival of terrace cultivation lies in its indestructibility,[1] that is, in other words, unless we had archæological evidence of it, we should never have discovered its existence in Britain. It is necessary to state the evidence in proof of the non-survival of the practice of terrace cultivation, besides which this will help us to form new conclusions as to its origin. Mr. Scrope's modern examples are not really examples, as Canon Jackson proves, of terrace cultivation. Mr. Tate says "they have been used down even to the middle of last century,"[2] and Mr. Lucas doubtfully suggests their recent use.[3] But such use as these remarks indicate does not really involve the question of a continuity of terrace cultivation. The modern farmer does occasionally use these parts of his holding for raising crops, but he is not thereby keeping up any traditional practice. Mr. Chambers, who observed them in Scotland, says "the country people have no traditions about them, and are even under an uncertainty as to their design and use."[4] A writer in *The Gentleman's Magazine* of 1796, speaking of the Wilts and Dorset examples, says "they are generally regarded in the neighbourhood as the offspring of human exertion in remote ages to facilitate and extend the dominion of the plough."[5]

[1] "English Village Community," p. 5.
[2] "Berwickshire Nat. Hist. Field Club," vol. iv. p. 448.
[3] "Studies in Nidderdale," p. 62.
[4] "Proceedings of the Society of Antiquaries of Scotland," vol. i. p. 130.
[5] *Gentleman's Magazine*, 1796, p. 821.

Thus it seems clear that in tradition there is nothing to prove the continuity to modern times of the true, as distinct from the partial, terrace cultivation, and accordingly we have thus far gained the right to appeal to archæology and to comparative custom for a solution of the problem.

3. We have therefore to consider now what evidence as to origin is to be obtained from their position and their structural formation. The face of the country has now so changed that it is difficult for the modern observer to arrive at correct conclusions when they so much depend upon a long previous state of things. But if we take note of the older authorities, we may obtain what may be fairly considered as echoes from the oldest times. Thus when Boate, in 1652, was observing the hill cultivation of Ireland, the topographical features of the country, much more than his own knowledge and ingenuity, suggested to him some ideas of considerable importance to the subject we have in hand. He says: "The inhabitants doe affirm that their forefathers being much given to tillage, contrarie to what they are now, used to turn all to plowland. Others say that it was done for want of arable, because the champain was most everywhere beset and overspread with woods which by degrees are destroyed by the warres. They say further that in those times, in places where nothing now is to be seen but great boggs of a vast extent, there were thick woods, which they collect from hence, that now and then trees are digged out there being for the most part some yards long and some of a very great bignes and length."[1]

Dr. Milne Holme observes of the district about Linhope, in Northumberland, that if corn was to be grown there in ancient times the most suitable spots would not be in the valleys, then covered with woods and liable to river-floods, but on the hillsides, which were free from trees, and at all events more easily cleared, and where the soil, consisting in great part of decomposed porphyry, must have been peculiarly fertile. These spots also had the advantage of being dry, and it appeared to him that in order to prevent the water running away the soil,

[1] Boate's "Ireland's Natural History," p. 83.

the ground had been formed in broad terraces more or less horizontal. Where the ridges and furrows slope down the hill there is to be observed, from the immense quantity of rushes and other aquatic plants, that the ground was full of natural springs, and if it was intended to keep the soil free from water, the mode adopted certainly was the best for the purpose.[1] Another writer on the subject says: "Such appearances of culture are referable to remote times, when, by reason of the valleys being overgrown with woods which were the haunts of wolves, bears, and enormous snakes, it was necessary for safety to retire to the tops of hills, and there cultivate those spots which still retain the appearance of human industry."[2]

What, then, does this accumulation of evidence point to? Certainly to no existing system of agriculture, and as certainly to a system belonging to a people occupying the hills in some force. Mr. Chambers concludes, mainly from the discoveries at Arthur's Seat, that to the era of the Bronze period "we must assign the examples of that peculiar mode of culture which have been noticed."[3] One important fact remains to be noted which comes out of the Scottish evidence, viz., absolute proof that the terraces are not produced by the plough, as Mr. Scrope, Mr. Seebohm, and others seem to think, but are artificially produced. Dr. Wilson observes of the Port Ellen terraces that they were retained by dwarf walls.[4] Although of one place Mr. Chambers states "there is no trace of masonry in their construction," he says of the group round Dunsapie that "it is quite evident that they have been carefully formed with a facing of wall composed of rough blocks, and the faces of some of them are so well defined and steep that it is barely possible to climb them;" and "the pastoral ground over which they extend has many rough blocks scattered over it."[5] Now, although there does not

[1] "Berwickshire Naturalists' Field Club," vol. iv. p. 244.
[2] Campbell's "Grampians Desolate," p. 167.
[3] "Proceedings of the Society of Antiquaries of Scotland," vol. i. p. 133.
[4] "Prehistoric Annals of Scotland," p. 123.
[5] "Proceedings of the Society of Antiquaries of Scotland," vol. i. p. 130.

appear to be any signs of such constructive evidence in the more southern examples, it is open to remark that the lapse of ages might account for the stone facing having been gradually removed, or that in some districts where stone was not plentiful some other material was used for the purposes of construction. For instance, of the Wilts example Mr. Scrope says the late Mr. Cunnington informed him that it was "a practice to dig in these lynchets for flints, and when engaged in this work the labourers have frequently found Roman coins, fibulæ, pottery, &c."[1] Mr. Scrope thinks this evidence is full proof that the ancient terrace cultivation was the work of the Romanized Britons, and this was the opinion of Gordon. The term Romanized Britons is a misleading one. *Romanized* Britons would not bury their "coins, fibulæ, pottery, &c.," in their tillage grounds; but after the departure of the Romans the un-Romanized hill tribes might very well have set to work again, upon their old sites building up their broken terrace-facings with flints from the deserted Roman sites, and thus unconsciously burying "coins, fibulæ, pottery, &c." Thus, then, the high position and structural formation of these terraces suggest that they were artificially formed, unconnected with and anterior to the open-field system, and that they must have been built up by a people unacquainted with the use of the plough, and who occupied the hills before the plains were cultivated.

4. We next want to show the connection between terrace cultivation and the other evidences of early hill occupation. This can only be accomplished by examining carefully their archæological surroundings. In some of the examples we have noticed this may be accomplished, and I select the following examples.

With reference to the Hampshire terraces it has to be noted that "at Woodcot, in Wallop Fields, on Sombourn Common Down, and elsewhere, they *are more remote from the village, and quite close to ancient earthworks.*"[2] At St. Mary Bourne the

[1] "Wilts Archæological Society," vol. xii. p. 192.
[2] *Antiquary*, vol. xvii. p. 51.

TERRACE CULTIVATION AND THE HILL-FORTS. 91

evidence is still more definite. Very near to the terraces at Linksfield have been found the relics of an old settlement, consisting of querns, pottery, and articles of domestic use, while at Hurstbourne siding have been excavated eight sites of pit-dwellings dug in the chalk, the floors of which were either pitched with flints or formed by the solid chalk, and outside of one was found a cooking hole. These were usually circular in plan, contained a central fireplace, and had sloping entrance passages. Their contents show them to have belonged originally to a neolithic people with traces of later occupation. Other remains of a prehistoric occupation exist, including an extensive camp known as Eggbury, which leads the local historian to the observation that "the district appears to be prolific in relics of a people who occupied the platform on which the camp is seated, and who most likely frequented it as a stronghold."[1]

On the top of Humbledon Hill one is standing in the centre of a British camp. Round two-thirds of the wide summit there is a circle of rude stones, themselves arranged into smaller circles, each representing the dimensions of a hut. As the walls have fallen the stones have become heaped confusedly together, but they always seem to have fallen outwards, so that the round plot of land which may have been the floor of each stone cabin is a clear green space. When the huts round the summit of Humbledon Hill were constructed, the terraces we have described above would be the only pieces of land in the neighbourhood which were capable of cultivation. The now fertile valley of Glendale might not then have safely been crossed even by a naked Briton on foot. Having to live, and to grow corn the inhabitants of these windy stone cabins would naturally level the sides of their chosen hill into fields, and in proof that they did so one seems to detect under the short grass the furrows of some ancient plough.[2]

With reference to the Heethpool terraces, it seems that the whole of this district, wherever the ground is sufficiently ele-

[1] Stevens, "History of St. Mary Bourne," p. 37.
[2] *Land*, May 5, 1883, p. 192.

vated as to be thoroughly dry, is covered with remains of prehistoric buildings. The sites show that the circular form seems to have been adapted for most structures. Three or four courses of very large stones, arranged in a circle 10 feet or 12 feet in thickness, formed the groundwork upon which the walls, made of smaller stones, were raised to a height of about 7 feet. In the instance of one fort, a circle of this description was 30 feet in diameter. Within it, also built in circles, were the habitations of those who defended them. In towns, or large assemblies of the same huts, the diameter of the circumvallation was correspondingly greater. Many of the habitations at Yevering were cut out of the hill-side. Encircling the summit of the Bell, a strong wall of the kind mentioned enclosed a space of twelve acres.[1] It was built of porphyry blocks without lime. There are four gateways, one on the west, one on the east, a third on the north, and the principal entrance on the south. This has a guard-house on its west side, of oval shape, 9 feet by 6 feet. All around the Bell, where the inclination is not very steep and craggy, fortlets and hut circles are traceable.[2]

At Greaves Ash, right in the centre of the Northumberland examples of terrace cultivation, and immediately adjacent to terraces which have been already noted, is perhaps the most perfect example of a prehistoric hill-town or settlement. Mr. Tate has described it in great detail, and I collect from his account the following salient features:—It is situated on an elevated platform on the southern slope of Greenshaw Hill, and consists of three principal parts, all defended by encircling walls. The western part is the largest, and connected with the eastern part by enclosures and a rampart; the third or upper part is north-eastward from the latter, and is connected with the others by a road and rampart. On the lower ground south-eastward of the outermost rampart several old walls form enclosures which, with the town itself, make up an area of about twenty acres. All the walls of the town, dwellings, and enclosures

---

[1] *Gentleman's Magazine*, 1862, part ii. p. 456.
[2] "Berwickshire Field Club," vol. iv. p. 434.

are built of the porphyry rock of the district, and no cement of any kind has been used in their construction, nor is any tool mark visible. The western part of the town consists of a number of hut circles and other inclosures surrounded and defended by two strong walls; on the south side the defence consists of three walls running parallel with, but a little distant from, each other, with the intervening spaces filled up with small stones and earth. The foundations of eighteen huts are visible, and traces of several more. They are quite circular, their diameters varying from 11 feet to 27 feet. Each has a regularly formed entrance, which generally faces the east or south-east. In the eastern part the hut circles are from 8 to 20 feet in diameter, and in the upper part are distinct remains of fifteen hut circles, besides obscure remains of other foundations. On the north side of the principal gateway to the western part is a rectangular chamber 12 feet by 10 feet, with an entrance from the gateway by a very rude passage; and from the position, this must have been a guard-house to the gateway. The entrance to the outer rampart is not opposite this gateway, but diagonal to it, being thirty yards to the southward. The principal roadway winds down the hill from the gateway of the western part; it is hollow to the depth of two or three feet, and defended on both sides by a mound of earth and stones. From the west side another road branches out, and this is defended by a stone wall. On looking at the position of the town with reference to the adjoining hill, we find it commanded by Greenshaw Hill. There is, however, no camp on this hill. These arrangements seemed to Mr. Tate to countenance the view that the camps and fortified towns in this district do not form a combined system of defence against a common foe, but that they are the works of independent tribes to protect themselves against the attacks of their neighbours.[1]

In some of the Scottish examples, Mr. Chambers has noted much the same phenomena that have been adduced of the

[1] "Berwickshire Field Club," vol. iv. pp. 294–303.

English. At Purves Hill the site of the ancient homestead is still to be traced. At Newlands Kirk "there were, till lately, the remains of an ancient house on the top of the hill, immediately over the centre of the terraced space. The farmer found many freestones among the ruins of this building, and a fragment of a quern." On Arthur's Seat "lumps of brass, mixed with the purest shell marl, human skulls and bones, large fragments of deer horns of uncommon size" have been discovered, which has led Dr. Wilson and Sir Alexander Dick to conclude that there was a settlement of the Bronze Age people.[1]

On the whole, it seems clear that the remains of terrace cultivation are intimately associated with the remains of primitive hill residences, and that these hill residences were occupied by tribes or clans, whose system of local defence shows that they had no idea of warfare, whereby a whole nation is involved against another nation, but that clan was pitted against clan—an important piece of evidence which tells us much of the degree of civilization to which these hill folk had attained. Canon Greenwell, from other evidence, has come to practically the same conclusion, and as the point is an important one when we come to discuss the position of these hill folk among the races of Britain, I shall quote the words of this great authority. In noticing some of the ancient grave hills in the North Riding of Yorkshire, Canon Greenwell compares them with the Northumberland mounds, and goes on to say that "in Northumberland every hill-end has its place of defence; in some instances two or three in connection, each one stronger than the other. They are provided with enclosures for cattle, and covered ways for concealed ingress and egress. These fortresses, in many cases not a mile apart, are so numerous, that in a day's walk some dozen or more may easily be visited. Can we come to any other conclusion than that we have in this the evidence of a number of small tribes living in a constant state of feud and warfare, probably about hunting

---

[1] "Proceedings of the Society of Antiquaries of Scotland," vol. i. pp. 127-133.

SUMMARY OF EVIDENCE ON TERRACE CULTIVATION. 95

grounds and pasturage; each tribe independent, to some extent, of the others, though possibly all, for certain purposes joined into a general confederation by some bond of political, and, therefore, at that time, of religious union?"[1] The importance of this evidence rests upon the nature of these defence works, the concealed ways of ingress and egress, each clan being defended against all the other clans, and the bond of federation being not political as Canon Greenwell suggests, but simply the loose dwelling together of people of the same ethnic stock.

5. We may now usefully summarize the results of the British evidence as to terrace cultivation. It seems that the most important of these terraces were artificially formed with stone-faced banks, or with flints, by a race of hill folk, who constructed these stupendous efforts of labour because of the impossibility of occupying the thickly-wooded valleys; that the residences of the hill men were strongly fortified and extensively occupied; that the system of occupation does not indicate anything in the nature of national efforts at settlement in a new country, but rather tribal and clan migrations taken step by step, and without eradicating tribal and clan feuds.

Our evidence so far pushes back the inquiry as to who were these hill folk, who constructed the cultivating terraces, to a pre-Teutonic period. I think it might be shown from the history of the village community that it also goes back beyond the Celtic period, but I prefer to bridge over this period by an appeal to the evidence of comparative custom.

6. The pre-Aryan races seem to have been essentially hill folk. They have attained their highest point of civilization in that wonderful country, China, and there, accordingly, we find terrace cultivation in perfection. The following account will serve to illustrate one fact, not easily understood by those who look at everything from the point of view of modern economics, namely, the expenditure of labour. "In South-west China there are two or three ranges between Ch'ung-ch'ing

[1] *Archæological Journal*, vol. xxii. p. 100.

and Lu-chou with summits about 2,000 feet above the sea, but little hills and narrow valleys form the distinctive features of the country. The rock is soft sandstone and shale, often much displaced. The softness of the stone makes terrace cultivation very easy, and this system is carried to greater perfection here than in any other part of China. Crossing one of the little cols, and looking over the valleys that break away from it, one is struck by the thought of the sum of human labour expended to bring rugged hills into such complete subjection, and one receives a most lively impression of the patient industry of this wonderful people. From peak to valley the whole hill-side has been levelled into terraces, so that not a foot of ground is lost. More than this, the terraces are cut up into fields—beds would be a better word—averaging 50 feet by 40 feet, perfectly level, and inclosed by narrow banks. The outside bank of each bed has a rough sluice to regulate the level of water, any surplus, after the ground is sufficiently covered for paddy, falling into the bed below, and so on till the bottom of the valley is reached. The result is that water lies at all levels, and appears to defy the law of gravity." [1] Another instance is supplied by the Karen rice country, adjoining the territory of the Shans, where the slopes of the hills are terraced for cultivation—the terraces being faced with stones, and each frequently 5 feet or 6 feet high.[2] This is an exact parallel of the Scottish terraces at Dunsapie; but in order to show the true relationship between the non-Aryan constructors of the hill terraces, and the Aryan holders of the valley lands, we must turn to an Aryan country. Fortunately in India the races have not yet become merged as they have in Europe, and I think I can produce from these a parallel to the state of things which must have existed in prehistoric Britain.

The village fields of the Khonds are formed in a succession of terraces, to which water is conducted with no mean skill.[3] The hill villages of Madras are surrounded by terraced fields

[1] Bluebook, "China No. 1," 1888, p. 2.
[2] Colquhoun, "Amongst the Shans," p. 65.
[3] Campbell's "Wild Tribes of Khondistan," p. 49.

running along the sides of the valleys.[1] "Native agriculture in Coorg," says Mr. Richter, "is still carried on as it was centuries ago. A system of rural economy, formed at a remote period, and transmitted for ages unchanged, is not likely to be disturbed by so conservative a people as the Coorgs."[2] This observation by a settlement officer, who has actual experience of the people he is treating of, is very important, and it emphasizes the significance of the Coorg custom of terrace cultivation, which takes place, we are told, in the narrower valleys near the Ghats, where the ground is terraced with considerable pains, the lower and broader fields having a rivulet running through them, and those terraced up along the sides being chiefly dependent upon the rainfall.

I could pause here and enter into a long description of customs and superstitions recorded of the Coorgs, which are identical with the customs and superstitions recorded in the folklore of these islands, and such a pause would be justified by the demands which comparative custom constantly interposes upon the scientific inquirer. But passing on with a mere statement that such a comparison might be instituted without difficulty, it is important to note another range of comparison between the structural methods of the hill folk of Coorg and of Britain. Mr. Richter, in seeking for language proper to describe the fortified positions of the Coorg hills, cannot find anything more adequate than the language used by Mr. W. W. Wilkins in *The Fortnightly Review* in describing early British fortified positions, and Mr. Wilkins says the organization of labour necessary for carrying them out evinces a condition of society utterly incompatible with the prevailing notions on the subject.[3] But this condition of society cannot be conceived by any one influenced only by modern economical conditions. To understand properly the position of affairs which allowed our prehistoric races to accomplish these feats of engineering skill, we must study the crystallized descendants

---

[1] Shortt's "Hill Ranges of Southern India," vol. ii. p. 76.
[2] Richter's "Manual of Coorg," p. 86.
[3] *Fortnightly Review*, April, 1855; Richter, *op. cit.*, p. 189.

of prehistoric races. Noting that the Coorg house, by its position, style of building, and the approaches, strongly remind us of small fortifications, while tradition points back to a time of general feuds when chief fought with chief, and clan with clan,[1] I will turn to another hill tribe of India, which presents us with the actual facts of which Coorg has only the tradition.

One of these, the Angámis Nágás, cultivate by terracing their fields. While some of the tribes follow the mode of cultivation known as júm, a system which necessitates fresh lands being taken up every two or three years, "in the higher ranges, where the hills have a gentle slope, the sides are cut into terraces from the base to the summit, and the same land is continuously cultivated."[2] These terraces are constructed, not made by the plough during a continuous period of cultivation, the only agricultural implements the people possess being a a heavy, long, square-headed dáo, or hand-bill, and a light hoe. The terraces are constructed "with wonderful care and skill in the valleys, and on the hill-sides ascending the latter for upwards of 1,000 feet each little field having its own retaining wall of stone 5 or 6 feet high. Water is brought round for long distances in channels cut with beautiful accuracy. The soil in the terrace fields is manured."[3]

This seems to present a very near parallel to the British evidence, and it is therefore worth while ascertaining what the villages of these Nágá terrace cultivators are like. They are invariably built on the very summits of the hills, and are strongly fortified with stockades, deep ditches and massive stone walls; the hill-sides being thickly studded with *pánjis*, a *chevreux de frise* of sharp-pointed bamboo sticks planted in the ground. In some cases, also, the slopes of the hill are cut away so as to form a perpendicular wall. The approaches to the villages are tortuous narrow *covered* ways only wide enough to admit the passage of one man at a time; these lead to gates closed by

[1] Richter, *op. cit.*, p. 128.
[2] Hunter's "Statistical Account of Assam," vol. ii. p. 185.
[3] *Journal Anthropological Institution*, vol. iii. p. 478; vol. xi. p. 62; Shortt's "Hill Tribes of South India," vol. v. p. 65.

strong heavy wooden doors with look-outs, on which a sentry is posted day and night when the clans are at feud. Very often these approaches are deeply scarped, and the only means of entry into the village is by means of a ladder, consisting of a single pole, some 15 or 20 feet high, cut into steps. The several clans, of which there are from two to eight in every village, are frequently divided off by deep lanes and stone walls. The cause of all this defensive work is a very well marked feature of early tribal history, when each tribe was composed of heterogeneous families, namely, the blood feud between clans. Accordingly, we very seldom find the whole of one village at war with the whole of another village, but almost invariably clan is pitted against clan. Thus a village is often split up into two hostile camps; one clan at deadly feud with another, whilst a third lives between them in a state of neutrality, and at perfect peace with both. The roads, connecting the several villages, as well as the paths leading down to their cultivation, are made with considerable skill; the more precipitous hills turned with easy gradients.[1]

Rude as all this unquestionably is, there is nothing in this description of clan life in India inconsistent with archæological remains in Britain. The fortifications described on the Cheviots are as complete and intricate as those now existing on the Nágá Hills. On Yeavering Bell, where terrace cultivation occurs, we find a guarded entrance remarkably like the Nágá. "The entrance of one fortlet is divided into two by a large upright stone placed jambwise in the centre of it, and in the thickness of the wall to the right of this entrance there is a chamber"[2] equivalent to the Nágá sentinel chamber. Another instance of tortuous protected entrances occurs at Hillsborough, near Ilfracombe, where, nearly at the end of the protecting banks, "the entrance presents a remarkable feature, for at the outer bank it makes a return at right angles to its general direction towards the inner, so that an enemy attempting to

---

[1] *Journal Asiatic Society, Bengal*, vol. xliv. pp. 315-324; Hunter's "Statistical Account of Assam," vol. ii. p. 183.

[2] *Gentleman's Magazine*, 1862, part ii. p. 456.

force an entrance would have to advance with the right side exposed to the defenders;"[1] while again at Linhope, in Northumberland, there "is a protected path leading down to the neighbouring stream."[2] It is impossible to do more perhaps than thus to indicate some parallels between the system of hill fortification in India and Britain, but this is quite sufficient to establish one more point of identity.

Finally, we have seen that the description of these hill fortresses reveals, in Britain as in India, protected clan homesteads, protected, therefore, because of clan blood feuds. Again, we must remark that there is nothing in the existing clan life of India inconsistent with the archæological remains at such places as Humbledon, Yeavering, and Arthur's Seat. And if we enlarge our outlook to places where the remains of hill settlements have been examined with some care, we shall find evidence which confirms this idea. Thus a part of Wansdyke presents a ditch and mound remaining very perfect. "In following the course of the ditch (where Wansdyke can just be traced to have entered the camp) round the western part, we come to a spot where the hard compact nature of the rock has been too much for the tools used in making the ditch, and where the original workmen have been compelled to leave it standing out of the ground. This shows that their instruments were small, and only capable of splitting the rock where it was already shivered and dislocated." And then we find that "the divisions of the settlement are still distinctly visible. Each family or clan had its allotted space, enclosed by a mound, which probably carried on it a palisade, somewhat after the manner of the divisions which exist in the pah of the New Zealander. Remains of hut circles may be closely traced in many portions."[3]

Thus step by step we have traced out the position which must be allotted to the remains of terrace cultivation in Britain, and it seems to me to be impossible to turn aside the evidence

[1] *Gentleman's Magazine*, 1840, part ii. p. 489.
[2] Ibid., 1865, part ii. p. 716.
[3] *Journal Archæological Association*, vol. xiii. pp. 104-107.

PARALLELS IN BRITAIN AND INDIA.

which has been derived from structural formation and position, and from comparative custom; all which proves the existence in Britain of a hill folk who bear a relationship to the Aryan occupiers of the valleys, exactly similar to that obtaining in India, where races have not lost their special characteristics, and are still marked off from each other instead of being crushed out by the greater weight of nationality. And when we come to test this evidence by the ascertained facts of man's early life in Britain, we are met by Mr. Boyd Dawkins' prehistoric farmer of the Neolithic Age, whose characteristics and position produced such vast changes in the history of prehistoric man, and whose descendants are to be traced in the surviving Iberic populations,[1] a remnant of which may still be

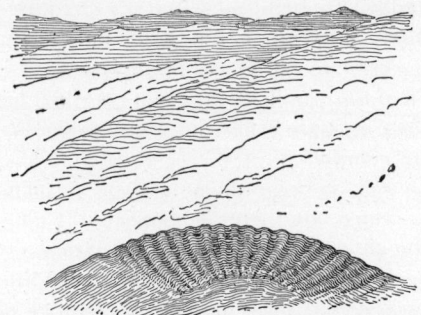

HILL CULTIVATION AT BRYNGLAS.

found in Britain, and types of which are represented by the hill tribes of Asia.

Another very interesting feature of agricultural usage may be mentioned here. "On the hill of Brynglas, between the ravines of Cwm Pysgottwr Fach and Cwm Pysgottwr Fawr, the hill rises in a portion of its line to a conical form, and here the corona is curiously ridged, and looks as if a furrow had been drawn at right angles across the apex; and then on each side of it other furrows made broad at the middle and gradually narrowing as they came near the central one, until at last they seemed to join each other and be carried continuously around

[1] Boyd Dawkins, "Early Man in Britain," pp. 247, 369.

the hill-top in an enlarging circle. They are considered to be remains of early ploughing; and Mr. Chidlow has met with other examples of the same kind on this extensive range. In connection with this it is interesting to compare what Sir John Lubbock has written in his chapter on North American archæology, relative to evidences of ancient agriculture in the state of Wisconsin. In many places, he tells us, the ground is covered with small mammillary elevations which are known as Indian corn hills. They are without order of management, being scattered over the ground with the greatest irregularity. That these hillocks were formed in the manner indicated by their name is inferred from the present custom of the Indians. The corn is planted in the same spot each successive year, and the soil is gradually brought up to the size of a little hill by the annual additions (Lupham, c. i. p. 19). But Mr. Lupham has also found traces of an earlier and more systematic cultivation. These consist of low parallel ridges, as if corn had been planted in drills. They average 4 feet in width, twenty-five of them having been counted in the space of 100 feet, and the depth of the walk between them is about 6 inches. These appearances, which are here denominated 'ancient garden beds,' indicate an earlier and more perfect system of cultivation than that which now prevails; for the present Indians do not appear to possess the ideas of taste and order necessary to enable them to arrange objects in consecutive rows. Traces of this kind of cultivation, though not very abundant, are found in several parts of the state. The garden beds are of various sizes, covering generally from twenty to one hundred acres; as a general fact they exist in the richest soil, as it is found in the prairies and the bunoak plains. In the latter case trees of the largest kind are scattered over them (p. 282). Arguing from such analogies as this we may infer that the remains on Brynglas belong to a very early period, and we are led to ask Whether they may not have been the work of the builders of the adjacent cairns, and of the occupants of the hut dwellings on craig Twrch? The entire absence of metal, and indeed of any implements whatever, removes them at once back beyond the range of history, and we can only assign them to the Stone Age."[1]

Thus, then, with the village communities dating back in documentary evidence to the sixth century, we have now turned by the aid of comparative custom to a still older period. And it seems probable that the village communities in the valleys and plains must have existed alongside of the ruder communities of the hills. Our next step is to see if, after the conflict between the two races (the non-Aryan and the successive waves of Aryan settlers) had been succeeded by settlement, amalgamation had taken place in Britain as it did in India. And it may be at once stated that there are many signs in Britain, as there are many absolute proofs in India, of this amalgamation. Mr. Elton has noted some rude and barbarous customs surviving in folklore which are non-Aryan; Mr. Beddoe has identified surviving types of non-Aryan physiognomy; General Pitt-Rivers has discovered a place of conflict between a short dwarfy people and the Romans; Professor Rhys not only points out some considerable remnants of the non-Aryan beliefs surviving in Celtic heathendom, but absolutely identifies Druidism as a non-Aryan cult; Professor Boyd Dawkins, as we have already seen, points out that the non-Aryan farmer introduced the cereals and some of the arts used by his Aryan successor; and I myself have sought to trace out evidence of the existence of totemism in Britain by its survival in folklore—totemism being primarily a non-Aryan cult, and obtaining among the hill tribes of India who helped to form the Hindu village community. As the archæological evidence in Britain reveals the existence of a hill folk constituted like the non-Aryan hill folk of India; as the points of contact between the Aryan and non-Aryan races are revealed in the structure of the Indian village community; and further, as the parallel between the Indian village community and the English village community is complete, it seems that we may quite properly turn to some

[1] "Archæologia Cambrensis," Fourth Series, vol. x. p. 60.

of the rural customs of England, and see if they do not reveal traces of their non-Aryan origin through the parallel they bear to the non-Aryan parts of the Indian village community.

Cæsar, describing the attributes of the Druids, includes some important characteristics which have a direct bearing on the proposition before us. "They decide all controversies, public and private; if a crime be committed, if a person be slain, if succession to property or the boundaries of land be in question, they determine the case and adjudge the awards and punishments" (lib. vi.). We see from this passage that the non-Aryan Druid caste performed for the village community the following functions:

(1) Settlement of controversies.
(2) Adjudging of crime.
(3) Settlement of succession [to property].
(4) Settlement of boundaries.

Now the appropriation of all these functions to a priestly or sacred caste is opposed to Aryan sentiment.[1] Certainly among the Hindus, the Greeks, the Romans, and, so late down as Tacitus, the Germans, the house-father was priest and judge in his own clan; and it is only amongst the rudest of the so-called Celtic tribes that we find this superimposing of an apparently official priesthood. But the suggestion of Professor Rhys that the cultus of the Druids bespeaks a non-Aryan origin, supplies the most perfect explanation as to why these functions should have been left in the hands of this caste. Compare them with what we have already seen were the functions of the Kolarian tribal priests, and with the functions of the aboriginal race of the lowest caste who always have charge of the boundaries of the village community in India, and the explanation is complete. They supply us, in fact, with the British evidence for what is so apparent in India, that the non-Aryan races have forced upon their Aryan overlords a position as priests to the still feared gods of nature. Some further details on this subject show us the means whereby the earliest non-Aryan settlers obtained a distinct place in the new life of

[1] Pictet, "Les Origines," vol. ii. p. 690.

the village community, when it had become an undergrade of Aryan institutions.

About one half of the agricultural population of Bonai, near the wildest part of Singbhoom, is of the Bhooya caste or race. They are doubtless the oldest settlers, and it was from their hands that the ancestor of the present Rajah first obtained his insignia as chief. The Bamra and Gangpore Rajahs are reported to have in the same manner derived their chieftainship from the Bhooya aborigines, and when a succession to the Raj takes place in any of these districts the acknowledged head of the Bhooya clan goes through a ceremony of making over to the new chief the country and the people. The Bhooyas also have charge of the oldest temples and shrines, and yet the temples are dedicated to the Hindu gods.[1]

The Kaurs (not strictly Hindus) have a yearly festival for each of the gods they worship—Shiva and Parvati—and in some villages there is a Baiga who offers sacrifices at these festivals, but the Baiga is not a Kaur. He belongs to one of the aboriginal tribes, and it is a remarkable feature in the religious ceremonies of the people of the Tributary Mehals that the aborigines should have a monopoly of such offices. The new settlers dread the malignancy of the local spirits, and to appease them naturally rely upon the aborigines who have longest known them.[2]

Among the Badagas of the Nilgiri Hills it is the custom for the low-caste Kurrumban to plough the first furrow, and give his benediction to the field, without which there would be no harvest, and he is again summoned when the season arrives to reap the first handful of corn.[3]

Sir Walter Elliot has described the festival of the village goddess, which is observed in every village of Southern India. The object of this ceremony is intimately connected with the preservation of boundaries, and it includes the sacrifice of a buffalo, and the burial of a piece of the sacred animal in the

---

[1] *Journal Asiatic Society, Bengal*, vol. xxxiv. (2), 2.   [2] Ibid., p. 20.
[3] Dubois, "Manners, &c., of the People of India," p. 343; King, "Aboriginal Tribes of the Nilgiri Hills," p. 43.

lands of each of the villagers. The officiating priests are the Pariahs, the low-caste tribe of village servants, who, on this occasion, are exempt from the degrading condition which excludes them from the village and from contact with the inhabitants, and who afterwards retire to their hamlet outside the town, and resume their humble servile character.[1]

It seems to me that these facts of Indian life, bringing into distinct prominence the influence of non-Aryan people upon the course of village history in India, should once more restore an ethnological meaning to some of the apparently meaningless customs of rural England. Confining ourselves simply to those that relate to the history of the village community, there are at least two curious features in early constitutional history and in surviving local custom which receive some kind of illustration from the Indian facts. The duality which everywhere seems to mark Teutonic and Celtic chieftainship extends from the village to the kingdom, and has attracted the notice of all our writers. The office was, on the one hand, hereditary—descending from the deified ancestor in the eldest male line; and, on the other hand, it was elective—chosen from the one god-descended family. This dual characteristic of chieftainship is represented in English manorial law where, as the last surviving example of Pamber in Hampshire fully shows, the lordship of the manor was elective as well as hereditary. Why may we not explain this dualism in custom by the dualism of race, each chieftain being (of course) hereditary so far as his own tribesmen were concerned, elective so far as his alien tribesmen were concerned? Such a hypothesis, reasonable in itself, is confirmed by many unnoted phases of peasant life which contribute much more information on the facts of unwritten history than is generally admitted. Some of these I shall proceed to note, but in the meantime I will draw attention to Dr. Hearn's strongly supported suggestion that the mass of the chief's dependents were not connected by any tie of consanguinity with the clansmen of pure descent, which helps to explain a very singular fact, the readiness with

[1] *Journal Ethnological Society of London*, New Series, vol. i. pp. 96–100.

which the Celtic peasantry transferred their attachment to new lords.[1]

We may now proceed to notice the many curious examples which occur in England of the election of a village officer upon some special day, and independently of the recognized officials. This officer is generally known as the mock-mayor. Examples are too numerous and too regular in all the details of old ceremonial observances to have arisen spontaneously all over the country merely from local caprice, or merely as the local expression on newly imposed institutions. They have no connection with a calendar festival, and they vary sufficiently to prove their antiquity in some now forgotten ceremony which once had a significance, the force of which is now lost. But the origin may be still traced if my reading of comparative custom be correct. If we examine some of the most curious examples, we are struck by the extreme closeness with which they parallel Indian customs.

One of the first objects on entering the village of St. Germans (East Cornwall) is the large walnut-tree, at the foot of what is called Nut-tree Hill. Many a gay May-fair has been witnessed by the old tree. In the morning of the 29th of the month, the mock mayor, who had been chosen with many formalities, remarkable only for their rude and rough nature, starting from some "bush-house" where he had been supping too freely of the fair-ale, was mounted on wain or cart, and drawn around it, to proclaim his pretended jurisdiction over the ancient borough, until his successor was chosen at the following fair.[2]

"Upon little Easter Sunday, the freeholders of the towne and mannour of Lostwithiel, by themselves or their deputies did there assemble, amongst whom one (as it fell to his lot by turne), bravely apparelled, gallantly mounted, with a Crowne on his head, a scepter in his hand, a sword borne before him, and dutifully attended by all the rest also on horseback, ride thorow the principal streete to the Church ; there the Curate in his best

[1] Hearn's "Aryan Household," pp. 256, 257.
[2] Hunt's "Drolls, &c., of Old Cornwall."

'*beseene*' solemne receiud him at the Church-yard stile, and conducted him to heare diune seruice; after which he repaired with the same pompe, to a house foreprouided for that purpose, made a feast to his attendants, kept the table's end himselfe, and was serued with kneeling, assay, and all other rites due to the estate of a Prince; with which dinner the ceremony ended, and every man returned home again."[1]

Ovingham Fair is on the 26th of April and the 25th of October. The day after the October fair is called "Gwonny Jokesane's day," why so is not known, and has been so called since the recollection of the oldest living. A mayor is elected, and carried in procession. On his advancing, his worship begins thus: "A yes! twe times a yes! an' three times a yes! If ony man, or ony man's man, lairds, loons, lubberdoons, dog-skelpers, gabbrigate swingers, shall commit a parliament as a twarliament, we, in the township o' Ovingham, shall hev his legs, an heed, tied to the cog-wheel, till he say yonce, twice, thrice prosper the fair o' Ovingham, on gwonny Jokesane's day."[2]

The ceremony of choosing a mock mayor was also observed at Penryn (near Falmouth), but it took place in the autumn, on a day in September or October, when hazel nuts were ripe, and "nutting day" was kept by the children and poor people. The journeymen tailors went from Penryn and Falmouth to Mylor parish, on the opposite side of the River Fal. There they made choice of the wittiest amongst them to fill that office. His title was the "Mayor of Mylor." When chosen, he was borne in a chair upon the shoulders of four strong men from his "goode towne of Mylor" to his "anciente borough of Penryn." He was preceded by torch-bearers and two town sergeants, in gowns and cocked hats, with cabbages instead of maces, and surrounded by a guard armed with staves. Just outside Penryn he was met with a band of music, which played him into the town. Bonfires were lighted, and fireworks set off soon

[1] Carew's "Survey of Cornwall," p. 322.
[2] "Jackson the Painter" in Hone's "Every Day Book," and see "Table Book," Leg. Div. iii. p. 198, &c.

after dusk. It was popularly supposed that this choosing of a mock mayor was permitted by a clause in the town charter.[1]

A very curious carnival was originally held under a Lord of Misrule, in July, on Halgaver Moor, near Bodmin, thus quaintly described by Carew: "The youthlyer sort of Bodmin townsmen vse to sport themselves by playing the box with strangers whom they summon to Halgauer. The name signifieth the Goat's Moore, and such a place it is, lying a little without the towne, and very full of quanemires. When these mates meet with any rawe seruing-man or other young master, who may serue and deserue to make pastime, they cause him to be solemnely arrested, for his appearance before the Maior of Halgauer, where he is charged with wearing one spurre, or going vntrussed, or wanting a girdle, or some such felony. After he had been arraygned and tryed, with all requisite circumstances, iudgement is given in formal terms, and executed in some one vngracious pranke or other, more to the skorne than hurt of the party condemned. Hence is sprung the prouerb when we see one slouenly appareled to say he shall be presented at Halgauer Court (or take him before the Maior of Halgauer). But now and then they extend this merriment with the largest, to preiudice of ouer-credulous people, persuading them to fight with a dragon lurking in Halgauer, or to see some strange matter there, which concludeth at least with a trayning them into the mire."[2]

On the third day of the patron festival at Polperro there is a "mayor-choosing, never a valid ceremony, but a broad burlesque. The person who is chosen to this post of mimic dignity is generally some half-witted or drunken fellow, who, tricked out in tinsel finery, elects his staff of constables, and these, armed with staves, accompany his chariot (some jowter's [huckster's] cart, dressed with green boughs) through the town, stopping at each inn, where he makes a speech full of large promises to his listeners, of full work, better wages, and a liberal allowance of beer during his year of mayoralty. He then demands a quart

[1] *Folklore Journal*, vol. iv. p. 241.
[2] Carew's "Survey of Cornwall," pp. 126, 127.

of the landlord's ale, which is gauged with mock ceremony, and if adjudged short of measure is, after being emptied, broken on the wheel of the car. Having completed the perambulation of the town, his attendants often make some facetious end of the pageant by wheeling the mayor in his chariot with some impetus into the tide."[1]

Other places may be noted as observing these singular customs. At Leigh, in Lancashire, near the church tower, on an open space, a townsman was annually chosen to be Lord Mayor for the day of election only, and he was carried through the town.[2] At Hanley,[3] and at Mold,[4] other examples occur. At Kidderminster formerly occurred a custom which, taking place at the election of Bailiff, falls into this group of customs. The town is for one hour in the hands of the populace, who meet and throw cabbage stalks at one another, and who afterwards gather together in order to pelt the newly elected bailiff and his official procession with apples.[5]

These customs, now reduced to the apparent foolishness of village frolics, will bear both scientific analysis and comparison. Although some of them are accounted for in the popular mind by some historical legend of lost chartered rights, this cannot account for all their peculiar characteristics. Not only do they present us with examples of the old village-moot assembling in the open air under a tree, and of the significant procession in the wain, but they parallel those significant ceremonies in India, when on special days the non-Aryan castes of the village meet together, elect their own leader, and take possession in wild and riotous freedom of the entire village. All the vagaries and nonsense practised at these festivals in India are so many symbolical expressions of the power of the non-Aryan tribes during the admitted period of licence. There is no reason why in Britain they should not express, in survival,

[1] Couch's "History of Polperro," p. 159.
[2] *Leigh Chronicle*, May 29, 1880.
[3] *Notes and Queries*, Sixth Series, vol. vi. p. 77.
[4] "Cambro Briton," vol. i. p. 259.
[5] *Gentleman's Magazine*, 1790, p. 1191.

the same village festival with all its significant ethnic symbolism. It would be impossible now to enter minutely into the comparisons these curious customs bear towards savage customs still obtaining in India, but I will give some few examples.

Grimm has dealt with the significance of the wain, or waggon, as a vehicle for some of the gods of heathen Teutonism;[1] but it is certainly older than the Aryan cults. In the Masulipitam district of Southern India the village goddess was carried round the boundaries in a car, each corner of which was surmounted by a sharp wooden spike, on which a lamb was impaled alive, and four sucking pigs in the middle.[2] This was one of the old village festivals where, as we have noted above, the non-Aryan, out-caste tribes, act as priests. Now, in the villages of Southern India, a sacred buffalo is dedicated to the village goddess, and its head is carried in procession, and Sir Walter Elliot points out how clearly this is a modification of the more primitive Khond practice of sacrificing a human being to the village goddess. Noting that the sacrifice of human beings has always been attributed to the Druid cult, noting, too, that sending the victim out to the mercy of the waves was a common form of such sacrifice, is it too much to suggest that the Polperro custom of wheeling the mock mayor in his chariot to the sea and there dipping him in is a modern relic of the more ancient sacrifice? Is it again too much to suggest that the attack upon the newly elected chief officer at Kidderminster is paralleled by similar customs recorded in ancient Corinthia[3] and in modern Africa?[4] When the history of the rise of the Aryan "lord" comes to be written, it will be found that such symbolic actions as this tell us much of his early power and position, which were derived not from his own tribesmen, among whom he was simply *primus inter pares*, but from those servile class of non-

---

[1] "Teutonic Mythology," vol. i. pp. 107, 213, 252.
[2] *Journal Ethnological Society*, New Series, vol. i. p. 100.
[3] Auban, "De Moribus Gentium." *Ulster Journal Archæology*, vol. v. p. 217.
[4] Du Chaillu, "Equatorial Africa," p. 19.

Aryans who assisted him towards an independent position in the community.

For further illustration of this subject it will be necessary to turn to another phase of the South-Indian village festival, where the non-Aryan tribes act as priests. The buffalo procured by the Pariah priest is thrown down before the goddess, its head struck off by a single blow, and placed in front of the shrine, with one fore-leg thrust into its mouth. Around are placed vessels containing the different cereals, and hard by a heap of mixed grains, with a drill plough in the centre. The carcass is then cut up into small portions, and each cultivator receives a portion to bury in his field. Afterwards a great number of buffaloes and several hundred sheep are slain as private offerings by the different families. On the last day of the festival the heap of grain deposited in front of the temple is divided among all the cultivators, to be buried by each one in his field with the bit of flesh. After this a distribution of the piled-up heads is made, a fearful scramble taking place among the candidates for the honour.[1]

Remembering that this festival takes place among the Aryan villagers of India, though the heads of it all are the non-Aryan out-caste tribes, we will now summarize its chief features:

(1) Sacrifice of the buffaloes and sheep.
(2) Dedication of cereals.
(3) Burial of flesh and cereals in the fields.
(4) Scramble for the head-trophies.

It is scientifically probable, and by the proof of examples it has been demonstrated, that folklore, if it retains any relics of such rude practices as these, might retain the several parts of the one ceremony at different places and under different conditions. It would be too much to expect that so savage a ritual could have survived in all completeness in English villages, though it has in Indian villages. But we may possibly pick up the fragments, and we proceed to show where these fragments may be sought for.

1. Adam of Bremen (iv. 27) mentions that at Upsala, the

[1] *Journal Ethnological Society*, New Series, vol. i. pp. 98, 99.

very centre of Teutonic idolatry, the heads of male animals were offered up to the divinities; and Grimm has many notes upon the practice. If we turn to the letter of Pope Gregory the Great to Bishop Mellitus, in A.D. 601, we find him saying that the English nation have been used to slaughter many oxen in the sacrifices to devils.[1]

2. Of the dedication of cereals there are too many well-known examples in English folklore to need setting down here, but their connection with animals was not so well recognized until Mr. J. G. Fraser pointed out the instances where the last sheaf of corn at harvest-time was sometimes known by the name of an animal.[2] What was the custom at harvest might well be duplicated from the spring festival.

3. In that curious piece of Anglo-Saxon ritual which explains how the restoration of fertility to land was accomplished by our ancestors, the ceremony was concluded by taking meal of every kind, baking it into a broad loaf, kneading it with milk and holy water, and depositing it under the first furrow[3]—practices which have survived among peasant beliefs to modern times.[4]

4. At the village of Holne, in Devonshire, is a field of about two acres, the property of the parish, called Ploy field. In the centre stands a granite pillar, 6 feet or 7 feet high. On May morning, before daybreak, the young men of the village used to assemble there, and then proceed to the moor, where they selected a ram, and after running it down, brought it in triumph to the Ploy field, fastened it to the pillar, cut its throat, and then roasted it whole, skin, wool, &c. At midday a struggle took place, at the risk of cut hands, for a slice, it being supposed to confer luck for the ensuing year on the fortunate devourer.[5]

From these folklore fragments I suggest we may yet discover and piece together the surviving relics of the savage

[1] "Beda," lib. i. cap. xxx.   [2] *Folklore Journal*, vol. vii. p. 48.
[3] "Anglo-Saxon Leechdoms," vol. i. p. 405.
[4] Gregor, "Folklore of Scotland," p. 181.
[5] *Notes and Queries*, First Series, vol. vii. p. 353.

ceremony which took place in Aryan village communities, because of their retention of the non-Aryan tribes in their midst. Collectively they afford a very near parallel to the South Indian practices when non-Aryan villagers are allowed to assert their old rights, and the suggestion is that they form the detritus in England of an old non-Aryan festival which has been preserved by these scattered fragments from absolute abolition.

Many parallels suggest themselves in the local festivals of all Aryan countries. Among classical references it is curious to note that in the Anthesterian Dionysia, called the waggon revel, the objurgations and abuse of the upper classes were delivered from a waggon; while a still more significant coincidence with the English survivals at Holne, in Devonshire, was the sacrifice of a kid or fawn, which was torn in pieces for some mystical or unknown reason. This Devonshire custom receives further illustration from another source. Referring back to the Badaga custom of the Nilgiri Hills, at the first ploughing, let us note how, with the addition of more minute details, it serves to illustrate the folklore of our island. Captain Harkness, in his account of the first ploughing, describes the low-caste Kurrumbar as setting up a stone in the midst of the fields, prostrating himself before it, and sacrificing a goat to it, of which goat he possessed himself of the head.[1] These details are not given by the other authorities; but it will be at once observed that they illustrate some of the details of the savage practice at Holne, in Devonshire, and possibly afford a clue to the origin of this singular custom, especially when we note from the evidence in Scotland that a grey stone is associated with the act of reaping.[2]

One further subject seems worthy of noting in this place. Mr. Seebohm has observed, as a common feature of English village lands, that little odds and ends of unused land have from time immemorial been called "no man's land," or "any one's land," or "Jack's land." I conceive these to be what

---

[1] Harkness, "Nilgherry Hills," p. 56.
[2] Gregor, "Folklore of North-East Scotland," p. 181.

Mr. Henderson has noted in Scotland, under a more definite category. Cloutie's croft, he says, or the gudeman's field, consisted of a small portion of the best land set apart by the inhabitants of most Scottish villages as a propitiatory gift to the devil, on which property they never ventured to intrude. It was dedicated to the devil's service alone, being left untilled and uncropped, and it was reckoned highly dangerous to break up by tillage such pieces of ground. In several places in Devonshire similar patches of ground are also found.[1] The explanation of them comes from the non-Aryan villagers of India. A surna among the aborigines of Gangpore is a fragment of the primitive forest left where the first clearance was made, as a refuge for the sylvan deities whom the clearing might have disturbed.[2] Every family among the Coorgs has some spot on the estate, in a retired part of the jungle land, where a sacrifice of a fowl is offered every year to the departed by the living members of the house.[3]

From all these subjects of investigation we have obtained, so far at least as my judgment goes, a not inconsiderable body of evidence as to the existence of a non-Aryan element in the village communities of Britain. Over and over again the certain evidence of these race distinctions which is forthcoming from the unamalgamated elements in Indian villages, finds a parallel among the existing archæological and traditional facts of English villages, and my contention is that the parallel must be true all along the line—must therefore tell us of the old race origins of the English village life. I do not, of course, suggest that the actual performers in these village rites are non-Aryan people, or the descendants of such. Blood descent from the old races cannot be identified except in some few isolated cases. But customs die hard: they continue long after their meaning and origin have been lost, and long after the descendants of their original performers have passed away from their class or caste, and become amalgamated with the nationality.

[1] Henderson's "Folklore of Northern Counties," p. 278.
[2] *Journal of Asiatic Society, Bengal*, vol. xxxiv. (2), p. 10.
[3] Richter's "Manual of Coorg," p. 164.

CHAPTER V.

THE HOMESTEAD OF THE VILLAGE COMMUNITY.

VERY little systematic attempt has been made to trace out the growth of the various beliefs among early man as to the sacredness of the homestead. One has to dig deep down in human history before coming upon the possible origins of such a cult; but it certainly appears as a special feature of Aryan religious thought that the homestead, containing the sacred hearth of the family, was a hallowed spot, where no one but members of the family might intrude, and where members of the family partook of their common meal, performed their common rites, and worshipped their common ancestor. Some of this old tribal cult has to this day survived among the peasantry of Britain.

It has already been noted that the Aryan house, in its primitive structural form, has survived in Britain, and I quoted the remarkable example in Gloucestershire as probably a perfect specimen. I shall have occasion to note hereafter some particular specimens of house-structure in connection with certain types of the village community with which we shall be dealing. But it will be best to collect in this chapter some few notes on the other examples of these primitive houses, for they mark the outward form into which the most important part of the village system fitted. The common fields and the pasture ground make up only a part of this outward form. Much more significant are the dwelling places, because they have a story to tell altogether independent of that told by the open fields around them, and relating to a phase of old village life which has to do with some of the most essential relics of primitive times. Before dealing with the house religion which made every village homestead its temple, we will examine some of the structural features of these homesteads. The importance of these in their relationship to the primitive house religion we shall presently see.

Much has been said about the lord of the village community. The extent of serfdom has been measured not only by its own characteristics, but by the power and position of the lord under whom and for whom the serfdom is supposed to have developed. Well, let us look at the lord in his village home. There is much to show us that his position was by no means one of undefined power: he had rights in the village but duties also. At Pamber, in Hampshire, the fact of his election as village chief was transmitted through manorial records to modern times. Mr. Peacock has noted instances in Lincolnshire where the lord was fined for non-fulfilment of his village duties, and Mr. Grange has given an example of how the fine was to be levied and how distributed.[1]

Apart, however, from these incidental evidences of his equality in the village system, the fact of his home being but little removed from the homes of his co-villagers is of great significance. The Gloucestershire example shows neither great wealth nor great advance beyond the primitive villager. Mr. Baring-Gould has given us further evidence by closely inspecting some fifteenth-century examples of domestic architecture near his own house—examples which show that a clay-walled cottage under thatch represents an ancient family mansion of a grand squirearchical race four hundred years ago. Mr. Baring-Gould goes on with his description of such houses in a manner which for my purpose does not bear curtailing, and I must quote a rather lengthy passage from him about a fifteenth-century example. He says it "has stained-glass coats of arms in the hall window. This house has been used as a farmhouse for three hundred years at least, but it was originally the seat of an influential county family. Now, what are its arrangements? There is a porch; from the porch you enter

[1] *Athenæum*, November 21, 1885; September 25, 1886.

the hall, with a huge fireplace and stained-glass in the windows; but do not imagine a baronial hall, but a low room, 7 feet to the rafters, unceiled. Behind this a lean-to back kitchen, which, I suspect, is a later addition. Beside the porch a dairy and larder. A winding stair of stone, and you reach the bedroom. I say the bedroom, because positively there was

A MANOR HOUSE, EARLY SEVENTEENTH CENTURY.
(*From a MS. in the Record Office.*)

only one, with a huge six-light window opening into it, over the porch, dairy, and hall. In the hall the family sat—squire, ladies, serving-men, and maids; upstairs—let us trust with some sort of screen between them—the whole community slept in one room. In Queen Anne's time this arrangement was too primitive even for the farmer, and an additional wing was erected, with a drawing-room below and a second bedroom upstairs. But no, I am, perhaps, wrong in thinking and asserting that the entire family of squire and retainers pigged upstairs in one room; on further consideration, I believe that the serving-men lay on the benches and in the straw on the floor, and slept about the fire of the hall; and very probably so did the sons of the squire. Upstairs he had his four-poster with curtains round, but the daughters and servant-girls had their uncurtained truckle bedsteads in the same room.

"An advance was made when partitions were erected, constituting a series of bedrooms; but even then all the rooms communicated with each other. Usually this was the arrangement—In the centre of the house, upstairs, at the stair head, slept the squire and his wife; on the right hand, through a door, marched the sons and serving-men to their beds; and through a door on the left hand trotted the daughters and the maid-servants to their beds.

"In a will in Somerset House as late as 1652 a gentleman leaves his dwelling-house to his son Thomas, 'and my will is that Joan, my daughter, shall have free ingress, egress, and regress to the bedd in the chambre wherein she now lyeth, so long as she continueth unmarried,' which is explicable enough when we understand how the bedrooms opened one out of another, and how the master of the house commanded the approach to them by sleeping at the head of the stairs.

"In the parish of Little Hempston, near Totnes, is a perfect example of a house of the time of Richard II. It was probably a manor house of the family of Arundell, but was given to the church and became the parsonage. It is absolutely unaltered, and is of extraordinary interest. It consists of a quadrangle, with building on all four sides, but the central court is only about 20 feet by 12 feet, into which all the windows look from sunless rooms. The only exception is the hall window, which has a southern outlook. The hall was heated by a brazier in the centre, and the smoke went out at a louvre in the roof. There was one gloomy parlour, with a fireplace in it, opening out of this hall. All the rest of the quadrangle was taken up with kitchen, porter's lodge, cellar, and stables. Upstairs, one long dormitory.

"The hall window for long remained a prominent feature. Often it forms a bay, and in the side of it may frequently be found a lavatory. The ladies of the house sat in this window at their needlework, whilst in the smaller houses the cooking went on at the hall fire. The hall served as kitchen, dining-room, parlour, and bedroom for the men. In Elizabeth's reign the bay of the hall window became more prominent, and was even sometimes cut off from the hall by panelling. The ceiling of this bay is low, whereas that of the hall is high. The ladies began to look to their comforts, but they had no separate fire in this bower. If their fingers became cold, they had to run into the hall and warm them at the common fire. Then, still later, came parlours as distinct rooms, generally on the side of the hall opposite to the entrance, and often forming a wing projecting at right angles.

"At first all houses of any consequence affected the quadrangle; but the dwelling-house formed only one side of the quadrangle; the other sides were occupied by stables, cow-houses, barns, and lodge. The windows all looked into the yard. When, however, this arrangement ceased to be necessary, because of the greater security in the country, the owners pulled down their farm buildings and reconstructed them behind the house, so that they might have a little sun look in at their windows, and a little prospect out of them other than at heaps of stable manure and the walls and roofs of cow-houses. There still remain, however, in certain districts on the borders of Dartmoor, a number of the early manor houses thus constructed and quite unaltered, left unaltered because their protection is needed from the boisterous gales. When the farm buildings before the house were removed, the house itself presented a perfectly plain straight front, occasionally with projecting porch, but not usually. The projecting porch was erected later, because the front entrance was exposed by the removal of the farm buildings. Eliminating these erections, the earliest houses of Henry III.'s reign were plain long buildings. Then a porch was added. Next, at right angles, a set of superior apartments, or a parlour, was erected, and the house was changed to the shape of a capital F. Increased wealth and need of accommodation, fashion, and compliment to the reigning Sovereign, made the house assume the shape of H or E. But the old quadrangles—very small— remain often where least expected. They have been glazed over and turned into a central staircase." [1]

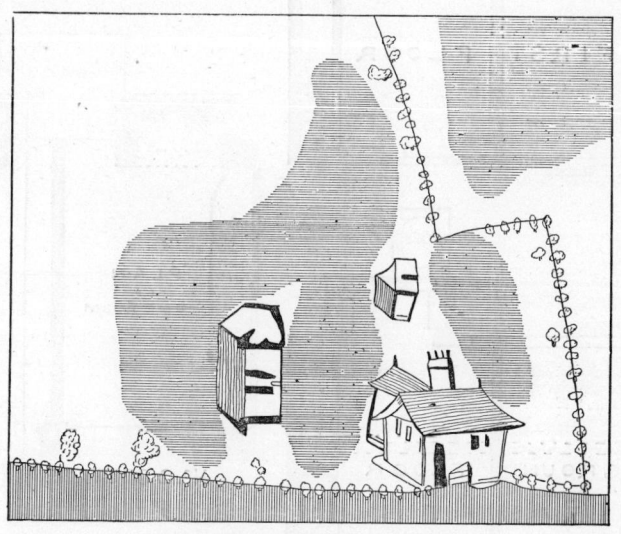

ELIZABETHAN COPYHOLD HOUSE.
(*From a MS. in the Record Office.*)

Such being the lord's homestead, we will now note those of the other villagers. Mr. Hubert Hall has reproduced from MS. sources elevations of old copyhold houses and barns from which it may be seen that the red-tiled, pointed roofs of our country villages are descendants of the earlier homesteads.[2]

---

[1] These facts may be further tested by reference to some well-known works on architecture, and I would refer to Mr. Niven's notes on houses in Shakspere's time, in Furnival's edition of Harrison's "Description of England."

[2] Hall's "Elizabethan Society," p. 36.

In southern and middle England these houses are all situated in villages. Thus an old agricultural writer says, "in Northamptonshire, as well as in the greater part of England, the farmers still live crowded together in villages or townships."[1]

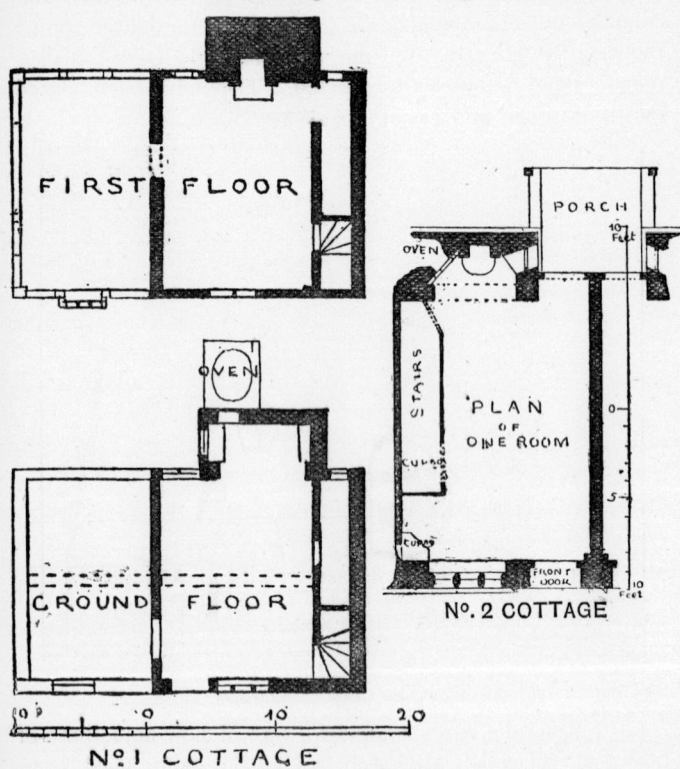

PLANS OF SURREY COTTAGES.

In Wiltshire "the houses are crowded together in villages. Every yard-land has its farm-house, its yard for cattle, its barns and its stables, and the owner resided upon it."[2] In Rutland

[1] Donaldson's "Agriculture of Northamptonshire," pp. 38, 43.
[2] Davis, "Agriculture of Wilts," p. 9.

"the houses are situated in townships, not upon the farms."[1] In Surrey the houses were always detached from the farm in townships.[2] In Lincolnshire the inhabitants were "collected in villages and hamlets, and almost every house you see is inhabited by a farmer, the proprietor of his farm, scattered about in the open fields" surrounding the village.[3] What these village houses were in construction may be gathered by turning to Mr. Nevill's recently published work on Surrey cottages, from which it appears that "the normal plan of the oldest cottages was a simple parallelogram containing one room on the ground floor, and one on the upper floor"[4] exactly, that is to say, the same as the plan and construction of the lord's house. A century ago, says another authority, many sets of farm buildings consisted of oblong blocks adjoining the farmyard, the dwelling being at one end of the block and separated from the out-buildings by a covered passage.[5] In Lancashire there seems to be some evidence that the houses were congregated together in enclosed folds for the purposes of defence. At a place called Tetlow fold, Mr. R. Wood has noted that the farmers seemed to combine for mutual protection, building their houses and farm buildings, so as to enclose them on every side, with the exception of a large doorway for access and exit. These buildings all faced inwards, and originally there were no back-doors, so that when the cattle were shut in at nights and a good dog left to watch, the inhabitants of the houses considered themselves tolerably safe. But if the marauders considered themselves strong enough to venture on a night attack, the farmers and their sons and servants and labourers would muster up twenty or thirty men, all trained to the use of the bow and quarterstaff, and it would take a much stronger force to drive them out of their den.

Bearing in mind what has been said about the mode of

[1] Crutchley's "Agriculture of Rutland," p. 21.
[2] Malcolm's "Compendium of Modern Husbandry," vol. i. p. 106.
[3] Stone's "Agriculture of Lincoln," p. 17.
[4] Nevill's "Old Cottage Architecture of South-west Surrey," p. 10.
[5] Dickinson's "Cumbriana," p. 197.

occupation of the lowland villages, this is remarkable evidence, and it will be borne out by some subsequent facts which are to be noted later on.

It will be anticipated that in Ireland this primitive state of things will be most fully represented. But I think the following account with its curious facts about the position of the fireplace and the absence of chimneys, will give us a clearer idea of the archæological value of this information than is generally recognized. "The term cabin is applied to houses of a single story, having one, two, and in some instances as many as four divisions on the ground floor, which is the only one. There is seldom more than one fireplace, which is commonly in the largest or family room. Sometimes the walls are formed of clay, sometimes of stones. About thirty of these cabins within the town of Boyle might be classed as destitute of chimneys, that is, of chimneys appearing above the thatch of the roof, and it was not easy to distinguish between those which had a hole cut in the thatch for the escape of the smoke, and those which had no passage for it but the house door or window." [1]

As evidence of the state of economical development, these village structures are extremely interesting; they show us the lord's place in the village system. Clearly he belonged to it and formed an essential integer in the composite system; he was not above it, belonging to another system. The examples hitherto examined explain to us the homesteads of the village community, and it is remarkable that when we examine the homesteads of the tribal community there is practically no difference in structure. The type house of the village community is square, and Henning has proved in his work, "Das Deutsche Haus," that the same type exists in Germany. The type house of the tribal community is also square, and Mr. Seebohm has pointed out its resemblance to the Gothic cathedral. There is one other feature to note, namely, that the homestead was composed, not of one house under one roof,

---

[1] "Statistical Survey of Roscommon," p. 189.

but of a group of houses under separate roofs, the principal house always being the living house.[1]

An example of the tribal homestead may be cited: "A farmer's *mains*, as they were called, consisted formerly of a set of low buildings in the form of a square. One side was occupied by the master himself, whose habitation was composed of two or three dismal apartments on an earthen floor, having a low ceiling and a few diminutive lights. On another side stood the barn; in which the roof timbers were built into the wall from the foundation. Opposite to the barn were the stables and the byre or cow-house. The cottages occupied the remaining side; in the midst of all lay the dunghill. These buildings were made of turf and stone alternating, or with stone, and clay for mortar—the roof of thatch, or of thatch and divot (turf or sods) intermixed. It was also very common to have a number of these farm-houses placed together in a village."[2]

It is the custom in some districts of Scotland for the people to retire in the summer to temporary residences or shealings for the purpose of herding the cattle at their summer pasturage. These shealings are commonly spoken of as beehive houses, and at one time were no doubt the permanent residences of early tribesmen. Dr. Mitchell has dealt with the subject of beehive houses in a very instructive manner in his excellent work, "The Past in the Present"; but he has not noted that they supply us with the necessary examples of the round structure figured on the column of Antoninus as typical of the Gaulish house, and on the column of Aurelius as typical of the house of the German barbarians. Not only do these shealings remind us of the shifting characteristics of tribal society, but they also appear to me to represent the stage of tribal development when the group living together were a band of descendants from a common ancestor. Thus they are often to be found, not singly and isolated, but joined together in groups.

[1] See Sullivan's "Introduction to O'Curry's Lectures," vol. i. p. ccc.
[2] Robertson's "Agriculture of Midlothian," p. 31; Lowe's "Agriculture of Berwick," p. 62; Smith's "Agriculture of Argyle," pp. 17, 19.

The first group described by Dr. Mitchell[1] consists of two beehive houses, making two apartments opening into each other. "Though externally the two blocks looked round in their outline, and were, in fact, nearly so, internally the one apartment might be described as irregularly round, and the other as irregularly square." The floor space of one was about 6 feet square, and of the other 6 feet by 9 feet. But this union of beehive huts is extended to a greater number than two. A remarkable instance of this is described and figured by Dr. Mitchell.[2] It has several entrances, and would accommodate many families, who "might be spoken of as living in one mound rather than under one roof." Looking at the ground plan of these beehive huts as figured by Dr. Mitchell, one cannot resist the conclusion that the cluster has grown up by accretion, as it were; that it has been added to by the beehive men to meet the increased wants of the primitive family who resided in it. One other form of the beehive hut I must notice here. Dr. Mitchell says the ruins of it are still older, still more complex, than any to be seen in South Uist. Its interior is round, and measures 28 feet in diameter. Within this area there are ten piers or pillars formed of blocks of dry-stone masonry. The stones are entirely undressed and of every possible size and shape, and there is no evidence of the use of any tool by the builders. This beehive house would accommodate from forty to fifty people.[3]

We are a long way from civilization in these summer shealings of eighteenth-century Scottish farmers. They represent in the most practical manner the force of traditional usage upon the ways of man when no disturbing force arises to break up such usage. But the history of the village community in Britain is not perfect if we do not consider their place among

---

[1] "Past in the Present," p. 69.   [2] Ibid., p. 64.

[3] Ibid., pp. 68, 69; for the sites of old villages of beehive formed houses, I would refer the reader to Boyd Dawkins' "Early Man in Britain," p. 267; *Archæological Journal*, vol. xxiv. p. 229; King, "Munimenta Antiqua," pp. 12–15; Rowland, "Mona Antiqua," pp. 25–27; "Archæological Association," vol. xviii. p. 119; Stevens, "Flint Chips."

the survivals which take us back to past ages. It may well be that the lowland types of the village community, as at Hitchin, at Winslow, or at those other places which we shall presently consider, have advanced beyond the most primitive type. They have been situated in the midst of the struggle which has led through feudalism to civilization. But on the outskirts of our land, village communities have remained crystallized, and they represent not only the degree of non-interference with primitive institutions which has been possible under the governments in Britain, but the point from which other survivals subject to much interference must have developed.

The internal home economy is just as simple and rude as the external structure. We read that "they had a window on each side, which they opened or shut as the wind blew, to give them light. These windows they stopped with straw or fern. When they kindled a fire they lived in a constant cloud of smoke. They had no standing beds, but slept on heath and straw, covered with the coarsest blankets, upon the floor. They kept their cattle in the same house with themselves tied to stakes in one end of the house. Their furniture consisted of stools, pots, wooden kogs, and bikkers. At their meals they eat and supped together out of one dish. Each person in the family had a short-hafted spoon made of horn, which they called a *munn*, with which they supped, and carried it in their pocket or hung it by their side. They had no knives and forks, but used their fingers."[1] This picture represents not a going back to barbarism, but an absolute non-advance from barbarism. It is this side of the question which must be considered most strongly in connection with our present subject. A group of men living under conditions of domestic economy and village or tribal economy which betray how they have kept themselves back during the time that others have been advancing, tells as much of the past history of the whole nation as the archæological remains which lie scattered on the hill-tops and plains. And we cannot ignore them in seeking for the origin of institutions in these

[1] Sinclair's "Statistical Account of Scotland," vol. ix. pp. 325-326.

islands. I have already stated that one of the subjects to be taken into account is the survival of the old domestic hearth cult which occurs in folklore, and which must have come down from the village community; and it appears to me we shall be less reluctant to admit the possibility of these survivals if we point to such surroundings as these we have just examined as the home of the old religion.

Some passages in Bede reveal the fact that the villages in his time were much as they have been described in the preceding pages. The story of Germanus having found shelter in a villager's house, and so preserved it from the fire which destroyed all the other houses in the village, reveals the collection of the homesteads into villages instead of in tribal homesteads (lib. i. cap. xix.); while the story of the sanctity shown by the earth taken from St. Oswald's grave not only shows us the village homestead, but reveals at least one important feature of primitive house life, namely, the situation of the central fire in the middle of the room (lib. iii. cap. x.)—an arrangement prevalent in Scotland so recently as the latter part of the last century.[1]

Following up this clue, it will be found that our examination of the village house structure in England leads us to perceive that it is intimately connected with the primitive Aryan principle of the sacredness of the homestead. The group of buildings making up the homestead is centred round that portion which contains the sacred house-fire, and it has been remarked with truth that "it is no fanciful metaphor to say that the house-fire is the seed out of which the house has grown." If the architecture of the old village homestead reveals this much to us, custom tells us something more. The preservation of the old chimney-stack of ancient dwellings while all else has been rebuilt and the right of house-bote attached thereto; the old tenure locally called "keyhole" tenure in Hampshire, by which, if a squatter could build a house or hut in one night, and get his fire lighted before the morning, he could not be disturbed; the demolition of

[1] Sinclair's "Statistical Account of Scotland," vol. viii. p. 510.

the homestead as a sign of loss of village rights,[1] taken in connection with a law of Canute which lays it down that housebreaking is an inexpiable crime, punishable only with death; seem to me to connect the house unmistakably with the old hearth cult. And the importance of this as a potent force in keeping together old forms of society may be to some extent measured if we bear in mind what Dr. Hearn has so strongly and ably set forth of Aryan society, that "it was not the tie of blood, or of family habit, or of superior physical force that held men together, but the far more potent bond of a common worship. Those who worshipped the same gods were relatives."[2]

We may now turn to another source of evidence—custom and usage—and see what relics have been preserved of the old hearth cult of the homestead.

Of the worship of ancestors as it affects the law of inheritance, Sir Henry Maine has already stated the principal features from the Indian evidence.[3] Mr. Elton has supplied much of the English evidence, concluding that "the oldest customs of inheritance in England and Germany were, in their remote beginnings, connected with a domestic religion, and based upon a worship of ancestral spirits, of which the hearthplace was essentially the shrine and altar;"[4] and he goes on to suggest an explanation of the prevalence of junior-right and its connection with the hearth cult, which is of peculiar interest to the view we have been considering as to the origin of the village community, namely, that this form of succession is due to a race of pre-Aryans, traces of which are still to be made out in the populations of Europe.

An analysis of the customs which attended the primitive hearth cult shows us that the sacred fire on the hearth was never allowed to go out; that the ritual attendant upon marriage, birth, and death centred round the sacred fire; that

---

[1] *Archæological Review*, vol. iv. p. 366.
[2] Hearn's "Aryan Household," p. 27. [3] "Early Law and Custom."
[4] "Origins of English History," p. 216; *cf.* cap. xxxviii. of Ine's laws, "Let the kin hold the homestead until it [the child] be grown up."

offerings to the ancestral god at the hearth were made from the food of the household; and that the hearth represented to its early worshippers the source of all their happiness and prosperity.

The Laws of Ireland have preserved for us the earliest relic of this cult, setting it forth that "the Brughfer should have an ever-living fire."[1] How this ever-living fire is represented in folklore I have already shown in my work on "Folklore Relics of Early Village Life." Spenser observes that in Ireland at the kindling of the fire and the lighting of candles they say certain prayers, and use some other [superstitious] rites, which show that they honour the fire and the light;[2] and an early writer of this century affirms the same of Scotland;[3] while in England the verse of Shakespeare, Herrick, and other poets has preserved the same practices. That the oldest rituals of the marriage ceremony, of baptism, and of burial were centred round the hearth in Britain, as also in India, is proved by frequent examples perfectly preserved in folklore, all of them together making up an exact parallel to those facts of the early Aryan world which Dr. Hearn has so well described from sources other than British. Among the Irish there is an expression "the breaking of cinders," meaning to charge and confirm guilt on a man at his own hearth, so that his fire, which represents his honour, is broken up into cinders—the trampling of a man's cinders being one of the greatest insults which could be offered to him, as it conveyed the idea of guilt, not only of the individual himself, but also of his family and household;[4] and when we note how this is parallelled by the English proverbial expressions preserved to us from Northamptonshire, "kill's a fire 'tween they two," and "the tow is in the fire," intimating the existence of great enmity between two persons,[5] there is certainly no room to doubt that the primitive

---

[1] Sullivan, "Introduction to O'Curry's Lectures," vol. i. p. cccxviii.
[2] Spenser, "View of the State of Ireland," p. 98.
[3] Wood's "Primitive Inhabitants of Ireland," p. 170.
[4] Sullivan's "Introduction to O'Curry's Lectures," vol. i. p. cclxxviii.
[5] Sternberg's "Northamptonshire Glossary," p. 58.

THE PRIMITIVE HEARTH CULT.

hearth cult of the Aryan village community is preserved among the traditional practices of the English peasantry alongside of the traditional agricultural practices.

It has not been found necessary to set forth the proofs of this early cult at great length, because this has already been done in a separate work, and writers have very frequently alluded to this most interesting survival. I think it may, on the whole, be considered as forming the most perfect survival preserved in folklore. But the point to insist on here is its close connection with the village community, and its bearing upon those other relics of the village community which have hitherto been made into an exclusive study. Clearly, as it appears to me, it points to the descent of the village community from primitive originals. The old worship, the old kinship, cannot be divorced from the concurrent agricultural practices, and in seeking out for origins we must group all these survivals together. As an old author puts it with force, speaking of the villagers he knew, "his religion is a part of his copyhold."[1] The peasants of Britain have preserved the whole group intact, during the time when the political rulers of the nation have been carving out a destiny for the country outside the conception of villagers. Let it be remembered that the documents which teach us of lordship and serfdom are drawn from the ruling class, possessed of national instincts and national hopes, whose terminology must frequently have been in advance of the facts. In the meantime it was the peasants who were preserving the history of the nation, which was thus changing and developing over their heads, and so often as the facts of this preserved history take us back to a stream from which flowed that great body of custom which tells us of a hearth-cult and a primitive system of agriculture, so often are we justified in the conclusion that this stream is the origin alike of Indian and British village life.

[1] Clarke's "Survey of the Lakes," p. 36.

CHAPTER VI.

TRIBAL COMMUNITIES IN BRITAIN.

WE are now able to examine the types of the village community which have survived in Britain to the present day. Our equipment for the task, as set forth at length in the preceding chapters, may seem to be very heavy; but it is quite certain that, looking at the facts in the history of the village community which I have there attempted to bring together, it is impossible to properly examine existing survivals without adequate knowledge of the facts which bring into relief all that such survivals mean in the history of institutions. A sudden plunge into manorial history has succeeded in bringing out certain economical features which are in strange contrast with the commercial economy of the age. It would also succeed in explaining that the works of our great political economists, from Adam Smith downwards, could only have been written after the manorial system had ceased to play any part, or at all events any important part in the development of the nation; and would enable us to trace in Adam Smith theories derived from the influence, dying as it was, of the manorial system, and to discover that these are just the theories which Mill and the later writers have rejected, not without some unwarranted feelings of scorn for the older master. Attempt to work this manorial system back through the centuries of English history, and we should find it fit in more nearly to the economical development of each age the further back we go. But on the great questions to be asked concerning it—Whence its origin? whence its long continuance? and what is its place among English local institutions?—we can get no sufficient answer, as it seems to me, by confining our researches to manorial history. Right athwart such an inquiry is the gap left by the absence of all detailed evidence in the early ages, the overshadowing influence of Roman history largely preserved by Roman historians, and the extreme difficulty of estimating or appreciating the accelerated force of the march of civilization, which makes each succeeding age so much in advance of what has gone before.

We have already noted that the two classes of communities —tribal and village — appear in all Aryan lands; that the former is the more primitive form, having been preserved by its home on the hills, and that the latter has resulted from a constant reception within its boundaries of swarms of new villagers whenever settlement has succeeded to conquest. We will now examine the survivals of tribal communities in Britain; and it will be found that these are invariably to be found in the hilly, or the outlying districts, difficult of approach and conquest, in contradistinction to the plains and valleys, easy of approach and conquest. Surely this is evidence enough of an origin due to causes which lay within the communities themselves. As we proceed I shall direct attention to the evidence which has already been shortly stated, that the hill communities, being difficult of access and difficult to conquer, remained in their primitive stage longer than the valley or plain communities, who always received the first shock of any conquest, and who had at successive eras to open their ranks and take in new villagers, who had first appeared as conquerors. Let me note that the late survival of the community constitutes the most essential part of the evidence. It is plain proof of the vitality of the communal principle as distinct from the national principle. Where Roman power was greatest in Britain was in the creation of a national government; if it had ever entered into the inner life of the communities, it would have burst the boundaries of such a localizing system, and the internal structures thus revealed would have become welded into a national system. That the community should have survived so late is the strongest proof of primitive origin.

I think there are few more archaic types of society than we

meet with in the Island of Harris in 1795. The higher order of tenants were mostly descendants of different branches of the chieftain's family, originally settled in patrimonial possessions on the estate. Many of these possessions had devolved in regular succession from father to son through a long course of ages. Subordinate to this grade were the small tenants. A small tenant farm was a little commonwealth of villagers whose houses or huts were huddled close together, "with too little regard," says Sir John Sinclair, "to form, order, or cleanliness." The lands belonging to these farmsteads were yearly divided by lot for tillage, whilst their cattle grazed on the pasture in common. Labour was performed by a class of cottar tenantry attached to the farmsteads, who were paid in kind and in land allowances, one day a week of their time being granted for their own use. Coarse flax sown in the ground was manufactured into shirts and other linens by the farmer's wife and daughters during the long winter evenings, and the farmer himself was clothed from the fleece of his little flock.[1] They ground their corn by means of the quern, *i.e.*, a couple of light millstones set in motion with the hand by means of a staff fixed to the upper stone. All the bread thus made was generally consumed by the month of June, and they then chiefly subsisted on their own sheep and the milk of their cows, with what fish they chanced to catch.[2]

Sir Arthur Mitchell has taught us the true archaic value of such domestic economy as this in his "Past in the Present"; but I much question whether the social structure to which it belongs is not of almost unique value. The strip of sea which separates the inhabitants from the mainland has preserved the form of society which has existed for centuries, and this little tribal community presents just such another picture as we obtain from the "Germania" of Tacitus, and from the early documentary evidence of Wales and Ireland.

We may sum up the constitution of this tribal community in

---

[1] Martin, in "Western Isles of Scotland," p. 57, describes a curious and primitive method of thickening cloth by the native women.
[2] "Statistical Account of Scotland," vol. x. pp. 352–370.

the exact words of the statistical writer of the last century, who notes that the whole "estate" is occupied by—

(1) Principal tacksmen or gentlemen;
(2) Small tenants;
(3) Cottars;

just the three classes which reappear in the village community wherever its traces are to be found in England. Now can we in this outlying island detect the race origin of these three classes?

It seems clear that the uppermost ranks of this community are the descendants of a band of settlers who, at the time of settlement, were organized upon the tribal system; for it is remarkable to note that the self-acting system of the Irish "fine," accounts not only for the organization of the first rank of this community as it appears in the eighteenth century, but will account for the existence of the lower rank of smaller tenants. The first step to take in order to show how this is so is to explain the system of tenure by which the lands of this community were held. This we can do by reference to an old account of the Highlands of Scotland which was published by Sir Walter Scott. We are told that "the property of the Highlands belongs to a great many different persons who are more or less considerable in proportion to the extent of their estates and to the command of men that live upon them or follow them on account of their clanship out of the estates of others. These lands are let by the landlord during pleasure on a short tack to people whom they call good-men and who are of a superior station to the commonalty. These are generally the sons, brothers, cousins, or nearest relations of the landlords. [Those sons who marry] are preferred to some farms. This, by means of a small portion and the liberality of their relatives, they are able to stock, and which they, their children and grandchildren, possess at an easy rent till a nearer descendant be again preferred to it. As the propinquity removes they become less considered, till at last they degenerate to be of the common people. As this hath been an ancient custom, most of the farmers and cottars are of the name and clan of the proprietor."[1] The shifting nature of this tribal tenure is explained very clearly in this extract, and it represents in survival the ancient practice which has been recorded in the Welsh laws and in the Brehon laws of Ireland,[2] the latter of which has been so much discussed. We shall have to revert to this again later on, but the point to note here is that a system of tenure depending upon the degree of propinquity to the tribal chief goes on uninterruptedly so long as there are tribal lands to meet the "going out" of sons from the chief homestead.

There now remains the cottar class of servile attendants. The position of the non-Aryan people, which, as we have seen, extended all over Europe and had to withstand the Aryan conqueror, might very readily be accepted as sufficient warrant for the origin of this cottar class, confirmed as it is by the analogy of the serfs mentioned in the "Germania" of Tacitus and of the most servile class in the Hindu village community. But in this case we may go beyond the argument of analogy, for there is not wanting evidence of the non-Aryan race element among the people of Harris. We first get at this by the physical characteristics of the people. They are described as of "small stature.... Scarcely any attain the height of 6 feet, and many of the males are not higher than 5 feet 3 or 4 inches. ... The cheek bones are rather prominent, and the nose is invariably short, the space between it and the chin being disproportionately long. The complexion is of all tints. Many individuals are as dark as mulattoes."[3] Then, if we

---

[1] Burt's "Letters from Scotland," vol. ii. p. 341.

[2] Compare Sir John Davies' account of the Irish sept, "Historial Tracts," p. 128: "If any one of the sept had died, his portion was not divided among his sons, but the chief of the sept made a new partition of all the lands belonging to that sept, and gave every one his part according to his antiquity." "Ancient Laws of Ireland," vol. iv. introduction; *Journal des Savants*, August, 1887.

[3] Dawson's "Statistical History of Scotland," p. 550. Mr. David MacRitchie, in the *Archæological Review*, vol. iv. p. 16, *et seq.*, has discussed this with other features of Harris ethnology with a view of establishing evidence of Ugrian blood in these islanders. *Cf.* Skene, "Celtic Scotland," vol. iii. p. 323.

look into some of their superstitions, we find them sufficiently near to non-Aryan beliefs to warrant the theory of a common origin. In an ancient chapel on one of the islands attached to Harris was "a flat thin stone, call'd Brownies stone, upon which the antient inhabitants offered a cow's milk every sunday,"[1] a custom which has its counterpart among the non-Aryan Todas of the Nilgiri Hills,[2] whilst the stone circles and the remarkable temple of "Annat"[3] afford other parallels to Toda antiquities and customs, and, what is more significant, perhaps, a total contrast to any of the forms of primitive Aryan beliefs.

It appears from this evidence that we may, in the outlying parts of our land, detect a still surviving specimen of the primitive tribal community, and that it enables us to retranslate Mr. Seebohm's famous formula of the manor with a village community in serfdom under it into a formula written on the archives of native history—the tribal community with a village of non-Aryan serfs under it.

It will be well, perhaps, before leaving this important type of the tribal community, to state shortly the proof that the Harris example does not stand absolutely alone. Let me, as a starting point, once more revert to the Toda people of the Nilgiri. Describing their dwellings, Colonel King says, "the walls are made of roughly-planed boards joined together with clay; the sides are not more than 3 feet high by about 12 feet long; ... the roofs are made of reeds and thatched with lemon grass. The whole structure is very substantially and neatly built, but there is no chimney, and the smoke from the fires pours out of the door and exudes from every crevice. The huts are built close together in clusters of three or four only, and not in villages, the family groups being called munds. The inhabitants migrate periodically from one to another for

---

[1] Martin's "Western Islands of Scotland," p. 67; cf. Pennant's "Tour in Scotland," vol. iii. p. 437.

[2] King's "Aboriginal Tribes of the Nilgiri Hills," p. 21.

[3] "Statistical Account of Scotland," vol. x. p. 375.

change of pasture."[1] Now, what Martin, in 1716, only saw in Harris a single specimen of, and describes in two or three lines,[2] Sir Arthur Mitchell has drawn with a master's hand, giving all the striking details.[3] Toda and Harris islander are clearly in the same stage of culture—tribal nomads living in clustered homesteads of the rudest fashion, so small, low, chimneyless, and uncouth as to show that the inhabitants lived in the open and sought only refuge in their huts.

Now let us turn to the mainland of Scotland. "Formerly," says Marshall, "sod huts were the common habitations of the tenantry of the central Highlands, and they are still (1794) in use in the more northern districts. Those huts were built with sods, or thick turf, taken from the pasture lands, and having remained a few years in the capacity of walls, were pulled down and spread over the arable fields as manure; another square of rock being laid bare and another set of sods piled up for the same purpose. The materials for the roof were used, and still are used, in the same intention; and perhaps the roof itself, in places where wood was plentiful and peats difficult to procure, was pulled to pieces for fuel, and a new one, culled from the nearest wood at the tenant's pleasure, set up in the form of a roof, to dry for a future store of fuel. At present the building material is stone; but no cement as yet is in use except in particular cases. The dwelling-houses are seldom more than five or six feet high, perhaps without glass in the window, and with door-way so low that even a middle-sized man must stoop. The roof is set on with 'couples' or large principal rafters, fixed in the walls two or three feet above the foundation, generally upon large stones set to receive their feet. Upon these couples lines of 'pan-trees' or parlines are fixed, and resting on these rough boughs (stripped of the leaves and smaller twigs) are laid rafter-wise and termed 'cabbers'; upon these 'divot' or thin turf laid on in the manner of slates; and upon this sod covering a coat

[1] King's "Aboriginal Tribes of the Nilgiri Hills," pp. 12-13.
[2] Martin's "Western Isles of Scotland," p. 67.
[3] Mitchell's "Past in the Present," p. 59, 63.

of thatch composed of straw, rushes, heather, or fern. The gables and the ridge are loaded with 'feal,' thick sods taken from the deepest best soil."[1]

These houses are tribal houses, not village houses. Studied by themselves they are extremely curious and capable of affording much insight into archaic society. But we can study them fortunately with the tribal community living in them.

After describing such stone and turf houses as these the agricultural report of Forfarshire by Mr. James Headrick (1813) goes on to state that a considerable number of them are commonly arranged together in clusters, with intermediate houses for their cattle, forming a sort of village without symmetry or plan. The inhabitants cultivated the contiguous land in the way called run-rig, that is, patches scattered here and there, with baulks or intervals betwixt them which received no cultivation, while their cattle and sheep grazed promiscuously on the neighbouring waste (pp. 128, 129). To these farmsteads were attached cottages collected in small villages called cot-towns, where they occupied a house and garden and sometimes kept a cow under the farmer. Their rent is paid in labour and services to their master (p. 137).

This is the type of tribal community to be met with in all the Highland districts. In Argyle, Inverness, Perth, Aberdeen, I have obtained specimens of this archaic society. The form of joint-tenancy has taken the place of joint-kinship.[2] All

---

[1] Marshall's "Agriculture of Central Highlands of Scotland," 1794, p. 20.

[2] Mr. Seebohm has remarked of the tribal community that "the evidence, as regards Scotland, is scanty" ("Village Community," p. 222), simply contenting himself with a reference to Mr. Skene's "Celtic Scotland." If we look for the tribal community in full archaic form, based upon kinship, I confess the evidence is not *direct*. In the first place, direct legislation has interfered to upset it. By the Act of 1695 run-rig *ownership* was abolished, and this at once cut at the root of the tribal community. As, however, it did not abolish run-rig *tenancy*, we have the exact date of the passing away of the old form of common ownership by blood relations, in favour of the new form of common tenancy by rent-paying to one landlord. My suggestion, then, is that joint-tenancy succeeded to joint-kinship without any break in the historical succession, and that evidence of the former is evidence of the latter.

the owners of the clustering houses just described were joint tenants of one landlord, each and all jointly responsible for the rent of the farmstead. At Caputh in Perthshire there were for the most part eight tenants in one farm, and the whole farm was in run-rig (Sinclair's "Stat. Acc.," ix. 494). This short but suggestive description is to be met with throughout the reports on Highland agriculture and parish statistics; and of course it carries with it all the extra particulars we have ascertained about Harris and Forfar. Now and again we obtain some interesting additional details of the system of dividing the lands. In Inverness the reports of the Board of Agriculture, 1808 (p. 334), state that the land is first ploughed without leaving any boundaries; then the field was divided by putting small branches of trees into the ground to mark off every man's portion before the field was sown. No man knew his own land till the seed was to be cast into the ground, and it became impossible for him to have the same strip of land any two successive years. At Kilmorie, in Bute, we get still more interesting particulars. "Nearly the whole of this tract was, till the last twenty-five years, in a state of undivided common, to which all persons, be they cottars or farmers, might send as many sheep and field cattle as they chose. . . . All the lands were undivided and unenclosed. Each farm was leased by a number of individuals, sometimes by as many as *ten and fifteen*, who were jointly and severally liable for the rent. Each farm was thus a *societas arandi* or township, containing as many families, having each an equal interest in its cultivation, each field being subdivided into as many strips, separated by a narrow ridge called a 'bone,' where the stones, weeds, and other rubbish gathered off the land were accumulated. These strips generally changed possessors every second or third year, according to arrangement of parties. The milch cows grazed in common upon the pasture lands which lay between the arable and the hill common; but when the crops were secured at the end of autumn, sheep, cattle, horses, swine ranged at large over the whole farm. . . . The arable land was divided into infield and outfield. The latter was exclusively devoted to white crop, which was taken off in succession, as long as it would return more than the seed, and then suffered to lie lea for six or seven years." [1]

The designation of the separate strips as "bones" enables us to carry on the examples to Ireland. We are told that in the hilly district of Kilkenny lands are held at will by tenants who generally live in scattered homesteads and hold in partnership. The custom is, when ground is to be broken for tillage, to divide it into shares, or what they call *lochs;* and they are so desirous of making the divisions equal in value, that each portion, though small, does not lie together, but is scattered in fragments. When the division is made out, lots are prepared; each man takes a bit of stick, or particular stone well marked; these are enveloped in a ball of clay, and a child or stranger is called to place each ball upon some one of the lots, by which each man's share is determined. These lochs in tillage are divided by ribs of sod left in the field, called *bones,* and are sometimes marked by stones. These ribs often produce a singularly striped and patched appearance in small farms.[2]

The townlands of Kilmactige, county Sligo, are divided into three or four portions, and each of these occupied by a certain number of tenants who hold in common, dividing the arable in equal parts, and appropriating the coarse ground and pasture in grazing; each having a right to put on a certain number of cattle, reckoning by their ages and kinds. Then we have a most curious primitive law of succession. Whenever a man has a farm or a part of an undivided farm, and has one or more sons to marry, he gives to each of them a division of his holding, making them subject to pay their proportion of the landlord's rent.[3]

In Roscommon are some examples of the farms in coparcency exactly similar to the Scottish examples.[4]

In these surviving types of the tribal community we are

[1] "New Statistical Account of Scotland," vol. v.
[2] "Statistical Survey of Kilkenny," p. 419.
[3] Mason's "Statistical Account of Ireland," vol. ii. p. 384.
[4] "Statistical Survey of Roscommon," pp. 475, 478.

clearly dealing with cases which have not met any great wave of opposition to their normal line of development. Gradually they have been hemmed in by the growth of surrounding populations; they have had less capacity for extension into wider areas; but no development of economical theory and practice, no conquest by tribal communities as rude as themselves, have occurred to turn their development into new channels. Constant repetition of all the details of life has succeeded in crystallizing these details into an unchanging form, and it is these crystallizations which we can study now as the best evidences of the past. The picture which Cæsar has presented to us of the constantly moving tribal communities, occupying some tract of virgin soil for one season and then moving to another tract (vi. 21-22), is not to be met with in surviving British custom, but it is, as we know, presented by modern Indian communities. On the other hand, the communities which Tacitus described, one hundred and fifty years later than Cæsar, as "dwelling apart and scattered as spring or plain or grove attracted their fancy," with villages containing those who were not free tribesmen ("Germ." xvi.), are to all extents and purposes represented in the tribal communities surviving on the borders of English civilization.

When we turn to the Welsh types, however, we meet with something over and above the tribal community. Like the Scottish and Irish tribal settlements, they outwardly exhibit the same characteristics, Leland long ago noting that "there is no place yn al these commotes where the people dwelle vicatim but al sparsim."[1] But this is not all. The artificial clustering of the homesteads into mathematically formed groups appears above the tribal communities themselves, and we recognize therein the iron-hand of the Roman tax-gatherer. While leaving untouched the internal structure of the community, the Roman power has diverted the outward form from its original type; and there being no later infusion of primitive tribesmen into the Welsh communities to uproot the influences of Roman imperialism, the Welsh tribal communities

[1] Leland's "Itinerary," vol. v. p. 54.

and their superstructure of taxation units remain in tolerable perfection for our observation.

The form of tribal community which we have described in the Island of Harris has now passed away, and private property in land has succeeded to it. It may therefore be suggested that, in the transition from tribal community to individual holding, the village community does not appear as a necessary term in the series of development; and that, therefore, in this case the ordinary course of events for the tribal community to develop into the village community, for the village to break up into families, and for the families to break up into severalty, has not taken place. But there is not wanting evidence that the normal transition, even in these remote islands, and under the enormous pressure which the influence of modern ideas has exerted in the contrary direction, did actually take place. Harris belongs to a group of islands known as the Outer Hebrides, and other islands, Lewis, North Uist, Long Island, possessed much the same kind of tribal community as Harris. But Mr. Carmichael, before the Crofter Commission, described the intermediate stages between this and private ownership to have actually survived thus: (1) the island of Heisgeir being occupied in run-rig wholly; (2) North Uist and South Uist in an intermixed system of crofts and run-rig; and (3) Barra, all divided into crofts, and no part being common. Now, if we examine the system followed in the island of Heisgeir, we find that it is occupied by one class of tenants only, equivalent to the lower tenants of the Harris community, and that these tenants work their farms on the principle, pure and simple, of the village community. Tenants of one lord, the tribal characteristics have all been swept away, and without the interposition of the manorial system we arrive at the village community—still tribal in one remarkable feature, the annual migration from village to hill for the pasture of flocks, but in all else belonging to the village type. So much is necessarily made of the manorial system in England, that it is important to observe similar results where the manorial system does not exist; and it strengthens a suggestion I am strongly inclined to make, that manors are the form in which the central government in England in the eleventh and perhaps late tenth century clothed the then existing village communities.

We may describe the Heisgier community as follows. It consists of ten tenants, or more properly, twelve, because two of the ten have two shares each instead of one: these I shall call the villagers. The dwelling-houses of the village are made of wattling, plastered over on both sides with boulder clay and whitewashed with lime. There are as officers of the community, the maor, the constable, and the herdsman. The maor is appointed by the lord's factor, and acts for the lord as a kind of sub-factor. The constable is elected by the villagers in a most primitive and interesting manner. The people meet together at a gathering called "Nabac" (neighbourliness), or if presided over by the maor, it is called mod, moot—the official title of the assembly thus following the official mode of meeting. The place of meeting is locally known as Cnoc Na Comhairle, the Council Hill, or Clach Na Comhairle, the Council Stone. The constable having been elected, he takes off his shoes and stockings, uncovers his head, and bowing reverently low, promises in presence of heaven and earth, of God and of men—*am fianuis uir agus adhair, am fianuis De agus daoine*—that he will be faithful to his trust. At Hallow-tide the villagers meet and decide upon the piece of ground within their mark which is to be broken up for arable cultivation, a different piece being selected every three years, and the old ground put under grazing as before. This land is called Scat, Clar, or Leob.

The allotment of the land is the next process. The constable takes a rod and divides the scot into each equal divisions. At the boundary of each division he cuts a mark in the ground, which is called by the curious name of Torc, and resembles the broad-arrow of the Ordnance Department. A man, probably the herdsman, is then sent out from the meeting, and each of six men then put a lot into a bonnet. The man sent out is recalled and the bonnet is handed to him. From this the man takes the lots and places them one after one on a

THE HEISGEIR COMMUNITY. 145

line on the ground, the order in which they thus stand being the order in which the owners of the lots stand to one another in the shares, each man knowing his own mark. The two tenants who have double shares retain their two shares each; the four other tenants subdivide their divisions with four other men, whom they thus represent at the division. These subdivisions are called Imirean or Iomairean, rigs or ridges, and each two tenants again cast lots for the subdivided rigs. A piece of ground is then set apart for their herdsman, which is the outside rig bordering on the grazing, and further pieces of ground are set out for the poor.

Having finished their tillage, the people go early in June to the hill grazing with their flocks. The different families bring their herds together and drive them away; the men carrying burdens of sticks, &c., to repair their summer shealings, the women carrying bedding, meal, dairy and cooking utensils. Barefooted, bareheaded comely boys and girls flit hither and thither keeping their herds together.

When the grazing ground is reached the huts are repaired outwardly and inwardly, fires are rekindled and food is prepared. Having seen to their cattle and sorted their shealings, they repair to their merry feast, *Feisd na h-imrig*, which consists chiefly of a cheese provided from last year's produce and shared among the neighbours and friends, as they wish themselves and their cattle luck and prosperity. Every head is uncovered, every knee is bowed as they dedicate themselves and their flocks to God, or in some touching dedicatory hymn invoke their patron saint.[1]

We have already seen what these summer shealings are and how entirely they take us back to the Stone Age for the origin of their structural features—unmortared sleeping-places made in the recesses of the thick wall, beehive in form, a low doorway just large enough to enter, everything bespeaking the primitive origin both of the shell which receives the human swarm and of the community which fits into the material shell.

---

[1] See "Report of the Crofter Commission," 1884, appendix xcix, paper by Mr. A. Carmichael, pp. 451–473.

The gathering of the moot at its open-air meeting-place, the election of officers and the payment of them by grants of land, the setting aside of land for the poor, and generally the combined action of the villagers, bespeak a close approximation to the village community. All these features we shall see repeated when we come to examine the types situated in the more thickly occupied lands of Southern Britain, where they form part of the so-called manorial system. That the manor does not appear as a term in the Heisgeir process of development is a point of some significance, and we must examine, if possible, any other transitional types that exist before proceeding to the latest forms of development in the village communities of Britain.

CHAPTER VII.

TRANSITIONAL TYPES OF THE VILLAGE COMMUNITY IN BRITAIN.

So long as we keep to the outlying lands which have been left untouched by commercial and political activity, we see the tribal community with its system of shifting homesteads, telling us of unlimited space for expansion and its villages of cottar serfs, telling us of the race it displaced. When we pass on to the lands occupied by the Teutonic tribes, we find evidence of a more restricted range of occupation land, and a development of the village principle. The Teutonic conquest was tribal, not political; and the tribes settled down side by side or in conjunction with the tribal communities of the Celts already settled. The Teutonic conquerors entered within the communal life of the Celtic conquered, and so drew tighter together the *local* bonds which kept each community together. There was less room for the tribal communities to expand with their principle of shifting homesteads; the tribal communities themselves were more closely packed because they had been compelled to open their bounds in order to admit new-comers. And this great change was marked by the homesteads becoming fixed.

It seems to me that the process by which this fixity of the homestead was obtained, is explained by the working out of the curious system of the " fine " recorded in the " Brehon Laws."[1] We have already noted how the system must have worked so long as there was territory enough to meet the constant "going out" of sons from the geilfine or original household. What we have now to find out is how the system

[1] " Brehon Laws," vol. iv. p. xciii.

would meet the closing up of the boundary of tribal territory, because of the pressure of other tribes all around. In the lowlands of Scotland and on the eastern coasts of Ireland this pressure was brought about by the invasion and settlement of new tribal hosts. When these Teutonic and Scandinavian conquerors took possession of the territory of Celtic tribes, or when they settled alongside of Celtic tribal holdings, the inevitable result was that the land had to support more people, and that hence there was no room for the old shifting of the homesteads, a system no doubt common alike to the Teutonic and the Celtic organization. Clearly, then, new homesteads must be built around the parent homestead, and gradually the group of homesteads would assume the characteristics of a village, the necessity of close habitation for purposes of common defence and the limitation put upon tribal boundaries both tending to produce the change from scattered to collected living.

If this is the correct explanation of the method of transition from tribal to village community, we ought to be able to detect some significant feature of the more primitive tribal system in some types which had not developed so far towards the final form of the village community as those which settled in the more thickly inhabited districts of Southern England. As a matter of fact we do meet with such types, and the feature which seems to me to stamp them as such is the shifting of the arable mark from place to place in the tribal territory. We will examine these types and see how far they conform to the theory. They must show, as at Harris, the race elements which are at the root of the village community; they must show, what cannot be seen at Harris, a closer assimilation of the whole community to the village system.

The first example we shall have to examine is the famous burghal community of Lauder in Berwickshire. This came under the notice of Sir Henry Maine, and he characterized it as perhaps the most perfect example of the primitive cultivating community extant in England or Germany. Sir Henry Maine obtained his information from a Parliamentary return of 1870, and he did not notice the decay which had already begun in the form of the community itself—a process which leaves the forms of land-tenure and the system of cultivation as archaic as we could well find them, while it leaves the social organism in the last stages of decomposition. But when we come to examine into this we find that it is possible to trace out its causes, so that we have in this example an almost perfect type of the tribal community in the stage of development which has been already explained. In the local reports of the Municipal Corporation Commissioners of 1835, we ascertain that the earliest recorded number of burgesses at Lauder was 315. A new division took place in 1744 and the number then was 105. In 1816 there were 48. In 1835 there were 25. We ascertain the reason of this from Kerr's " Report on the Agriculture of Berwick," 1813. The burgess acres, it is there stated, "are subject to private sale, disposition, or inheritance like any other private property," and it goes on to say that " from the heritable and transferable nature of the burgess lots, it has necessarily happened that several have been concentrated into the possession of single individuals, and it may happen that the whole may ultimately fall to one proprietor, who will then become the corporation " (p. 80). It is perfectly clear that the causes which are bringing about this state of things belong to modern and not to ancient history. We see the community in process of decay, but this also enables us to see the original from which it is the lineal descendant. Camden notes that in his time " Lauder had 40 houses and cottages, all according to the universal practice, sashed" (iv. 43). The increase of the community beyond its village capacity brought about the new tenure of village lands, and so we lose all traces of kinship and of clan relationship except one very important relic, namely, that the right to hold burghal lands depends upon the possession of a homestead in the village. When we consider that the extent of the parish is 34,981 acres, while the burghal community now holds only 1,700 acres under a tenure which is rapidly passing them into personal property, we may gather some idea of the former condition of things of which we are now only examining the relics.

But if the community itself has thus died away, its old system of land cultivation has survived, and this we proceed to examine. There are 105 separate portions of land called Burgess Acres. These vary in extent from one and a half acres to three and a half acres. To each such acre there is a separate progress of writs, and these "Acres" are the private and absolute property of individuals. . . . No one has hitherto been admitted a burgess of the burgh who has not been an owner of one of these Burgess Acres. The lands of the burgh consist of . . . Lauder Common, extending to about 1,700 acres, which has, from all time of which there is any record, been possessed thus : A portion of it has been set off periodically, say once in five or seven years, to be broken up and ploughed during that time, and at the end of the time fixed has been laid down in grass, and grazed along with the other lands; when another portion of the common was, in the same way, broken up and ploughed, and again laid down in grass. The portion of the common so broken up and ploughed at a time, has, of recent years, been about 130 acres in extent. An allotment of this portion of the common has been given to the owner of each of the 105 burgess acres, whether he happened to be a burgess or not, one allotment for each acre. The portion laid off for cultivation is, in the first place, cut into the number of allotments required, and the share of each person is decided by lot. The conditions attached to the taking of hill parts have been—compliance with a system of cultivation prescribed by the town council, and payment of a small assessment, generally just sufficient to reimburse the burgh for expenses laid out in making drains, roads, &c., to enhance the value of the land for cultivation. These allotments have been called "hill parts." The whole of the remainder of the common has been used for grazing purposes, and has been utilized as follows :—Each burgess resident within the bounds of the burgh has grazed on the common two cows, or an equivalent, and a certain number of sheep—at present, and for some years, fifteen ; and each widow of a burgess, resident in the burgh, has grazed on the common one cow, or an equivalent, and a certain number of sheep—at present, and for many years, twelve.

The chief points to be noted in this extremely archaic mode of cultivation are, first, the arable mark being cultivated under rules prescribed by the town council; secondly, the arable mark being shifted periodically from one part of the domain to another; thirdly, the assignment of parcels within the cultivated area to members of the community by lot; fourthly, the right to land for purposes of tillage being inseparably connected with the ownership of certain plots of land within the township; fifthly, the right to pasture on that part of the common in grass. All these features of the modern Scottish burgh are features also of the primitive village community, and they are not repeated in any of the examples nor in any portion of the voluminous chronological evidence which Mr. Seebohm has collected concerning the village community in Southern England. And yet there is this to note. The Roman roadway passes through the parish, and a little to the west of the village—evidence of contiguity to Roman influences, which elsewhere is held sufficient to prove the Roman origin of the village community in serfdom under a lord. There is absolutely no such evidence here. The seven round camps within the boundary of the parish tell us of old conflicts and old tribal settlements, and the village of Addinston tells us of the subjected race ousted from their once supreme position. But the village in serfdom is not under a lord—it is under a community which has, even in this century, something to tell us of its old tribal organization.

The next example is in Ireland, namely Kells, County Meath. The constitution of the corporation is extremely interesting. It is a place of considerable antiquity, and certainly existed as a walled and fortified town during the long occupation of the district by the Danes. When the English first conquered the country Kells was at once made a centre of operations, and its importance to them is shown by the grant of a charter by Richard I.

This charter not only marks an important epoch in the

political history of Kells, but the circumstances attending it lead directly up to the question as to the source of the constitution which reappears under its provisions. It is said to be the means by which the corporation obtained its landed property;[1] but this distinctly legal way of stating the case is shown not to be historically true by the charter of 2 Richard II., wherein an inspeximus of the charter of Richard I. is said "to have been made at the request of the then burgesses;"[2] in other words, the royal sanction was given to an existing state of things. This is shown to be equally true of the charter of Richard I. by the terms of that document which granted "three acres in the fields to each burgage"—a form which, in the first place, leads to the conclusion that burgages already existed, and in the second place that the grant of three acres was in addition to a territory which already existed.

Of the unquestioned influence of the Danes there is some interesting evidence to be obtained from the agrarian condition of the county—a condition which supplies us with the same terminology as that existing in England, certainly as early as the time of Domesday.

The full organization of the community does not appear from the only sources of evidence at command, but one or two details connected with the later system of borough government indicate an archaic origin. Thus one very important feature of the village community is to be found in the provision that freemen are not allowed to enjoy their shares of the common lands unless they are resident. Traces too of the old system of kinship are recognizable in the provision that widows of freemen do not retain any portion of their deceased husbands' rights in the arable allotments, though they enjoy a right of grazing upon the common pasture. One further archaic feature in the organization of the community exists in the custom of setting apart a portion of the common field, generally five or six acres, for letting and utilizing the rent thus obtained to pay the tithes and taxes of the entire community. These scraps of information, however, do not enable us to

---

[1] "Mun. Corp. Com. of Ireland," vol. i. p. 181. [2] Ibid.

build up the old organization of the village community with any degree of certainty, but they are necessary preliminaries to a consideration of the evidence supplied from other sources. Leaving this portion of the subject we will turn to the system of cultivation, one portion of which will afford an interesting and valuable clue to the original organization of the cultivators.

The system of agriculture adopted at Kells is the same as that at Lauder, namely, that known as co-aration of the waste. It has held its own at Kells, not because of the unlimited amount of land belonging to the community, but by the constant limitation of the members of the community. The details of this interesting system are thus described by the Municipal Corporation Commissioners of 1835:—"The 312 acres in possession of the corporation are divided into six fields and thus used. The fields are broken up in rotation one at a time, and tilled during four years. Before the field is broken the members of the corporation repair to it with a surveyor, and it is marked out into equal lots, according to the existing number of resident members of the body. Each resident freeman gets one lot, each portreeve and burgess two lots, and the deputy sovereign five lots. The members hold their lots in severalty for four years and cultivate them as they please; and at the expiration of the fourth year the field is laid down with grass and a new one is broken, when a similar process of partition takes place. The other five fields are in the interim in pasture, and the right of depasturing them is enjoyed by the members of the corporation in the same proportion as they hold the arable land; that is to say, the deputy sovereign grasses five heads of cattle (called 'bolls') for every two grazed by the portreeves and burgesses, and for every one grazed by the freemen."[1] Mr. Thompson in his statistical survey of Meath, 1802, adds that three yearling calves, or one yearling and a two-year-old, are considered equal to one beast[2] —a method of calculation which obtains from the earliest times.

[1] "Mun. Corp. Com. of Ireland," vol. i. p. 181.   [2] Ibid., p. 123.

This system exhibits all the main features of the primitive village community. There is the shifting of the arable mark; there is the division of the arable land by lots every fourth year, and then the return of the whole into common and a re-division in another part; there is the right of pasture regulated by the holding in the arable field—a form which is scarcely to be distinguished from its archaic original, which regulated all rights according to the homestead.

Now that we have the whole facts before us, we may look a little closer into the working of this system to see if something more may not be discoverable concerning the homestead and its position in the tribal organization. The division of the whole territory into six fields, only one of which is allotted for arable culture, the other five remaining in common pasture, has a strangely artificial appearance. Why should the common pasture be divided into five fields? There is nothing in the archaic systems of cultivation to explain it, and unless it represents the survival of an older state of things by an unmeaning adhesion to custom no longer observed in its original form, there is no explanation that I know of for it. Apart from the extreme improbability of it having been invented to meet some modern contingency no longer discernible, there is evidence to suggest that it represents the result of an old racial conflict when the new-comers did not carry out the complete system of the conquered, though they did not upset it entirely.

It will be, in the first place, advisable to point out why these five fields were used as pasture. They were no doubt taken into pasture when the old pasture lands of the community had become alienated. In 1802 it was observed that "about 100 acres which *had not hitherto been enclosed*" were to be enclosed and improved forthwith.[1] This was clearly original pasture land. On the map of the Down Survey there is delineated a portion of ground amounting to 37 acres and known as the "White commons of Kells," but which, says the Municipal Corporation Commission, "are not now in possession of the

[1] Thompson's "Statistical Survey of Meath," p. 124.

Corporation;"[1] and again the same authority asserts that "it was stated that a denomination called 'Sherries' containing upwards of 90 acres and now in possession of Lord Headfort, formerly belonged" to the Corporation.[2] These examples of alienation do not, it is true, account for a very large extent of pasture land; but they serve to show that outside the area of the "six fields" there once existed lands which were utilized by the community as pasture; and my suggestion is that when these old pasture lands were given up, a portion of the "six fields" was used in exactly the same way and for exactly the same purpose as the original pastures. It is fortunate that the force of custom had become so established as to bring about the performance of the same rules within a restricted area as once obtained in a larger area, otherwise this extremely archaic survival would have perished.

If the evidence is admitted to be sufficient to allow this conjectural explanation of a state of things not otherwise explainable, we may go a step further, and say that originally the whole arable mark, was shifted about periodically from one part of the waste to another as it is now within a very restricted area, and that it was divided into six fields—that is, the whole of the present six fields was formerly cultivated as arable land, and the pasture land was outside of it. What, then, is the explanation of this division of the arable mark into six fields? It was no longer of any definite meaning to the Corporation of Kells. But a reference to the organization of the tribal community will enable us to detect in these six fields at Kells the arable allotments of six tribal homesteads into which the tribal community at Kells was originally divided. The Danish settlers would not accept the Celtic division of the tribe, though they did not break up the Celtic division of the land, and thus we are able to detect the two race influences stamped on the surface of the land, though originating in the organization of the community.

With these two examples of Lauder and Kells as transitional

[1] "Municipal Corporation Commission, Ireland," vol. i. p. 181.
[2] Ibid.

types between the tribal and the village community, we must for the present be content. They show us in the shifting of the arable mark the adhesion to old tribal institutions; they show in the fixity of the homestead the development towards village institutions.

CHAPTER VIII.

THE FINAL TYPE OF THE VILLAGE COMMUNITY IN BRITAIN.

WE have now examined two types of the village community as it has survived in this country—the tribal community in its most primitive form, and in its transitional form towards the village type. We have next to examine the survivals of the village type. Let it be remembered that we are examining survivals only. The famous example of Hitchin which Mr. Seebohm has brought forward, and from which he started in order to proceed back through records and chronicle history to the centuries during which English history was still unwritten, does not stand alone, and I suggest that the methods of comparative custom impose upon the inquirer into this subject an examination of a wide group of survivals. We have said that the plains of India give us examples of a village community into whose bounds are gathered the relics of old race conflicts, one chief relic of which is the serfdom of the conquered aborigines. We have pointed out that evidence is not wanting of aboriginal race elements in English local customs and thought. We have noted that in the extreme parts of our land where successive conquest and settlement could not have taken place so frequently, tribal communities have survived, and in the archæology of hill cultivation, traces of non-Aryan tribal settlement are to be found. We have, finally, suggested that the parallel types of village community in India and in England may very well indicate a parallel origin. It therefore remains for us to examine those types of the village community which surviving in the lowlands and districts most easily settled by succeeding waves of new-comers, may indicate to us, roughly it may be, but still sufficiently, that they originate in a primitive system which is recovered from the lost history of our race by the aid of comparative custom.

The peculiar tenure of the lands in the manor of Aston and Cote is well known to students. It is quoted in text-books on real property law and in books dealing with the early history of land holding, but I do not find that the evidence it affords upon the history of the village community in England has ever been considered. This can only be done by a critical examination of the chief points in the history of the manor, and until this is done this famous example of an ancient system of society will not be properly understood, and will not therefore receive its rightful place in the early history of English institutions.

The manor of Aston and Cote is a sub-manor of the manor of Bampton, and is situated in the parish of Bampton in Oxfordshire. Our first step will be to consider the evidence as to the earliest occupation of this district. There is, first of all, evidence of a British occupation at Bampton in "Lew Barrow," a mound about 15 feet high and of proportional dimensions standing on the highest point of the Lew Hills,[1] but there is no Roman roadway or evidences of Roman occupation. We next turn to the Anglo-Saxon period. In 614, the Welsh, making a raid on the valley of the Cherwell, struck over the Cotswolds by Cirencester,[2] and proceeded to Bampton, probably to their old settlement at Lew. There they were met by Cynegils and Cwichelm, who slew three thousand of them,[3] and probably after this decisive victory the conquerors resolved at last to settle and build up a home for themselves.

This conclusion seems to be confirmed by the name of the town itself, which implies what modern tradition confirms, the tree-town, or "Bampton-in-the-Bush,"[4] that is, a settlement

---

[1] Giles, "History of Bampton," p. 110. The "Low Barrow" is most likely Saxon.

[2] Green, "Making of England," p. 239.

[3] "Anglo-Saxon Chronicle," A.D. 614.

[4] Giles, *op. cit.*, p. 15. It is marked as "Bampton in the Bush" in the map attached to Young's "Agriculture of Oxford."

carved out of the unoccupied woodlands. There are other place names which unquestionably give evidence of its Anglo-Saxon origin. Thus among the names of the lands we have, as noted by Mr. Williams,[1] the Byttam=byht-hàm, from byht,[2] a corner or bend; the "hucket"=a hooked field from hock or hó; the Stew meads and the Steway, probably from *stig*, "a path"; the Edy-Garston or Gaston, Blechingworth, the Stathe (a bank), Stadge, Bosengay, Mallenge, Sinderworth, Sinbury Hàm, and the Woo. We have therefore, first, traces of British occupation, later on there are traces of Danish occupation,[3] but we may fairly conclude that the predominant influences of the Bampton settlement were Anglo-Saxon.

The spot on which this Anglo-Saxon community settled was one well suited to them. It is perfectly flat except towards its most northerly portion, where there is a gradual rise towards a line of low hills. On these low hills it reaches its highest elevation at Lew Barrow and again falls gradually away on all sides.[4] Upon such suitable territory as this they settled, and how completely the community was isolated in its inter-village independence is witnessed by a fact which has gone far to preserve to this day the remarkable archaic survivals we shall presently have before us, namely, that no stoned road of any kind led from Bampton to the neighbouring towns and villages, travellers of modern days even being compelled to strike across the common which surrounded the town, and thence to find their way to Witney, Burford, or Oxford as best they could.[5]

[1] *Archæologia*, vol. xxxiii. pp. 269-270.

[2] Examples of this word in place names are collected from the "Codex Diplomaticus" and other authorities in Toller's edition of Bosworth's "Anglo-Saxon Dictionary," *s.v.* byht.

[3] Traces of Danish influences are observable at Bampton; see *Archæologia*, vol. xxxvii. p. 382.

[4] Giles, " History of Bampton," pp. 17-18.

[5] Giles, *op. cit.*, p. 17; *cf.* Young's "Agriculture of Oxford," 1813, p. 324, for the general condition of Oxford roads. How remarkably parallel the state of things at Bampton is to the village community in India may be seen by referring to Sir John Phear's " Aryan Village Community in India and Ceylon" p. 4, "there exist almost no roads . . . only irregular tracks, sometimes traversable by wheels, along the balks which divide the soil into small cultivated patches."

Scarcely anything could be more indicative of archaic village life than this absence of roads, and I wish to draw special attention to it. One other fact which has helped to preserve the archaic social group at Bampton is that, abandoning whatever chances might have existed for carrying on a manufacturing occupation, the people almost wholly engaged in agriculture.[1]

The initial facts in the history of this district are, therefore, all in favour of producing a good example of the village community, and we will now endeavour to ascertain whether the organization of the manor, as known to us in later times, may be taken to be a survival of the more archaic institution. Let me recapitulate what these initial facts are—there is evidence of Celtic occupation, no evidence of Roman occupation, there is isolation of the district consequent upon there being no roads, there is a very late and exclusive agricultural industry.

The superior manor of Bampton had under it several sub-manors, one of which was Aston and Cote; and to the facts of this sub-manor we shall now pay exclusive attention. I have made an extensive search through the calendars of the deputy-keeper of the Public Records and other MS. sources of information, and have not been able to light upon any information relative to Aston. We have, therefore, to rely for the principal evidence as to the organization of the village community at Aston upon a "case" which the lord of the manor

---

[1] Giles, *op. cit.*, 72. Mr. Ashley, "English Economic History and Theory," has sufficiently pointed out the nature of English trade and commerce down to the fourteenth century. "What existed," he says, "was scarcely more than a trade between certain towns, an inter-communal or inter-municipal commerce" (p. 102). Bampton carried on this feature of early English village life longer than other parts of the country. Plot, writing in 1677, says there are in Witney "a great many Fellmongers, out of whom at the neighbouring towns of Bampton there arrises another considerable trade, the Fellmongers' sheep skins after dressed and stained being here made into wares, viz., jackets, breeches, leather linings, &c., which they chiefly vent into Berkshire, Wiltshire, and Dorsetshire, no town in England having a trade like it in that sort of ware" (Plot's "Natural History of Oxfordshire," p. 280).

stated to Sir Orlando Bridgman and Mr. Jeffrey Palmer, on the 30th of November, 1657, and which has fortunately been printed by Mr. Giles as a supplement to his "History of Bampton." The importance of this document is greatly enhanced by its having been written for the purpose of getting legal opinion upon the lord's rights and the rights of the manorial courts as opposed to the organization of the tenants. It was, in point of fact, an attempt on the part of the lord to take over to himself the free institutions of the community. On the one hand, we have a statement of what were considered to be the lord's rights; on the other hand, we have a statement of what were considered to be the tenants' rights. While these two contrasting statements enable us to obtain a lurid view of the organization of the agricultural community in the seventeenth century, they also afford us very valuable evidence as to one of the modes of transition from village rights to lord's rights—evidence which has never yet been brought to bear upon the history of the village community in England. And when we consider how extremely difficult it is to meet with such evidence, it will be recognized that in this example we must be careful to note every step of the process, so as to gain a complete knowledge of details, which will serve as a guide to many phases of our local institutions, the origin of which cannot easily be established for lack of evidence. Not only does it afford an almost unique example of the process by which the lord of the manor sought to obtain rights that almost everywhere else we find him in full possession of; but by the successful resistance to this claim it affords a very late example of the village community in England with much of its archaic structure and archaic methods of government and cultivation of land left intact. If the lord had succeeded in his claim, the Manor of Aston and Cote would not probably have been distinguishable in its customs from other manors; that he did not succeed has preserved for us a type of archaic village organization not to be matched elsewhere in manorial history.

The manor consisted of sixteen hides. To each of these hides were attached four yard-lands—making altogether sixty-four yard-lands belonging to the sixteen hides. Confining ourselves, in the first place, to the structure of this social organism, it was stated by the lord of the manor in 1657, that "there hath been a custom time out of mind that a certain number of persons called *the sixteens*, or the greater part of them, have used to make orders, set penalties, choose officers and lot the meadows, and do all such things as *are usually performed or done in the Courts Baron of other manors.*" This is the free democratic assembly, and its title, the Sixteens, as well as its constitution, takes us back to primitive times.[1] Nor is this all. From the body of "the sixteens" are elected four of "the most influential persons" as grass stewards. These represented the manor of Aston and Cote at the superior court of the manor of Bampton, and are thus brought into close parallel with the four best men of the Anglo-Saxon township.[2] The archaic nature of this village organization and its entire independence of political thought and action, are also shown by the fact that for the purpose of taking combined action, it met in the open air, like the assemblies of all early social groups before they have become associated with higher organizations leading on to the nation.[3] The meeting-place of the Aston and Cote Assembly was the cross situated in the centre of the village,[4] and though the custom had already fallen into desuetude in 1848, Mr. Horde, in 1657, sufficiently attested its importance by the assertion that its orders "if proclaimed from the Town Cross are binding upon the inhabitants."[5]

Over and above the extensive system of self-government

---

[1] See *Archæologia*, vol. xxxiii. p. 269; Gomme's "Primitive Folk-moots," pp. 119, 120. We may compare this court of sixteens with two other similarly named and similarly constituted courts, namely, those at Ditmarsh and Corbey.

[2] Stubbs' "Constitutional History," vol. i. p. 90. The "four best men and the reeve" are the full representatives. Still the analogy is curious enough to note.

[3] See "Primitive Folkmoots," p. 119, *et passim*.

[4] Giles, "History of Bampton," p. 78.

[5] *Archæologia*, vol. xxxiii. p. 274.

which this community exercised upon its members, including all those numerous powers conveyed by the possession of pillory, ducking-stool, &c., it retained some functions which are of special significance to our present inquiry. The Sixteens were bound to provide at their joint expense four two-year-old bulls every season to run on the common pasture; at the end of the season they sold them for their own benefit, and during the season they claimed a fee for every cow that fed on the common.[1] Comparing this with the municipal custom at Marlborough,[2] the gild custom at Leicester,[3] and the manor custom at Hitchin,[4] it may appear that we have a clue to the origin of the lord's bull. If the Sixteens and their powers had passed into the hands of the lord of the manor in 1657, the village bull would have been indistinguishable from that at Hitchin, and Mr. Seebohm's conclusions as to its origin could hardly have been shaken. As it is, we have clearly in this instance one of the duties of the community at large for the benefit of the individual members; and it is in the hands of the community, not in those of the lord.

The other function of the community to which special reference must be made in this place is the appointment of officers. These are made known by the names of certain "town-hams" set forth by Mr. Horde in 1657 as follows:— In the Out-Mead—Brander Ham, Bull Ham, Hayward's Ham, Water Steward's Ham; in the Inn-Mead—Water Hayward's Ham, Homage Ham, Constable's Ham, Penny Ham, Herd's Ham, Smith's Ham, Grass Steward's Ham, Another Grass Steward's Ham, Wonter's Ham, Worden Ham. Mr. Benjamin Williams has investigated the titles of these officers, comparing them with the officers mentioned in "Rectitudines Singularum Personarum," with some very useful results, into the details of which it will not be necessary to enter now.[5] But

[1] Giles, "History of Bampton," p. 78.
[2] "Municipal Corporation Commission," 1835, p. 83.
[3] Thompson's "English Municipal History," pp. 51, 52.
[4] Seebohm's "English Village Community," p. 11. See also Nelson's "Lex Maneriorum," 1726, app. p. 28.
[5] *Archæologia*, vol. xxxiii. pp. 276-278.

the point to which attention must be drawn is that they supply a very full complement of village officers exactly on a parallel with the village officers in the communities of India. Then there is the still more important custom of allotting land to them for their services.[1] With such a set of officers the village was independent of other villages with respect to all the labour necessary for the support of its members; and with such a method of payment, identical with that to be found extant in all early types of the primitive village community, it was independent of any fiscal considerations outside the most perfect village economy.

Then the Sixteens in their corporate capacity held lands for the benefit of the community. These consisted of "several leyes of greensward lying in the common fields two years mowed and the other fed, viz., Catmore leyes, other greensward, and bushes on Claywell Hill, No-man's Plot, Holliwell Green, the Ham Ways, Trueland's Plotts, and some other." Besides these were the Hams above-mentioned, which were not allowed to officers, namely, the Homage Ham, and the Penny Ham; and Mr. Horde, in 1657, said that these hams "are disposed at the discretion of the Sixteens, some for the public use of the town, as for making of gates, bridges, &c., and some sold to make ale for the merry meeting of the inhabitants." Alike in the providing of the bull, the appointment and payment of officers, the possession of lands for public purposes, we find these "Sixteens" exercising important corporate functions as a self-governing community.

We now pass on to a consideration of the methods of holding and cultivating the lands. The whole district is divided into three parts—(1) common field; (2) common meadow; (3) common pasture—the three parts, in fact, by which the economy of early agricultural society is almost everywhere represented. This is distributed as follows:—Each proprietor of a yard-land, or originally each member of a homestead, who, it will be remembered, owned four yard-lands, possessed

---

[1] *Cf.* Gomme's "Municipal Offices," pp. 34, 35; Maine's "Village Communities," p. 126.

about thirty acres, which were divided among the three above-named sections of the territory. In the first place, he had twenty acres of arable land in the common field, from which he obtained wheat, beans, and other similar crops; then he had four or five acres in the common meadow, which he made into hay for feeding his cattle in the winter; lastly, he had the right of feeding either eight cows or four horses, at discretion, on one part of the common pasture, and sixteen sheep on that part set aside for sheep.[1]

In the common field every occupant knew his own land. The whole of the field was divided by landmarks, and each strip always belonged to the same owner. All the owners adopted the same mode of cultivation according to the four-year course, leaving always a fourth part fallow. This fixity of ownership is only a development from one of the chief features of the common-field system, for in 1577, when a terrier was taken which is still extant, the land was intermixed in small portions of half an acre or less,[2] each yard-land thus representing a bundle of acre strips scattered over the common field.

The common meadow was laid out by boundary stones into thirteen large divisions technically called "layings out." These always remained the same, and each, laying out, in like manner was divided into four pieces called "sets"—first set, second set, third set, and fourth set. Recourse was then had to lots; and the following mode was practised. From time immemorial there have been sixteen marks established in the village, each of which corresponds with four yard-lands, and the whole sixteen consequently represent the sixty-four yard-lands into which the common was divided. A certain number of tenants therefore have the same mark which they always keep, so that every one of them knows his own. The use of these marks

[1] Mr. Williams adds that the right of pasture was for "8 rother beasts, or 4 horses and 32 sheep, but formerly of 12 rother beasts and 40 sheep." Rother is from Anglo-Saxon *hyrther*, "horned cattle" (*Archæologia*, vol. xxxiii. p. 271).

[2] *Archæologia*, vol. xxxiii. p. 271.

was to enable the tenants every year to draw lots for their portions of the meadow.[1]

When the grass was fit to cut, the grass stewards and Sixteens summoned the freeholders and tenants to a general meeting, and the following ceremony took place. Four of the tenants came forward, each bearing his mark cut on a piece of wood, which, being thrown into a hat, were shaken up and drawn by a boy. The first drawing entitled its owner to have his portion of the common meadow in set one, the second drawn in set two, &c., and thus four of the tenants have obtained their allotments. Four others then come forward, and the same process is repeated until all the tenants have received their allotments. When the lots are all drawn, each man went armed with his scythe and cut out his mark on the piece of ground which belonged to him, which in many cases lied in so narrow a strip that he had not width enough to take a full sweep with his scythe. A single farmer might have to cut his portion of grass from twenty different places, though the tenants frequently accommodated one another by exchanging allotments when it was convenient for parties to do so.[2]

The common pasture has already been sufficiently described. Mr. Horde adds to his other valuable information about the state of things in 1657 that the manor had fishing rights as well. He says, "It hath been long accustomed and known by repute that such a part of the fishing of the river belongs to such tenants, and in all or most part of the old deeds or leases of the several tenements are granted the fishings thereunto belonging; those parts of the river called 'several waters,' and then there are other parts of the river called 'common waters,' though every man knoweth his part of the ridding

---

[1] Mr. Williams, in *Archæologia*, vol. xxxiii. p. 275, gives a description of these marks as follows:—Each of the hides of land has its distinctive mark, as the one thwart over —, the two thwart over =, the three thwart over ≡, and Mr. Giles, in his "History of Bampton," p. 79, adds the following examples: the "frying-pan," the "crane's foot," the "bow," "the two strokes to the right and one at top."

[2] Giles' "History of Bampton," pp. 75-80.

thereof, in which is pretended a liberty for all to fish without control."

Such is the main outline of the Aston village community and of its self-governing powers, which had not disappeared from legal observation in 1657. Mr. Horde, "for the better understanding the meaning of the sixteens" as they existed in his time, gave the archaic account of them which has just been described. If we now proceed to contrast this description of the old state of things with their exact condition, as Mr. Horde himself observed around him, we shall find some explanation of the changes which had come about; the changes are significant rather than sweeping, and from them, I think, can be ascertained a very important period in the history of manors.

The yard-land, in 1657, was the unit of holding. Of the 64 yard-lands, the lord held 40. Of these 40, 12 were "estated out to several tenants for lives by copy of court roll, 22 yard-lands are let by lease to several tenants for 99 years if certain lives so long live, and 5 yard-lands are let by several leases to several tenants for several terms under rack rents, so as there is now no parcel of the said manor in the lord's hands." Of the remaining 24 yard-lands out of the total of 64, "*about* 12 yard-lands thereof was ancient freehold, not holden of the manor of Aston Boges, nor paying any rent to the lord thereof, or doing any suit to the courts there; 9 yard-lands more were heretofore parcel of the manor of Shifford; and 4 yard-lands residue do belong to the manor of Bampton Deanery."[1] How it came about that the yard-lands once belonging to other manors were included in the government of Aston manor, is far from clear. Shifford was a manor from an early date, as there is a charter giving its metes and bounds in 1005,[2] but it is certain that the 9 yard-lands said to have

[1] It will be observed that 39 yard-lands out of the 40 held by the lord are accounted for, and that for the 24 out of the lord's hands 25 are accounted for. I have no means of correcting this error in the figures, but it does not affect the argument.

[2] "Codex Diplomaticus," No. dccxiv. The place is called Scypforda in the charter, and it is not identified with Shifford in Mr. Kemble's *index locorum*, but I think there is no doubt that Shifford in Oxfordshire is meant.

once belonged to it, were in 1657 locally situate in Aston and intermixed with the other lands there.[1] And the statement as to them originally belonging to Shifford advanced by Mr. Horde, does not obviate the very significant fact that the owners of these yard-lands took part with the other owners of yard-lands in the government of the manor of Aston and Cote; so that the true state of the case may possibly have been that at some time previously a re-arrangement between the lords and tenants of the several manors subordinate to Bampton had taken place, by which Aston still kept up its traditional constitution, and released or exchanged lands in return for the nine yard-lands obtained from Shifford.

But, however this may be, and the point is not very material, it will be seen, upon closer examination, that the village organization, the rights of assembly, the free open-air meetings, and the corporate action incident to the manor of Aston and Cote in reality attach themselves, not to the 64 yard-lands, but to the sixteen hides, because although these hides had grown in 1657 into a considerable tenancy, fortunately as a tenancy they kept their original unity in full force and so obstinately clung to their old system of government as to keep up by *representation* the once undivided holding of the hide. If the organization of the hide had itself disappeared, it still formed the basis of the village government, the sixteen hides sending up their sixteen *elected* representatives.

How the tenancy grew out of the original sixteen homesteads may perhaps be conjecturally set forth. We shall presently come upon other survivals of the village community in England which give clear evidence of the steps which accompany the growth of an increasing tenancy. In the meantime it may be seen that the owners of the yard-lands succeeded to the place originally occupied by the owners of the sixteen hides. Instead of the original sixteen group-owners we have therefore 64 individual owners, each yard-land having remained in possession of an owner. And then at succeeding stages of this dissolution we find the yard-lands broken up

[1] *Archæologia*, vol. xxxiii. p. 269.

until in 1848 " some farmers of Aston have only half or even a quarter of a yard-land, whilst some have as many as ten or eleven yard-lands in their single occupation."[1] Then disintegration would proceed to the other proprietary rights, which, originally appendant to the homestead only, became appendant to the person and not to the residence and are consequently "bought and sold as separate property, by which means it results that persons resident at Bampton, or even at great distance, have rights on Aston and Cote Common."[2] And finally we lose all traces of the system, as described by Mr. Horde and as depicted by the representative character of the Sixteens, and in its place find that " there are some tenants who have rights in the common field and not in the common pasture, and *vice versa* several occupiers have the right of pasture who do not possess any portion of arable land in the common field,"[3] so that both yard-lands and hides have now disappeared, and absolute ownership of land has taken their place. Mr. Horde's MS. enables us to proceed back from modern tenancy-holding to the holding by yard-lands; the right of election in the yard-lands enables us to proceed back to the original holding of the sixteen hides.

This process of evolution of the tenancy of the manor of Aston from an original division into sixteen hides enables us to suggest that we have in this instance stumbled upon a very late survival of ancestral shares in the village community. Turning back to the Indian example quoted in the second chapter, we must perhaps pass over the singular parallel it affords by the division into sixty-four shares, because at Aston the process seems to have been from 16 to $16 \times 4 = 64$, whereas at Pudu Vayal the process seems to have been from 4 to $4 \times 16 = 64$. But knowing that the hide was the original holding of the family, knowing that the law of succession in England is stamped in its early stages with one of the most significant marks of early Aryan life, namely, the undivided family as the owner and the prohibitions against partition of the family homestead, it is a reasonable hypothesis

[1] Giles' " History of Bampton," p. 76.   [2] Ibid.   [3] Ibid., p. 79.

to put forth that this Aston community has preserved by means of its elected representatives in later ages the original constitution of the community by ancestral units. Like the Indian example, the ancestral shares at Aston have stamped their imprint upon the land so unalterably that though subdivision has gone on through succeeding ages still the history of the original settlement is to be traced. This history tells us of (1) the original sixteen families forming a community of hereditary villages;[1] (2) the periodical allotment of land on the basis of the original ancestral shares and the subdivision of each ancestral share among the under-shareholders; (3) the peculiar method of allotment according to marks belonging to each of the ancestral shares; (4) the holding of land by the community for the benefit of the villagers generally; (5) the corporate assembly of the villagers in the open air and the rights of government by this assembly; (6) the position of the lord as holder of village lands bound to conform to village rights, and unable to translate these as lord's rights; and (7) the position of the cottar tenancy as servants of the community. And finding all these phenomena repeated in the Indian example which has been put forward, we may suggest that they are due to causes which are adequate to explain both the Eastern and Western village community.

Before passing away from the Aston village community it may be well to point out that its typical division into sixteen and sixty-four units is parallelled by an example from Scotland, namely, at Elgin. Unfortunately all the details of this case are not to hand, still there are enough to make the parallel exceedingly interesting. In the first place, we get the assembly of the Burgh in the churchyard of St. Giles in the open air.[2] Secondly, there are the burgh-lands, the tenure and management of which are

[1] The permanency of the original shares in the village is a well-ascertained fact of Indian village communities, and Professor Haussen has dealt with the German evidence.

[2] See a charter printed in Macphael's "Religious House of Pluscardyn," dated 1272, pp. 210, 211.

described sufficiently to indicate their origin in the primitive village community of the Aston type. "There is a large field of arable land to the west of Elgyn divided into what are called auchteen parts, but consisting of sixty-four which vary in extent from four to six acres each. Originally they belonged to sixty-four distinct proprietors, burgesses of Elgyn. They lie in run-rig, and so disjoined that different portions of the same lot may be almost an English mile asunder. They still are the property of a number of different persons, though many of them have been acquired by one individual."[1] And finally there are traces of the settlement having been formed by the admixture of different races. The final settlement was probably Scandinavian, the district having been conquered by Sigurd, the Norwegian Earl of Orkney, in 927. But on a hill called Tor Ruadh, a little east of which is Gallowhill, both significant names, has been found a splendid hoard of bronze implements.[2] Perhaps still more significant of the ancient race distinction, and parallel to the facts already noted of the tribal communities, is the situation of the village of Lossiemouth within the parish bounds of Elgin, and since 1694 belonging to the burgh corporation.

In this case of Elgin we have perhaps some remnant of the original ancestral shares (represented at Aston by the sixteen hides) in the so-called auchteen parts. I will now turn to an example where we are face to face with yard-lands only—a type which has been taken by Mr. Seebohm to be the type of the village community in England. I shall describe its chief characteristics so far as they are discoverable from the scant evidence to hand, and I shall suggest that these characteristics are sufficiently near to those belonging to Aston to conclude that we have in this example an instance where the higher organization into ancestral shares or hides has been cut away during the lapse of ages.

Rothwell in Northamptonshire contains about 3,000 acres.

[1] Sinclair's "Statistical Account of Scotland," vol. v. pp. 17, 18.
[2] "Proceedings of the Society of Antiquaries of Scotland," vol. ix. p. 428.

Of this 600 acres were enclosures near the town, and the remaining 2,400 acres open common lands in three distinct fields of about 800 acres each. These fields contained a considerable breadth of grass land never in tillage. In round numbers there were 600 acres of arable land in each common field and 200 acres of grass land.

First, we note the organization of the village. The farm houses and offices were congregated into a village which was situated at one end of the cultivating lands, so that the parish being some four or five miles long and one to one and a half broad, each owner of the lands possessed portions two or three miles from home. The greater number of the tenements were built with mud and covered with thatch.

Next we note the tenure of the lands. A farm was what is called four yard-lands, and contained about 120 acres of open land and 30 acres enclosed. Five horses, 18 head of cattle, 96 sheep, 24 sheep being attached to each yard-land. This describes very succinctly how rigidly exacting and artificial the yard-land system had become, and yet in the grouping of four yard-lands to each farm we can detect the last faint relics of the original ancestral shares or hides.

There are curious details of the method of occupation. The common field was occupied in yard-lands. There were altogether in the parish eighty yard-lands, each comprehending about thirty acres of the common field, with a right of pasturage for four heads and a half of cattle and twenty-four sheep to every yard-land. The cattle were kept in two distinct herds of about one hundred and eighty in each, and pastured on different sides of the parish, attended each by a herdsman and assistant. They were driven home at night through the summer, separated, to each one his own, confined in yards or home closes during the night, and sent out again in the morning to pasture in the grass land of the common field. After harvest they were left at large in the common field till wheat seed-time. The sheep grazed promiscuously on the grass plots of the fallow field; or, if the owner thought proper, on his own enclosures during the day time, and every night were folded on the fallows, each one's

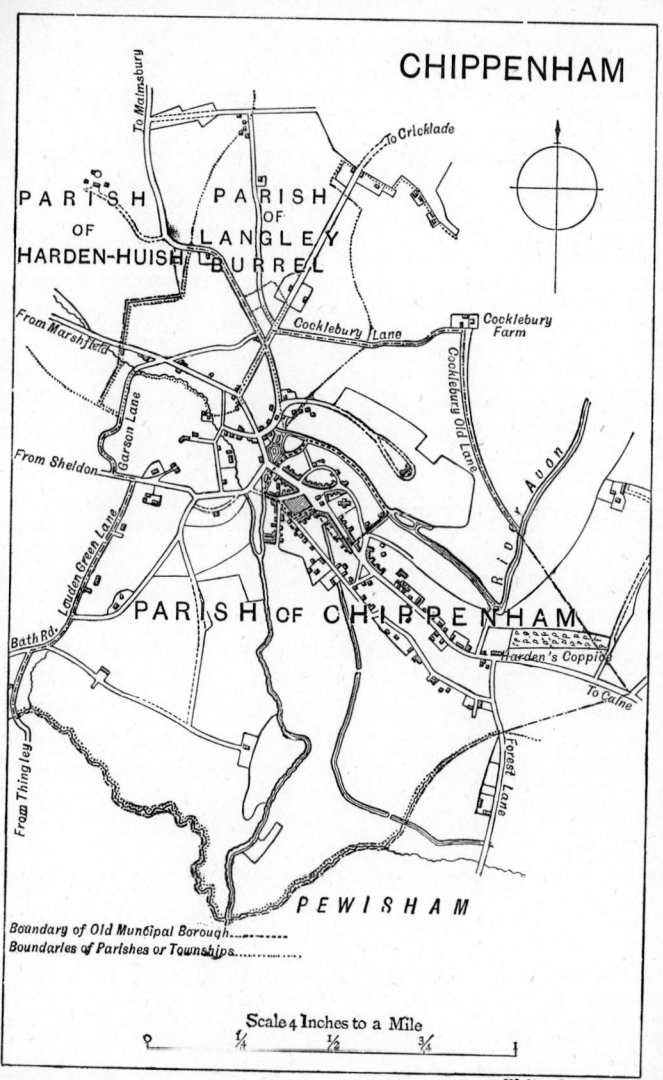

THE CHIPPENHAM VILLAGE COMMUNITY.

flock on his own land, the distinct occupations being dispersed and intermixed throughout every part of each field, and every occupier having land in all directions.[1]

One thing cannot fail to be noted here, that the manor is not a necessary factor in the history of this community. If it exists it is shut out of sight by the organization into "farms of four yard-lands each"—the farmer taking his place in the village in lineal succession to the village owner of the homestead. The farms are not broken up into manorial tenancies of single yard-lands or half yard-lands, each tenant performing his *pro rata* service to the manor; but each bundle of four yard-lands is preserved in the farmstead as in the hide at Aston in the seventeenth century and at Thorp in the thirteenth century.[2]

We may now turn to a Wiltshire example of the village community and the survivals of its archaic origin still obtaining—namely, Chippenham. We will consider first the basis of membership.

The homestead is clustered together in a village. The plan of Chippenham shows us that through the centre of a tongue of land formed by the windings of the River Avon, a roadway from Bristol to Calne was cut, and along the sides of this roadway, in English fashion, the village community of Chippenham constructed their homesteads.[3] These formed the initial points of all rights, and this archaic rule left its imprint on municipal custom, when in 1835, it was reported that the freemen are "those who occupy what are now called burgage tenements,"[4] and "if a burgess ceases to reside in the town, it is usual for him to resign."[5]

What kind of tenements these were, and how nearly they answered to the description of the homesteads of the archaic community, can fortunately be ascertained from a document to

[1] Pitt's "Agriculture of Northamptonshire," pp. 25, 27, 36, 64–67.
[2] Seebohm, "Village Community," pp. 52, 53.
[3] Compare the description given by Davis in his "Agriculture of Wilts" of the situation of Wiltshire villages in general, p. 9.
[4] "Municipal Corporation Commission."   [5] Ibid.

be presently more fully quoted, dating from James I.'s reign. It is there stated that "no inhabitant or householder within the said borough taking or who is to take any benefit of the said borough lands by virtue of these presents, shall at any time hereafter divide his tenement house or habitation into divers parts or habitations, or into more habitations than one."[1] Clearly therefore we have here as the homestead of King James's time, something far larger than the ordinary village or town house;[2] and it is not too much to suggest a comparison with the enclosed homestead and its "gerstun," "stôdfald," "oxena gehæg," "sceap-hammas," "flax-hammas," which Dr. Nasse has collected from the charters,[3] and which are within recent times typical of Kentish farm-houses.[4] It appears, then, that Chippenham was, so recently as the early seventeenth century, a collection of farm homesteads rather than a town in the ordinary sense of the term.

In order to obtain some idea as to how this cluster of homesteads in a village held together before the days of chartered privileges, we must turn to the name of a portion of the land still held by the corporation. This land is called "Englands," and is situated very near to the town, and close to the site, or reputed site, of the King's Villa, which tradition assigns to the spot now occupied by the premises adjoining the new county court, including perhaps the Angel Inn.[5] In a survey of Chippenham, dated 1275 (i. Edward I.), this land is called "Hinlond," and Canon Jackson very appropriately identifies this with the *inland* or home ground of the Anglo-Saxons. Dr. Leo says of this word "an Anglo-Saxon estate was usually divided into two parts; one of which was occupied by the proprietor or usufructuary himself with his establishment, and

---

[1] "Municipal Corporation Commission."
[2] This may be compared with the burgage tenements of other municipalities. At Westbury there were "61 burgage tenements covered by 140 houses," and other examples occur of a like nature.
[3] Nasse's "Agricultural Commmunity of the Middle Ages," pp. 16, 17.
[4] "Arch. Cant.," vol. iv. p. 217.
[5] Jackson's "History of Chippenham," p. 16.

the other was ceded to the greater part of the servants in return for rent and service, as a reward for their assistance, or as the means of support to those who were not freed men. The portion so surrendered was called *útland*, and that occupied by the owner himself *inland*, or *hláfordes inland*."[1] This is of course in accordance with Mr. Seebohm's reading of the evidence, when he points out that "the lord's demesne land was called in the Exon Domesday for Cornwall, the thane's *inland;* so, too, in a law of King Edgar's the tithes are ordered to be paid 'as were on the thane's *inland* as on geneat land,' showing that the distinction between the two was exhaustive."[2] But our evidence proves that in modern times, that is, certainly since the reign of Queen Mary, this inland, translated so freely by the authorities just quoted as lord's demesne land, belonged at Chippenham to the village community itself without the interposition of any manorial lord. The only question is then, did it belong to the village community at any earlier period, and especially at a period which enables us by strong historic probability to suggest that it had so descended age after age from the date when the market village first carved out its clearing in the forest? Such a period is represented by the Domesday survey. What is recorded there Mr. Seebohm proves is true of the early Anglo-Saxon period.[3] In Domesday, then, Chippenham is termed a "manerium."[4] The king held it, and it provided one night's entertainment with all its customs. Here is the community acting in its corporate capacity. It was, moreover, absolutely free—*non geldavit, nec hidata fuit*. Its land consisted of 100 carucates; in demesne were 16 carucates and 28 serfs, the villani (48), bordarii (45), cotarii (20), and swineherds (23), holding, *inter omnes*, 66 carucates.

[1] "Local Nomenclature of the Anglo-Saxons," p. 54.

[2] Seebohm's "English Village Community," p. 135. and *cf.* p. 150. The passage cannot be identified in the Exon Domesday, but I have let the quotation stand.

[3] See cap. iii. of the "English Village Community."

[4] This term is an important distinction from the other term used in Domesday for a community, villa. See Ellis's "Introduction to Domesday."

There were also 12 mills and 100 acres of meadow, wood 4 miles square, and pasture 2 miles long and 1 mile broad. We have here a description of the "inland," the "outland," and the surrounding meadows, pasture, and wood. The survey goes on to say that Bishop Osbern held 2 hides, Ulviet 1 hide, Edric half a virgate, and in other folios it is recorded that Roger de Berchelai held 1 hide, ½ virgate of the demesne, and Rainald Canut held 1 hide of the king. Now, these special holdings were certainly taken from the demesne lands: in one case it is expressly said so, and they therefore represent the earliest transfer of lands held in common to a tenure in severalty. But however early this tendency to break up the old system was, these grants did not exhaust the 16 carucates of the demesne or inland; and the holder of the remaining lands must therefore have been the manerium in its corporate capacity. One expression in the Domesday account of Chippenham indicates the existence of group holding as distinct from individual holding, namely, *inter omnes*, by which term the holding of the 66 carucates of the villani, &c., is recorded. I am inclined to think that this and other similar expressions in Domesday meant a holding in common, not a quantity of land held by many individual tenants; and therefore if we translate this method of holding into its proper historic equivalent, we get the individual group [of kinsmen] holding their possessions in lineal descent from those times when to divide a family holding was almost the last, not the first, resort of the co-heirs of an estate. And hence the suggestion that the manerium of Chippenham held the demesne lands as a group-holding is borne out by Domesday evidence itself.

Our next point in this survey of the community is to ascertain whether the same continuity of custom which marks the method of holding lands and of cultivation, and which thereby tends to show that the charter of Queen Mary did not create the institutions it legislates upon, marks also the system of self-government existing at Chippenham. Before the reign of Mary there is evidence that within the manor and under the jurisdiction of the Bailiff there was not only a pillory and a prison, but also a gallows.[1] And when we come to the byelaws enacted after the granting of the charter, there is exactly the same species of jurisdiction, though nothing in the charter but general clauses grants or suggests the powers assumed to exist. The system of self-government of Chippenham alike before and after incorporation was practically the same, and it bears further witness to the archaic origin of the community. In the 39th of Elizabeth a set of byelaws was framed by the bailiff and burgesses, "with the consent of the chief commons," a consent which certainly takes us back for its origin to a time prior to the charter. These byelaws provided, *inter alia*, under penalty of fine and disfranchisement, for the attendance of all the inhabitant householders on the bailiff and burgesses when summoned for the composition and maintenance of good order within the borough. Offenders were interdicted for transgressing against the regulations for buying or selling within the borough on pain of fine and imprisonment. Bakers offending against the assize were to be set in the pillory; every tippler setting up a tippling-shop to be bound by recognizances; and there were also similar regulations for butchers, brewers, chandlers, and others. Every burgess was required to have in his house a staff and a club, and every other inhabitant householder a club, to come forth whenever need should require. No inhabitant within the borough was allowed to "seek for reformation or justice to be ministered in any matter touching good order in the borough" at any court other than that of the bailiff and burgesses "upon pain every offender to lose his and their whole freedom."[2]

These enactments are curious, and as evidence of archaic continuity of self-government are of great value. But the true force of their evidence as to archaic origin lies in the sanctions enforcing the law. These were not dependent upon the national executive, but were strictly communal in their character, and one of them, "that the offender should also be debarred of all

[1] Jackson's "History of Chippenham," p. 20.
[2] "Municipal Corporation Commission," vol. ii. p. 1247.

benefit out of the borough lands until he submit himself," has its counterpart all over India and among other peoples who live in village communities.

Thus far, then, the community of Chippenham presents an interesting example of the archaic village community, independent of any special manorial influences. The period which witnessed its probable spoliation of lands kept alive the archaic customs of holding and cultivating lands, and with these kept alive its connection with the lands themselves. And hence without any real break in the continuity of its history as a landowning and land-cultivating community, we can now pass on to consider the exact nature of the customs which regulated its internal economy.

The lands set out in Queen Mary's charter are as follows:—

A messuage, the moiety of a yard-land and four parcels of land called Poxes in Rowder Down ...	120 acres
Arable land in the common field of Chippenham ...	21 acres
A mead called West Mead	30 acres
Close of pasture called *Englands*	17 acres
A close in Chippenham called *Burleaze*	4 acres
A coppice called *Rowder Down Coppice*	21 acres
	213 acres

Pasture in Chippenham called *Boltscroft*, admeasurement not set out.

These lands, however small in extent, represent the full requirements in kind of a village community of the most perfect type, and it is suggestive that the community of Chippenham should thus have obtained in the reign of Queen Mary so archaic a provision.

Turning first to the arable land it is surely significant that the old bundle of acre-strips knows as a yard-land should appear among the lands. If the yard-land here was the same as it was in other manors nearly all over the country, the villagers of Chippenham possessed one relic, at all events, of the most ancient form of holding land.[1] They evidently carried out the archaic practice most fully in their twenty-one acres in the "common field of Chippenham." It must be remembered that the limited body created by the charter, and not the general body of freemen known by prescription only, enjoyed this arable land; and when they cultivated their own scattered strips they were mixing with others who were likewise engaged, but who represented the descendants of the once undivided ownership of the common field of Chippenham. In later times this partial survival of archaic custom had passed away, for in 1835 there was no mention of the arable land in the common field, but in its place appears "about six acres of land which the corporation have of their own property" and from which they received rent.[2]

The meadow land was used even so late as 1835 in a very archaic fashion. From the Commissioner's report it appears that the land, called "West Mead," was laid down in meadow, and the grass divided annually among the bailiff and burgesses and the ninety-seven first freemen on the anciatry. An acre was first set out for the bailiff and twelve burgesses, and the remainder was then divided into quarter-acres called "farthing-doles," and each of the ninety-seven freemen was entitled to one. None were allowed to enter the mead until the bailiff had cut his acre; but after the bailiff had carried away, any one was at liberty to cut his farthingdole when it suited himself, and application was made to the sub-bailiff who, if necessary, trod down a path to the specified farthingdole. The freemen were said to be much attached to this mode of occupying their property.[3]

Now observing from what has already been said that the bailiff was the "headman" of the Chippenham community, the archaic significance of his cutting the first acre is best shown by some Hindu customs. At the chief Hindu festival connected with agriculture the Raja goes through the form of

---

[1] The meaning of the term yard-land in Wiltshire and its archaic provisions, is recorded in Davis, "Agriculture of Wilts," p. 268.
[2] "Mun. Corp. Com.," vol. ii. p. 1248.   [3] Ibid.

ploughing and sowing before any one else commenced these operations, and this was considered to take away the sin which tilling the land is supposed to convey.[1]

After the grass is cut in the West Mead the whole is stocked in common by the freemen and freeholders, the freemen paying 4d. to the corporate fund for every beast which they put in, and the freeholders putting in three beasts for every acre free of any charge.

Besides this pasture the land known as *Englands* was stocked by the freemen each putting in two horses or six beasts; and, probably, this took the place of the older pasture ground called *Boltscroft*, which is now lost to the corporation, though by what means is not now ascertainable. Then there is the forest or woodland, which is represented by the coppice called *Rowder Down Coppice* and the *Burleaze* close. Further evidence of this is to be obtained from the Hundred Rolls (ii. p. 506), where we have the following curious and valuable entry, "communa de Chippenham habet in bruariis viii quarant in longitudine et in latitudine iiii quarant; eadem villa habet in morisco," &c.

Thus, then, the arable land with its relics of archaic allotment into yard-lands, the meadow land with its still surviving custom of tribute by the headman, the pastures and the forest held in common, make up together the exact requirements in kind of the ancient village community. That in extent they were far short of the requirements of the ancient village community is due to the conflict between archaic rights and more modern necessities.

We have noted that the evidence points to Chippenham as an example of the free village community, and Professor Nasse quotes the Hundred Rolls as being one proof out of many that "it is not to be seen who could have been lord of the

[1] Biddulph's "Tribes of the Hindoo Koosh," p. 106. Such a ceremony by the headman is by no means confined to the agricultural community of the Aryans, as may be proved by the feast of the Zulus, when the king sacrifices a bullock, and so renders it lawful to cut the new-ripe mealies (*South Africa Folklore Journal*, vol. i. p. 134; *Antiquary*, vol. v. p. 138).

manor on this pastura communis, and we may assume that the common pasture must have belonged actually to the villata, *i.e.*, either to the possessors of the different feoda or to all the libere tenentes," a conclusion coinciding remarkably with all the other evidence here drawn together that in Chippenham we have an example of a village community not under the dominion of a lord.

When we come to gather up the facts for a comprehensive view of the community of Chippenham we see plainly enough that it passed through several stages of decay or disruption until finally it was broken up, leaving only the mosaics of its original constitution, which we have now examined. From these facts we discover three very important stages in the process of breaking up. The evidence is to be derived from the settlement of a dispute in Chancery in the reign of James I., the charter of Queen Mary, and Domesday; and I represent these to myself as epochs in the history of the Chippenham community when the force of outside events had produced internal disruptions—a state of things which, if read by the light of comparative history, will reveal to us several important features in the transition from the village community to an organization which would meet the requirements of an advanced commercial society.

The document dating from the reign of James I. is a decree of Chancery settling a dispute which had arisen between the inhabitants of one portion of the then borough and the borough authorities as to who were entitled to enjoy the borough lands. Finally it was settled that all the tenements which then stood within the borough were in future to represent the initial rights of the community to the exclusion of all tenements which might subsequently be created. Here it will be seen that in the village itself first commenced the process of decay: the old homesteads did not suffice for the growing population, so long as group-living did not obtain. But this decree not only reveals where the decay had set in; but where the natural development of the primitive community was arrested. The original democratic constitution of the old community is revealed by the struggle which took place before it was possible to create tenements which did not carry with them the rights of burghal freemanship; and this sudden stoppage of a development from a democratic village community to a democratic burghal community is the fact which marks the break-up of the older organization of the village.

But if in the reign of James I. it had become necessary to resort to the law courts to obtain an arrest of the natural growth of the community, may we not assume that the previous charter of Mary had been obtained for a somewhat similar object? Up to that date Chippenham was unchartered. Whatever rights and privileges it possessed, had descended with its old position of a village community or, to speak technically, a manor; and for it to have suddenly obtained the position of a chartered borough, without possessing any great commercial activity which needed protection, betokens that something was going on which threatened its existence as a corporate body. This is what appears to me to be fairly deducible from the legal operations of King James and Queen Mary. And this inference is borne out by some facts which are presented to us from other sources, and which show that the danger to be met was the transfer of the village lands into holdings in severalty.

In early days the Bailiff of Chippenham had struggled hard to maintain the old land-rights of the community;[1] in the days of Mary it would appear, if we take the charter to represent the whole facts of the case, that the community was almost landless. It might be argued from this that the community of Chippenham had lost its lands during the disruptions which enabled the Lords of Hungerford to grasp at all they could lay hands on. But it does not at all follow that the grant of Queen Mary suggests that Chippenham possessed no lands other than those then bestowed. The alienation of the corporation lands has been enormous since this period,[2] and this

[1] Jackson's "History of Chippenham," p. 21.
[2] For instance, the "Municipal Corporation Commission" shows that over 86 acres of the chartered lands were "missing" in 1835.

alienation may well have been from lands held by prescriptive rights, which would be more readily disposed of, while the charter-granted lands, possessing a more definite and publicly-known title, could not have been so readily alienated. This view of the case is confirmed by a very curious piece of evidence. Some land called the West Mead is granted by Queen Mary's charter. The extent of it was then stated to be 30 acres, and it still remained in the hands of the corporation in 1835, its exact acreage being 30 ac. 3 r. 15 p. But in the occupation of this mead, which is cultivated as we have seen in an extremely archaic fashion, are associated several individual freeholders who hold their portion of the common "in the same manner as the corporation hold theirs."[1] Who, then, are these individual freeholders? They must have been small holders, as their whole possession did not amount to more than thirteen acres, and their intimate association with the corporation lands is most significant. Surely we have something more here than a merely convenient arrangement for agricultural purposes? My own suggestion is, that they are descendants of original members of the community who before Queen Mary's time had transferred their temporary rights in the land to a holding in severalty. If this is the right reading of the evidence, we may go one step further, and say they represent the last of a series of transactions which had been going on from time to time since the days of the first carving out of the market village in the forest, and which will fully account for the necessity of converting the prescriptive village community into a chartered burghal community.

Taking into account, then, that the community was already in possession of some lands at the time of Queen Mary's grant, our next point is to consider the nature of this grant. The lands granted to the newly-made burgh had belonged to Walter, Lord Hungerford, beheaded by Henry VIII. They were in temporary possession of the Crown, until the heir came of age, which event happened within twenty-three days after the date

---

[1] "Municipal Corporation Commission."

of the charter.[1] And the reason for cutting off from the possessions of Lord Hungerford lands which made up a great part of the parish of Chippenham seems to me to rest, not so much in the caprice of the sovereign, as in the asserted rights of the community which had at one time or other been despoiled of these very lands. For there are two very important facts which suggest such a state of things. The first and most important is that when the new corporation began to utilize their newly chartered lands, they did so in a thoroughly archaic fashion, and not in the spirit of the charter, nor of the transactions in King James's reign. This gives us evidence of the continuity of the methods of holding and cultivation, and hence it goes a long way towards establishing a continuity of the holding itself; for why should a community suddenly created by a modern charter proceed to exercise its rights in the fashion it might have done if its lands had descended uninterruptedly from the earliest times? It certainly could not have invented the traditional customs of a bygone age, and the tradition could scarcely have survived without the aid of the lands which supported it. Secondly, the evidence of Domesday proves that at the time of the Norman conquest, the community possessed the lands subsequently granted to it by Queen Mary out of the possessions of Lord Hungerford. Taking into account what we have noted of the survivals of archaic custom and the evidence of Domesday, it appears that Mary's grant may be interpreted as representing the asserted rights of the community based upon their continuance from early times. The evidence on the whole, therefore, seems to prove that the period which witnessed the inauguration of the new borough witnessed, too, the last stages of the village community. The old democratic and archaic constitution was not suited to the times which recognized landed property as one of the chief means of individual wealth. The village community, therefore, passed on into the burghal community, and in its new capacity re-asserted some of its old rights. It obtained some

[1] Jackson's "History of Chippenham," p. 23.

of these rights in the charter-granted lands, and by retaining with these the old methods of cultivation, we are able to identify them as remnants of a once more extensive land community.

Finally let us note some of the race elements in the early settlement, for here, as in our other examples, it will be found that Saxon and Celt have settled side by side. There is some evidence that the Britons had one of their forest homes not far from the present site of the town of Chippenham. Turning up from the river Avon through a narrow roadway indicative enough of early occupation is a farm now known by the name of Cockleborough, and Aubrey has preserved for us a tradition of his time that this place was once a "borough."[1] The thick woods of a forest, which can even now be traced in the forests of Braden, Calne, and Bowood, Pewsham Wood, Blackmore, Selwood, Groveley, Gillingham, Cranbourn Chase, and New Forest,[2] hemmed this place in and made it a stronghold such as Cæsar tells us that the Britons retreated to. That this British stronghold guided the settlement of the English on the river Avon, there is no evidence to tell; but the process may be pictured by what we know of the doings under similar circumstances in other lands. The holding in the forest is traditionally recorded in the rhyme preserved by Aubrey, who, noting that "this towne did stand in the Pewsham forest before it was disafforested about the year 16[30], the people made this rhyme:

> "'When Chipnam stood
> In Pewsham Wood
> Before it was destroyed
> A cowe might have gone for a groate a yeare
> But now it is denayied'"—[3]

and the ancient way to the forest is even now marked in the place-names of the modern town by the name of Forest Lane.

[1] Aubrey's "Collections for Wilts," p. 10.
[2] Rev. Canon Jackson, "History of Chippenham," p. 2.
[3] "Collections for Wilts," p. 8.

Bearing in mind what Mr. Kemble has to say about the gradual encroachment of the communities on the mark, "when once the surface of a country has become thickly studded with communities settled between the marks, and daily finding the several clearings grow less and less sufficient for their support,"[1] we may turn to the evident origin of the name Chippenham as the market village for our next guidance. Dotted here and there in the ancient forest lands of middle England are market villages whose history is of considerable importance. By the side of Chippenham in Wilts we must place Chipping [Campden] and Chipping [Sodbury] in Gloucestershire; Chipping [Lambourn] in Berks; Chippenhurst, Chippinghurst, and Chipping [Norton] in Oxfordshire; Chipping [Wycombe] in Bucks; Chipping [Warden] in Northamptonshire; Chipping and Chipping [Barnet] in Herts; Chipping [Ongar] in Essex; and Chippingham in Cambridgeshire. All these were carved out of the forest land of the early communities. This crucial fact enables us to take an important step in ascertaining the origin of these market villages. "In order to understand what a market originally was," says Sir Henry Maine, "you must try to picture to yourselves a territory occupied by village communities, self-acting, and as yet autonomous, each cultivating its arable lands in the middle of its waste, and each, I fear I must add, in perpetual war with its neighbour. But at several points, points probably where the domains of two or three villages converged, there appear to have been spaces of what we now call neutral ground. These were the markets. They were probably the only places at which the members of the different primitive groups met for any purpose except warfare, and the persons who came to them were doubtless at first persons specially empowered to exchange the produce and manufactures of one little village community for those of another."[2] Of course in this passage we have a picture drawn rather from India than

---

[1] "Saxons in England," vol. i. pp. 48, 49.
[2] "Village Communities," p. 192.

England, but we know that much of it is as true of the past state of one country as of the arrested stage of the other.

Thus, then, we have the market village of Chippenham, situated conveniently on the banks of the river Avon, which helps to show us that the Wilsetas understood the art of settlement, a fact which is abundantly evidenced by the situation of their towns throughout the county—a situation which led the rural economists of last century to speak so eloquently about them.[1] When next we come to the period when the kings of Wessex possessed a hunting seat at Chippenham, and the Latin Chronicles begin to style it "villa regia,"[2] we are dealing with the accidents of its early history. That the Danes encamped here for a short time, that one of their chieftains found his last resting-place in a tumulus still called after him "Hubba's low," are facts of more pregnant importance, because where the Danes settled, there, as a rule, they stamped the mark of their occupation.[3]

In considering the settlement at Chippenham therefore there are the following interesting facts to note: There is evidence of contact with the Celtic settlement in its neighbourhood; and there is absolutely no trace of any town or even occupation-land having been on this site during the Roman period.[4] So much has occurred to disrupt the course of its history that we do not find that the traces of the old Celtic tribal organization remain alongside of a later Saxon organization; but we find, as at Aston, ample evidence as to the evolution of a tenancy in severalty from an original communal holding in the village.

We next come to Malmesbury; and turning first to the

[1] See Marshall's "Rural Economy of the Southern Counties," vol. ii. pp. 307, 308.

[2] Canon Jackson's "History of Chippenham," p. 7.

[3] That the Danes had some degree of influence at Chippenham is shown by the Domesday record of "Rainaldus Canut," who held there one hide of the king. Canut is certainly a Danish name, and he held lands nowhere else in Wiltshire.

[4] Jackson's "History of Chippenham," p. 3. The nearest evidences of Roman occupation are at Studley, Bromham, Lacock, Box, and Colerne.

structure of the community itself we will consider it under the heads of (1) the basis of membership; (2) the rights of membership.

The basis of membership has some features which are of almost unique importance. Our knowledge of them is chiefly to be obtained from an account in *The Gentleman's Magazine* of 1832, which is copied from a manuscript dated 1685–6. What this manuscript is, and where it is, I have failed to discover, but that the extract I am going to use is original cannot for one moment be doubted: "Being to mention Malmesbury often in the ensuing narration, I have thought it not unfit, to say something of the policy of that auntient Corporation, which by the justice and clemency and liberality of former Kings, hath not only retained its auntient forme of Government, but hath been inriched with great quantitys of land, which are disposed amongst the Freemen and Guildeners, by very just and prudent methods. The Borrow of Malmesbury is situated in two parishes, that of Malmesbury properly, and that of Westport. The Commoners and Guildeners of Malmesbury are divided into sixe centurys or hundreds or tribes, and every Commoner is reduced under one of these tribes, and inrolled in a large skin, under the name of a tribe or hundred, so that there are six columns of names, all which persons have right of Common in the large portion of grounde called King's Heath, given to them by Charter, in reward of faithful services done to King Athelstan, whose monument is yet extant in Malmesbury, by that magnanimous King, but wisely limited, so that every Commoner hath an equal advantage by it. Now the 48 names which by antiquity or seniority come to be next the names of the respective centurys or tribes, are termed the 48ths, and have an Addition of Land in a Common Field, belonging to that Corporation, as a Corporation. There is also a superiore order of 24^s, which are elected ever out of the 48 by the majority of the 24^s, who doe not always respect seniority, but the tribes of the persons. There is also another order, which consists of 13, who by the majority of the 13, are ever elected out of the majority of the 24^s onely, in which

Election seniority is also not always regarded. Three persons of this 13 are yearly presented to the Commoners by the rest of the 13, who choose out of them an Alderman for the ensuinge yeer, which Alderman is a Justice of the Peace for the Burrow; and hath power to nominate a Deputy, who is to act onely when the Alderman is out of the Burrow. These 13 have also large Meadowes or Pastures, none lesse than £8 nor none worth more than £16 per ann. to each one, but under penalties of waste, so that these grounds are not empayred, altho they pass thorow many hands."

We have to deal with modern phraseology in considering the extent to which the Malmesbury community is indebted to blood relationship for its basis of membership; but in spite of this we can detect, I think, the archaic original which preceded the record as it has come down to us. The mode by which persons can become free burgesses was settled in 1821, and this was preserved by an Act of Parliament then obtained for the enclosing of the borough lands. It is thus given by the commissioners of 1835: "Every son of a free burgess or commoner in his own right, he being at the time of claiming admission of the age of twenty-one years and married, and also a parishioner of one of the parishes within the borough, and likewise at the same time an inhabitant householder in an entire tenement (and not an inmate) within the borough, is entitled to be admitted a free burgess or commoner of this borough. Every man who has married a free burgess's daughter, he being at the time of claiming admission so married and his wife living (but not otherwise), he being also of the age of twenty-one years and a parishioner of one of the parishes within the borough, and an inhabitant householder in an entire tenement (and not an inmate) within the borough, is entitled to be admitted a free burgess or commoner of this borough; but a free burgess's daughter having once married cannot communicate to a second husband a right to admission; nor will such subsequent marriage give to the sons or daughters of such husband by another wife any right to admission. No son of a free burgess born before his father shall have been admitted in court a free burgess is entitled to be admitted a free burgess. No daughter born before her father shall have been admitted in court a free burgess can communicate to or invest any husband with any right or title to be admitted a free burgess."

Disqualification and causes for rejection and amoval are (1) conviction of felony; (2) not being at the time of admission, or at any time after admission ceasing to be an inhabitant householder in an entire tenement within one of the said parishes within the borough.

Blood relationship is by this constitution absolutely the basis of the Malmesbury community,[1] and even where it oversteps the line of male descent, it runs parallel to the archaic system, where, as in some tribes in the Punjab, the daughter may bring her husband to fill up the ranks of the community, failing through disease or any other calamity.[2] We even have preserved in this curiously constructed system of municipal freedom the archaic succession of all the sons—"every son" being entitled to take up his freedom upon coming of age. There is also the practical prohibition against widow marriage which is parallelled in Hindu usage.

The regulation of the affairs of the community was determined by an assembly composed of all its members. The report of the Municipal Corporation Commission of 1835 describes the assembly at Malmesbury as follows: "An assembly composed of the alderman, capital burgesses, assistant burgesses, landowners, and commoners, has the privilege of deciding on the title of claimants to a share in the Corporation lands." The commissioners of 1876 obtained the information that there are four courts during the year— one for the appointment of officers, one for the swearing in of officers, one for admission of commoners, and one for the turning out of commoners upon disqualification. We do not know sufficiently the details of the proceedings of this

[1] The evidence of Mr. Player before the Commission of 1876 illustrates how actual was the kinship basis of the community. See Question 6318 *et seq*.
[2] Tupper, "Punjab Customary Law," vol. ii. pp. 74, 75.

assembly to pick out all the points of contact with the assemblies of early social groups; but Mr. Trice Martin has preserved in his preface to the "Registrum Malmesburiense" (vol. iii. p. xliii) an interesting archaism which accompanies the delivery of the allotted portions of land to the commoners. Seizin was given by the transferring of a twig and the repetition of the rhyming formula—

> " This land and twig I give to thee,
> As free as Athelstan gave it me,
> And I hope a loving brother thou wilt be."

The appearance of the rhyme at once denotes that we are in the presence of archaic custom,[1] and the last line recalls that "common brotherhood" which is a typical feature of early communities, and of which we have already had some evidence in the kinship which underlies the constitution of the Malmesbury community. Further than this is the significant practice of the delivery of the twig. Comparing the method of allotment adopted at Aston and Cote, we have seen that the allotment of the land is made by means of curiously formed twigs,[2] a twig being placed on each strip of land, and corresponding twigs being cast into a hat, from which the various members of the community draw. The twigs so drawn denote the piece of land which each drawer is to have for the coming year. With these interesting facts before us I suggest that in the rhyming formula still surviving at Malmesbury we have a relic of the periodical redistribution of land by the assembly of the community.

We have next to deal with the rights of the community. The rights of membership at Malmesbury, governed by that intricate system which has already been noted, are entirely of an archaic order. There is the tenement or homestead. There

---

[1] I have given some details of this interesting subject, rhyming formulæ, in an article in the *Antiquary*, vol. viii. pp. 12-15.

[2] See also *Archæologia*, vol. xxxvii. p. 383.   symbols of transfer generally, consult Spence's "Court of Chancery," vol. i. p. 22.

is a right to land "in a common field," that is, land held in common by those bundles of strips of acres or half-acres which Mr. Seebohm has made so familiar to us. There is the common pasture attached to the arable lots. In 1835 the Municipal Corporation Commission thus described this land: "The property of the Corporation consists of about 516 acres of land, divided among the entire body in the following proportion: 280 commoners, about 1 acre each; 48 landholders, about 1 acre each; 24 assistants, about 2 acres each; the alderman and eleven [twelve] senior capital burgesses, 140 acres between them" (see "Report," vol. i. p. 77)[1]—but the Commissioners of 1876 obtained much more valuable information. This information I summarise as follows, the reference figures being the number of question and answer in the evidence:—

1. The homestead, which gives in primitive times the right to land allotments in the common lands, is represented by thirty-nine properties, which belong to the alderman and capital burgesses (5487–5500).

2. The allotment of lands.—No one can hold land unless he be a freeman of the borough either by right of birth or marriage (5415). This enables them to take up their right as commoners (5420), and they take common as a vacancy occurs. The commoners then succeed by rotation to a vacant acre held by the landholders. The mode of succession to this higher body is regulated by custom. The custom is, that the whole common is divided into six "hundreds," each hundred part having a particular name (5433–6), though the names are not of much significance in their present form. The commoner draws lots upon one or more of these six "hundreds," and enters himself as a candidate for vacancies as they arise (5411). He cultivates or lets his allotment, which is not marked out by boundaries or by fences (5531). The next grade is that of assistant burgess. To become a member of this grade the

[1] This is the same as recorded in the preamble of the local Act 1 and 2 Geo. IV. cap. 34, and it is interesting to note this as an instance of archaic custom being recorded in a modern statute.

candidate must first give a "seeking feast" to the body of twenty-four (6293), and then take up his allotment upon the death of a present holder. Then from the assistant burgesses are elected the capital burgesses, who have each a burgess part in the lands of the borough (5470).

Now this remarkably intricate custom has many features common to the primitive agricultural holdings, some of them of special interest. The village tenements, the arable allotments, the common pasture, are all characteristics that do not belong to modern times. Rotation by death or seniority replaces the annual allotment of primitive times. And this slight deviation is quite capable of historical explanation (see Laveleye's "Primitive Property," p. 93), besides which we may compare this succession to long-established allotments to the Punjab custom of succession to ancestral shares.

Another fact it is important to note is the use of the word acre in its archaic sense. The common land is divided out into lots or "acres." These, it was explained to the Commissioners of 1876 (Q. 6491), are not statute acres, some being half and some three-quarters of an acre, and it is these nominal acres which form the holding of the members of the hundreds.[1]

Now, the area of land belonging to the modern corporation has admittedly diminished. The Commissioners of 1876 obtained from one of the witnesses evidence to the effect that, "by reputation," they had lost some lands, and do not know where they have gone to, and they possessed "old deeds relating to property" of which they do not know the existence. If we turn to the doings of the abbey, as chronicled in the "Registrum Malmesburiense," we can obtain some explanation of this. The enclosure of the common lands round Malmesbury, says Mr. Trice Martin in his preface to that volume, furnishes the subject of many of the documents. Fouleswike

---

[1] This naming of the holdings by the term "acres" led to a wrong statement of the area of the corporation property. In 1835 it was stated to be 516 acres (see above), but there were really 516 *lots*, which represented 800 statute acres, if not more. See Commission of 1876, Question 32,613 *et seq.*

and the Rowmerse, which are frequently mentioned in this connection, are probably what is now known as Bird's Marsh, about a couple of miles north of Chippenham, on the Malmesbury road. Portmaneshethe recalls the familiar Portmeadow of Oxford, and was the property of the burgesses, as well as Barndehethe or Burntheath, which the Malmesbury people are fond of telling strangers was granted to their ancestors by Athelstan for help given in the battle against the Danes.[1]

Turning to the documents, they tell us the same story which we may learn from other parts of the history of Malmesbury. The lands are intermixed allotments in a common field, and held by their various owners in bundles of acres. It will be sufficient to quote one or two examples to prove this; and I will select the documents dealing with Thornhill. This is the name of one of the six "hundreds" into which the lands of Malmesbury are divided; and I think we have here not only evidence of the ancient mode of culture and holding, but of the once wider extent of these "hundreds." The first document is a grant of "tres acras terrae cum omnibus pertinentiis suis in campis de Thornhulle, quarum duae acrae jacent juxta tenementum quondam Roberti le Charpenter versus occidentem, una dimidia acra extendit se versus terram Willelmi Parcarii inter terram Willelmi le Frere et Ricardi Pinnock, et alia dimidia acra jacet in campo de Borghtone qui vocatur le Ham, inter terram Roberti Woderove et terram Aliciae de la Grene."[2] Here we have two acres lying together, and two half-acres lying between the acre-strips of other holders. The next document relates to an exchange of land at Thornhill, consisting of "illas septem acras terrae arabilis quae jacent in campis de Boruhtone et Thornhulle,"[3] of which two acres and two half-acres are the same as described as above, and the remaining four acres are scattered in parcels, two of one acre each, and the remaining two acres together. The last document relating to this district is the grant to the abbey "totum tenementum

---

[1] "Registrum Malmesburiense," vol. ii. p. xliii.
[2] Ibid., vol. ii. p. 184.   [3] Ibid., vol. ii. p. 230.

meum et terram meam apud Thornhulle, cum domibus, gardinis, curtillagiis, pratis, pascuis, et pasturis."[1]

The documents of Malmesbury Abbey show us very clearly how the abbey gradually gathered into its hands tenements in the town and large tracts of land without, which once no doubt belonged to the community. And when we come to the charters of John, which granted the town to the abbey in feefarm, and gave them absolutely the castle, the Norman successor of that ancient British castellum which was the centre of all civil rights in Malmesbury, we know quite well that the stage when old communal lands were to be transformed into church lands had been reached.

Looking at the evidence thus, I do not think it is too much to suggest that the community of Malmesbury was once a community independent of the national economy for its support, obtaining its own food and its own clothes from the lands and flocks which it owned. One special illustration of this view is the custom of granting land for the support of the village officers. We have already drawn attention to this point,[2] and its bearing upon the independent economy of each settlement. That we have a survival at Malmesbury in the annual grant to the alderman of a piece of land known as the "Alderman's kitchen" is evidence of a once existing system of economy which did not extend beyond the community itself.

And I would venture to suggest a survival of the duty of the free tribesmen "to join the chief's host in his enterprises," in the "Domesday" record that "when the king was going on an expedition, whether by land or sea, he was either wont to have from this borough twenty shillings for the support of his sailors, or took with him one man for each honour of five hides."

It will have been seen from these details of the village community surviving at Malmesbury that they are far more than ordinarily complicated, and it becomes a question whether by attempting to unravel some of the complications we can arrive at any clear data as to the origin of the community.

---

[1] "Registrum Malmesburiense," vol. ii. p. 349. [2] *Ante*, p. 163.

We find it divided into four classes, as we may call them, and also into six hundreds or tribes; and it is to be noted that these are concurrent divisions and not subordinated the one to the other. The first thing is to distinguish between the four classes as representing one group of custom and the tribes or hundreds as representing another group of custom; for, looking at these two classifications of the community how we may, it is clear that they do not belong to one system, and must therefore come from different origins.

Confining ourselves at first to the three classes of thirteens, twenty-fours, and forty-eights, what is the evidence to be derived from the remarkable document quoted above? The answer is to be found by ascertaining the constitution of the Welsh tribal communities, which can readily be done by turning to Mr. Seebohm's "English Village Community" (pp. 181–206). Mr. Seebohm is there treating, not of the late survivals, imperfect in form and twisted from their archaic originals by the forces of modern politics, but of the early tribal communities as seen from the evidence of laws and other early authorities. And though I shall not suggest that we can absolutely identify the Malmesbury community, with its "hundreds or tribes" and its "thirteens," with the "tribes" and "thirteens" of the Welsh system, yet I shall urge that the archaic arithmetic of the early Welsh tribes has unquestionably survived in the curiously complicated system of the Malmesbury community. "Without pretending to have mastered all the details," says Mr. Seebohm, "of these obscure [Welsh] tribal arrangements, the point to be noted is that the scattering of the tyddyns all over the country side, and the clustering of them by fours and sixteens, or twelves, into the group which was the unit paying the gwestva or tunc pound, and again into clusters of twelve or *thirteen* under a maer as the unit of civil jurisdiction were obviously distinctive features arising from the tribal holding of the land."[1] Apply this statement to the con-

[1] "English Village Community, p. 205. Mr. Seebohm quotes from the "Gwentian Code," p. 375, the following: "There are to be thirteen trevs in every maenol, and the thirteenth of these is the supernumerary trev."

dition of things at Malmesbury, and what do we find? Except that there was no "scattering of the tyddyns all over the country side," Mr. Seebohm's summary of the early Welsh tribal constitution holds good as a summary of the late Malmesbury constitution.

Of course, it is not to be expected that the structure of the community in the seventeenth or nineteenth centuries was exactly the same as the original from which it descended. But the twisting which has taken place, owing to the operation of modern economic laws, is wonderfully small. I have elsewhere entered into the details by which this is proved;[1] but I will deal here with the evolution of the landholding body.

The Malmesbury constitution may be grouped thus:—

1835.	1685.
Per Municipal Corporation Commission.	Per quotation from *Gentleman's Magazine*.
280 commoners 48 landowners 24 assistants 12 capital burgesses and 1 alderman	The forty-eights The twenty-fours. The thirteens.

It will be seen by this that the 280 commoners are the outcome of the period between 1685 and 1835, and as constituent portions of the community must be struck out of our present consideration. But, what is much more important, we must strike out, too, the "titles" of the other bodies, and substitute for them the extremely archaic titles derived from the number comprising the body. There thus remains the three bodies of the forty-eights, the twenty-fours, and the thirteens. Now, if we eliminate from these the body of "twenty-fours," we are enabled to make a tolerably perfect comparison of the Malmesbury community with the South Wales tribal system; and I

[1] *Archæologia*, vol. L.

would suggest that we may well consider this body to have been the creation of the fifteenth and sixteenth centuries, just as the 280 commoners are proved to have been the creation of the seventeenth and eighteenth centuries. If this is so, we have left as representatives of the archaic tribal constitution of Malmesbury, the forty-eights and the "thirteen"; and my suggestion is, that in these two bodies we have the twelve tyddyns, and one supernumerary tyddyn, with their corresponding four erws (or acres) each, or together, 48 erws.

We will deal first with the 48 erws, or acres, belonging to the tyddyn, and endeavour to ascertain how they helped to form the group of "landholders" who became an integral part of the community. Mr. Seebohm points out the difficulty attending the curious geometrical system of the early Welsh tribes, unless we adopt the shifting characteristics of a pastoral people; and he states that, long before the fourteenth century, the households were settled in their homesteads, geometrical regularity had ceased, and the land was divided and subdivided into irregular fractions. I suggest we have in Malmesbury a curious example of these irregular fractions. When the tyddyns lost their archaic nature, they could no longer keep to the old laws of succession by undivided groups, and hence at some period when the pressure of population began to tell, the question of the succession to the communal property began to arise. To meet this state of things the then possessors of the 48 erws, or acres, belonging to the tyddyns, were allowed to keep their holdings, and in virtue of them to become the basis of a new class in the community, just as at later periods the same question would arise, and additional classes such as the "assistants" and "commoners" subsequently succeeded to the inheritance of the once undivided households of the original tribal holdings.

We have next to deal with the "thirteen," and I may advance the suggestion that the close analogy it bears to the group of tyddyns in the old Welsh tribal system considerably strengthens the perhaps somewhat speculative considerations I have put forward as to the origin of the other bodies. The group of tyddyns was made up of twelve, plus one supernumerary tyddyn, making together thirteen. And so the "thirteen" at Malmesbury were composed of twelve, plus one supernumerary. This important fact did not appear until 1876 when evidence was taken before the municipal commissioners.[1] Nor is this all. It was one of the features of the tribal system, as we see it in Ireland, that "the families of free tribesmen did not always occupy the same tyddyn, but were shifted from one to another whenever the dying out of a family rendered needful a redistribution to ensure the fair and equal division of the tribal lands according to antiquity and their rank under the tribal rules."[2] The holdings of the "thirteen" at Malmesbury were likewise at one time, though not now, subject to a re-allotment whenever a new member was admitted upon the death or removal of an old member.[3]

Whether this be the correct explanation or not of the curious classification of the Malmesbury community, one thing seems very certain, namely, that the thirteens and the two other classes do not originate from the six tribes or hundreds, and in point of fact appear to have the hundreds superimposed upon them. These three classes have their special holdings in the land as we have seen, but the hundreds themselves also have rights in the land, each of them having a portion of the common land allotted to it. Now we have noted that at Kells in Ireland the division of the community was into six groups, and if these groups at Malmesbury similarly represented the old ancestral shares stamped upon the land by some later comers into the community who did not at the same time stamp out thereby the old divisions of the Welsh tribal system, we have an explanation which does to some extent answer for the curious dual constitution which appears to have obtained with this community. We are, by the evidence of analogy,

[1] See "Municipal Corporation Commission," 1876, part ii. p. 836, "There is always one capital burgess who has not a 'burgess part'; he is paid money out of what is subscribed by the other capital burgers."

[2] Seebohm, "English Village Community," p. 236 ; see *ante*, p. 135.

[3] See "Municipal Corporation Commission," 1876, part ii. p. 833.

which has been put forward throughout these pages as our guide, prepared to find such curious divergencies as these, and we would *ex hypothesi* attribute them to race influences. In this particular instance there is much in the history of the district which would enable us to identify some of the race conflicts and race settlements of early days when Malmesbury was at the head of a wedge-like area of Celtic occupation surrounded on either side by Anglo-Saxons. The conflict took place at Malmesbury, and the records of the settlement may still be read, the only points of which that need be mentioned here are the surviving strongholds of the early races, namely, at Caer Dur, which the Celts had formed, and at Brokenburgh, the work of the Saxons.[1]

In the cases which we have now examined the one phenomenon which appears common to them all is what I have already termed the evolution of a numerous tenancy from an original community based upon kinship. At Aston, as at Malmesbury and Chippenham, we meet as the latest form of the community a body of men entitled to share in the land privileges of the community who have succeeded to a much smaller body who are dimly discernible in the remote past. In the case of Aston we have seen that the evolution had proceeded so far as to practically dissolve the community, leaving only its imprint upon the land. In the cases of Malmesbury and Chippenham we have seen that the more modern features of municipal life arrested the progress of this evolution at a certain stage which is almost everywhere to be recognized in municipal history, the stage, namely, where the burghs passed from their earlier democratic constitution to their late mediæval constitution of close corporations. In no case, however, is this so peculiarly exemplified as in the Scottish burgh of Newton-upon-Ayr, and it is a case well worth studying. It presents us with phenomena which are perfectly familiar to settlement officers in India, and which have been presented to the student in

[1] I have detailed these facts from my point of view in *Archæologia*, vol. L.

that somewhat remarkable collection of Punjab customary law published by the Government of India under the superintendence of Mr. C. L. Tupper. The gradual individualization of original communal rights has proceeded upon lines which have left marks on the history of villages in India, and these lines are parallelled in a remarkable manner by the evidence which Newton-upon-Ayr supplies, supplemental to that we have already noted in other examples.[1]

The constitution of Newton-upon-Ayr is thus described: "The number of freemen or burgesses is limited to forty-eight, which compose the community. Each of these freemen possess what is called a lot or freedom, containing about four acres of arable land, besides the common, on which the burgesses have an exclusive right to pasture their cattle. No houses are annexed to these freedoms; but every burgess must reside in the burgh, or possess a house as his property, which he may rent to any of the inhabitants. The community meet every two years to elect their magistrates, and at this election every freeman has a vote. . . . The right of succession to these freedoms is limited. A son succeeds to his father; and a widow, not having a son, enjoys the property of her husband as long as she lives. But as the female line is excluded, the lots of freedom frequently revert to the town, who dispose of them to the most industrious inhabitants of the place, on their advancing a certain sum of money which is placed in the public fund."[2]

We can pick out at once in this example the safeguards against the decay of the community, and these safeguards all belong to archaic law. Every landowner is also a house-owner; the right of succession is based upon kinship, and limited; when the right of succession fails the land reverts to the community. With these provisions in force, the community of Newton could not, like the communities of Lauder and Aston, revert to a single individual. There is life and means

---

[1] See Tupper, *op. cit.*, pp. 44-50; and *cf.* Fenton's "Early Hebrew Life," p. 71.
[2] Sinclair's "Statistical Account of Scotland," vol. ii. pp. 263-4.

of continued life in the system. But Newton, like Lauder and Aston, has had to fight against the encroaching powers of modern economical laws, and, as in every other case, archaic legal rules have had to give way. Newton has retained the old forms of her community, but she has given up the old forms of her land tenure and cultivation.

The first cause of the decay was the fatal practice of selling the "freedoms." No such right existed in early times, and the Commissioners of Municipal Corporations of 1835 report that few instances occurred till within the last half-century. But even in these there is a safeguard based upon the archaic rules of early society. A freeman wishing to dispose of his right renounced it to the community at a fixed price, who resold it to the purchaser. Beneath this legal fiction we can easily perceive that the lands were not the freeman's to sell; they belonged, as in archaic times, to the community.

But a far more powerful cause than this put an immediate end to the archaic rules obtaining with reference to the burghal lands of Newton. They were originally divided out into separate holdings every year, and returned into common after the harvest had been gathered in. The departure from this plan is recorded in the reports of the Municipal Corporation Commissioners, and the whole extract is so curious that I must be pardoned for giving it in full (vol. i. pp. 92-94).

It appears that the community or freemen of the burgh had, from a very ancient period, records of their own, separate from those of the council. These records were relied on by the freemen as establishing the following points:—

1. That prior to the date of the existing charters the territorial possessions of the burgh were enjoyed by the individual freemen patrimonially, each having in old times had his own "daill" given to him at the periodical partition of the lands "according to the auld ordour use and wont."

2. That the right of a freeman in this burgh was heritable as well as patrimonial, inasmuch as sons—whom failing, sons-in-

law—were entitled to succeed to the right of their father's demise, and to enter to the freedom in his stead.

3. That the number of freemen entitled to "daills" of the common property was limited, and in 1604, the date of the first "daill" after the existing charters, the limitation was held and understood to be precisely forty-eight, which is said to have been agreeable to the established law and custom.

The "daill" of 1604 was declared to subsist for eleven years, or till 1615, at which period a new division must have occurred, but of this there is no direct evidence.

On the 8th of December, 1642, a resolution is passed to "daill" to each freeman the east side of the moss, but on the 5th of November, 1644, this part of the common property "befoir dealt" is "with consent of the hail counsale and communittie" set to the two bailies. This transaction does not seem to have been approved of, for on the 8th of May, 1648, the bailies renounce their right, and this property is again ordained to be dealt to the freemen.

At successive periods, extending to seven years each, during the whole time between 1655 and 1764 inclusive, the allotment of "daills" is entered in the minute-book. The next "daill" occurred on the 21st of November, 1771, when, to remedy the evils experienced from the short periods of possession for which the casts had hitherto been made, it was resolved that the casts or divisions of the lots or daills "shall endure and continue for fifty-seven years from this date."

The period of this last division expired in 1828, when a new division of the property by lot fell to be made, and at the community meeting of the 23rd of January, 1829, the report of the committee was approved of, which recommended the continuance of the lot assigned to the individual burgesses at that cast or division to be for nine hundred and ninety-nine years after Martinmas, 1828.

More recently it appeared to the freemen to be desirable that their several possessions should be vested in them by "charter and sasine," and it was resolved by the community on the 10th of April, 1833, that the magistrates and council should grant feu rights of their lots to such of the freemen as might wish to hold their lands in that manner.

The patrimonial rights thus vested in the forty-eight freemen were never, until the attempts in 1829 and since, the subject of separate titles in their persons. Under the charters and the immemorial usage of the burgh the entry as burgess and freeman formed of itself the evidence of the freeman's right to his share of the common property, and the record in the community books of his entry and of the right thereby acquired by him to a "daill" constituted his only title. Non-residence in the burgh was in early times declared to nullify the right. The right, when freedoms fell in from any cause, was at the disposal of the community.[1]

I know of nothing to equal this in the history of the village community in the British Isles. It places absolutely at our disposal a complete record of the means by which lands originally held of the community for the temporary purpose of one year's cultivation became the private property of individuals; and in travelling back along the lines which these burghal documents point out to us we arrive at the most perfect evidence for ascertaining the several stages in the development of freehold property.

There are two other points yet to be noted about this Newton-upon-Ayr community. The assembly of the freemen, as we have seen, was in many respects peculiar, and it was composed, as the assemblies of all archaic societies are composed, of the men who possessed tenements in the village and allotments in the village lands. It is interesting to note that it bore also a very significant name—the "Beltan Court"; and I would venture to throw out a suggestion that this name gives us some traces of older race origins than the purely Teutonic name of the town. Secondly, there is the status of the widow. It cannot be one of the accidents of burghal custom that, like

[1] See reports of the Municipal Corporation Commission, vol. i. pp. 92-94; and compare "New Statistical Account of Scotland," *sub voce* "Newton-upon-Ayr."

many of the manorial customs in England, Newton has preserved in its rule that widows shall hold for life, if they have no children, one of the oldest of Aryan customs, and the history of which, as Sir Henry Maine has so remarkably proved, bears very closely upon the early history of women in relation to law.[1] And I will add in passing that there seems great need for a re-examination of burghal rights and of the means of their transmission. The surrender of manorial lands in the lord's court has been held to be a peculiar mark of serfdom, but at all events we have in this example a case of surrender, not to a lord, but to a community.

In the same county occurs an example which illustrates some of the same facts as at Newton. The burgh of Prestwick, in Ayr, contained in 1794 about sixty-six dwelling-houses and two hundred and sixty-six persons. There were thirty-six freeholders in the burghs whose freeholds had the privilege of pasturage for seventy-two soums of sheep upon the common, five sheep being reckoned to a soum. Sometimes poinds were driven and executed at the cross of Prestwick. A freeman, when incarcerated, could not be confined with locked doors; but if he came out he lost his freedom, unless liberated by the judicial sentence of the magistrates. None could sell their freedom but to the community, who have power to sell it to whom they please upon paying the agreed price. Males and females equally succeed to the freeholds. . . . The enclosures were few, the tenure by which they held their freedoms being unfavourable to such improvements, being subject to a revolution every nineteen years, when they cast lots for the respective freedom each freeman is to possess.[2]

I will mention two other examples which illustrate this portion of our subject. The first is that of the village of Crawford in Lanarkshire. Sir John Sinclair's "Statistical Account of Scotland" (iv. 512) thus describes this remarkable village community: "It consisted of about twenty freedoms,

---

[1] "Early History of Institutions," p. 334; *cf.* my paper in *Archæological Review*, vol. ii., on Widowhood in Manorial Law.

[2] Sinclair's "Statistical Account of Scotland," vol. xii. pp. 396, 397, 398.

which were in the form of run-rig. Besides the masters of these freedoms, who were called lairds, and their wives ladies, there was a subordinate rank, who feued ground for a house and a yard. Each freedom consisted of four or five acres of croft land parcelled out in all the different parts of the town, with a privilege of keeping a certain number of sheep, cows, and horses on the hill, or common pasture. This little republic was governed by a *birley* court, *in which every proprietor of a freedom had a vote.* If the proprietor resided not in the place his tenant voted for him. The great business of the court, which was held weekly, was to determine the proportion and number of sheep, cows, and horses which the respective proprietors should keep on the common pasture."

There is scarcely anything wanting in this example to absolutely identify it with the most archaic type of the village community. The village itself is the centre of all the rights; the assembly is composed of men possessing land rights; the allotments are determined by the assembly; and the nature of the cultivation is also thus determined.

In many respects this bears a close resemblance to another archaic type, namely, that of Whitsome in Berwickshire. I cannot help drawing attention in this instance to one remarkable fact, viz., the meeting of the village assembly, called, as at Crawford, the birlie court. In the "New Statistical Account of Scotland" it is recorded that till the middle of last century a mound was visible called the Birlie Knowe. Thither the villagers usually repaired to submit their petty grievances and to ask redress; and there the birlie-men, after hearing parties, pronounced their cheap and sapient decisions (vol. iii. p. 172). The system of landholding at Whitsome is thus described: "To convey some idea of Whitsome as it was, it may be noticed that the range of land on the north side of the village was divided into several small portions, still denominated 'lands.' Hence the possessors or occupiers were styled 'portioners.' 'The ten lands' formed the southern part of the present farm of Ravelaw; and 'the nine' and 'the eight' lay east from the preceding, and are included in the farm of Leetside. The southern side was parcelled out in like manner. The space between the two ranges, of considerable breadth, and upwards of half a mile in length, was enjoyed in common."

At Chirnside in Berwick the line of the village runs in two rows of houses east and west over the broad summit of the hill to the length of more than half a mile. Another row of them, not so compact, descends the hill in a southerly direction. Departing from the former at an opening near the middle, called the Corse, and properly the Cross, it has the church for its termination. Before the division of the lands of the barony into the separate shares of its proprietors in 1740, the village houses made that mean appearance common to the others in the country. Until 1745 no edifice of modern structure was to be seen in the whole parish. The village comprehended all the houses and cottages appertaining to the several proprietors, great and small. Adjacent to the mansion house of some of the large proprietors there was what was called the mains farm, or that of his domain or household. During the continuance of the blended property of the several heritors the further extension of farms and steadings was prevented by the common property they had in the out-fields. Of these the only use which could be made was that of a pasturage for all the cattle and sheep of the village. Besides the common moor adjacent to the village, a commonalty, running in a certain track several miles into Lammermuir, appertained to the barony of Chirnside. The acres and smaller lots of the arable were laid out in such a manner that balks or strips of untilled ground being interposed between every five or six ridges, a waste of the best land was thus made for the sake of marches not only between the grounds of the different proprietors, but amidst the lots and subdivisions of acres into which they were cast. The husbandmen had certain days or weeks at least marked out, especially in the spring season, for commencing their labours. The tradesmen in the village had portions of acres in the fields.[1]

[1] Sinclair's "Statistical Account of Scotland," vol. xiv. pp. 8, 10.

As we move on from one example to another we should be able to show again and again that in the survivals of the village community in Britain there exist, sometimes in one place and sometimes in another, facts parallel to the village community in India, all of which bear upon the suggestion which has been made throughout these pages, namely, that in Aryan custom and in the contact between Aryan and non-Aryan custom must be found the true history of village institutions in this country. In a succeeding chapter I shall collect some few fragmentary survivals of various details of the village community, and I shall suggest that they represent once complete examples. We have met with serfdom, we have met with dues to the lord, but neither of these two important characteristics of the survivals of the village community in Britain are necessarily connected with the manor, nor do they connect themselves with the ascertained facts of the Roman occupation of our country.

In the meantime it is important to have before us, if possible, evidence of the close contact between Roman institutions and the village community. Which is the intruding element—the Roman town constitution intruding into the villages, or the village community intruding into the towns? The continuity of Roman occupation is far from certain even in such cities as York and London; but if it be granted for the latter city, and it may well be so, we may perhaps ascertain whether the influences of Roman London penetrated into the village communities which settled, as we have already seen, in close proximity to her walls, or whether, on the contrary, it was the village communities which penetrated into the city. If the Romans could not keep the Saxons out of Londinium they could not overlord the Saxons in the country. If the Saxons, with their old Aryan instincts, could settle down alongside of the Romans in London, and could for a time dominate the city, they could much more settle alongside of Celtic villagers and never lose their hard-won overlordship, typified by their dominant name of Englishmen.

London stands out as absolutely unique throughout her

long and glorious history. She is unique in two ways—at the commencement and in the present stage of her history. As the hill-fort of the Romans, standing out above swamp and waters, and yet commanding such an important position, she is unique in origin; as a city, whose suburbs have outgrown and almost hidden from sight and knowledge the parent urbs, she is unique in her later and present history. And whether we approach her early history from one side or the other, up or down the stream of time, difficulties clog the way. If we stand on the Roman oppidum and attempt to penetrate onward from thence there is the shock of Teutonic conquest to meet, there is the rapid commercial prosperity, there is the strong mediæval power; if, on the other hand, we stand in the modern Guildhall there is the vast stretch of houses and streets obscuring the topographical outlook, and hiding in almost impenetrable gloom that view of London from extra-London which is so valuable to the archæologist. We can see Colchester and Dorchester and Winchester and Chester and even York from points of vantage which lay outside the borough walls; but where are we to go if we want to see London in the same way? At Breakneck Steps we may see with Mr. Waller the old course of the Fleet river;[1] in this alley or that court we may select the last remnants of ancient land or water marks; but everywhere vast buildings shut out that view of ancient London which would have shown her standing in the midst of country fields and country scenes; which would have shown the gathering in of her citizens to their town homes, and the wandering forth of her citizens to their country haunts and walks. For when the citizen lived who came into contact with the early municipal history of London he walked out of a city gate into green fields—to Finsbury archery-butts, to Moorfields, to the fields where churches came to be built dedicated to St. Giles and to St. Martin; or maybe he walked along the narrow trackway by the river which led to the little village of Charing and to the king's city of West-

[1] "Transactions, London and Middlesex Archæological Society," vol. iv. p. 96 *et seq.*

minster. This is the citizen with whom we must converse of the older history which he is still in touch with; and this is the London which must be asked to give up its tale of older days.

Thus as the starting-point for any consideration of the early municipal history of London we meet with the strongly contrasted positions of *Roman London*, the centre of commerce situated on great highways which connected her with Europe; and *Saxon London*, first hemmed in by small agricultural settlements, then overcome and occupied by these bands of fighting agriculturists. And the question before us may now be asked in the following terms: What is the evidence that exists as to the descent of Roman municipal custom: what is the evidence of Teutonic village custom; and, finally, in what relationship do they stand towards each other?[1]

Modern inhabitants of the great city, and students of her history as well, are apt to think of municipal London as a London of chartered rights, of lord mayor's shows, aldermanic banquets, guild festivities, and common council debates; and that beyond these facts there is nothing in her history or her customs which need trouble the historian. But fortunately chartered rights do not by any means express all the rights appertaining to municipalities: there is a vast body of custom and unwritten law which tells us more than even chartered rights can tell, and it is with this that I shall now have to deal.

Now the mere grouping of London municipal customs into Roman and Saxon origins will not establish at least one important fact, namely, the intrusion of Saxon customs upon Roman customs. Our next question is which system of polity predominated in the government of London? If we see one group of customs becoming distinctly and clearly recog-

---

[1] "I shall next take notice of some ancient customs which had their original from the Romans (as I take it) . . . and if a collection of all of them were drawn up and published together I am apt to think that it would be very useful as well as a pleasant undertaking, and conduce in a great measure to the clearing of many particulars of Roman history" (Bagford's letter in Hearne's Leland, vol. i. p. lxxiv.).

nized as municipal law, and so losing its historical origin in its later utility, and if we see another group of customs delegated to municipal usage only, having no force as municipal law, we may be reasonably sure as to the method of fixing upon the dominating power. The men who practise customs because their fathers practised them, though they have a historical continuity of race origin, have no historical continuity of power if they have not succeeded in getting those customs promoted to the dignity of legal sanction. The case here put generally is applicable to the early municipal history of London: we see municipal law and municipal custom side by side; the one with a legal or political sanction at the back of it, the other supported by social effort only. I have succeeded in collecting what I shall venture to characterize as a remarkable collection of customs practised in London far down in the mediæval ages, and which are unquestionably of Teutonic origin. But I have not found this body of custom recognized or codified. It obtains in one locality and not in another; it is mentioned incidentally by one authority and not by another; it is practised by one body of citizens and not by another; it has no cohesion one item with another, no systematic codification into municipal law; it is, in short, the sport of an undercurrent life of the citizens, and not the outspoken action of the dominant life. And hence I conclude that this Teutonic custom existing here in the midst of mediæval London had met with a power with which it was hard to fight. That power could not have been Norman, because the Normans, partly Teutonic themselves, would have legalized or chartered their innovations. And the London charters of Norman times are distinct and definite in their formal recognition of existing municipal law. If it was not the Norman, then, who fought with the Teuton and relegated his barbarous law into municipal custom, it must have been the Roman. The Roman, with his precious gift of commercial insight, with the growing powers of wealth, stood firm to his old ways; and while the Saxon Londoners kept their folkmoots, drowned their criminals, pilloried their minor offenders, tilled their lands, the Roman merchants kept to their own laws, until they ultimately superimposed them upon the whole community.

Now, the Anglo-Saxons, as masters of London, would introduce the village system, or its central ideas, into the government of the town: these would be, the village tenement, the communal lands around, the common pasture beyond these.

Commencing, then, with the subject of municipal polity, let us see what evidence there is of old village life as the basis of later municipal life in London. Every free villager was an owner of a tenement within the village, and the possession of such a tenement was the basis of all his political and social rights. Mr. Coote draws attention to the fact that the citizens of London were landowners,[1] and he specifies two remarkable instances, namely, Becket's father and Osbern, who in later days held many possessions.[2] Mr. Loftie does something more than suggest that, in the oldest days, the aldermen were the owners of their respective wards;[3] and the process by which this ownership was obtained is an interesting feature in London municipal history. Looking at the earlier times by the light of later events, the facts appear to shape themselves somewhat as follows: The Saxon intrusion upon the old Roman site was not of the same nature as an ordinary village settlement in the open country. The citizens did not cluster into one space, with their lands stretching round them. The Roman wall dictated a boundary to their settlement which they could not and did not ignore; and, therefore, great open spaces of unbuilt land separated the tenements of the new settlers. Such open spaces could not be used for agricultural purposes, and they became the means of starting in London the wide-reaching powers of economical laws which proclaim that private ownership, not collective ownership, is the means to national prosperity. These ward-owning aldermen followed without a break the model, if not the personality, of the Roman

[1] "Romans of Britain," p. 377.   [2] Ibid., p. 389.
[3] "History of London," vol. i. pp. 158-161.

citizen, and they sealed the fate of the smaller tenements which existed all around. Mr. Riley, in his introduction to the "Liber Custumarum," has summarized from the text of that remarkable volume several instances of public land, that is, land belonging to the municipality, having been appropriated and built upon.[1] We get a glimpse of this corporation property, too, from the Chronicles of the Mayors and Sheriffs of London. At page 35 of Mr. Riley's edition we read how Henry III. issued letters patent restoring the right of the citizens, among which it is said that "they shall have all issues of rents arising from houses and tenements as well in the city aforesaid as in the suburbs thereof." And again, at page 83, we read how the populace, in 1262, "endeavoured to throw open lanes, which, by writ of his lordship the King, and with the sanction of the Justiciars Itinerant, the community assenting thereto, had been stopped up and rented to certain persons;" and again: "King Henry III. in 1265 came to London and gave away more than sixty houses belonging to the citizens, they, with all their families, being expelled" (p. 59).

These facts show us, I think, a departure from the primitive system of village ownership; the struggle which they indicate could not have resulted from the existence of a Roman municipal polity, which fully recognized individual ownership, whereas they present to us a picture of the growth of individual power converting village tenements into personal property. But this process was arrested before it finally swept away the last remnant of old constitutional life; and the possessions which now remain in the hands of the City Corporation, situated in the neighbourhood of Broad Street, New Broad Street, Broad Street Fields, Fenchurch Street, Aldgate, and the Minories, testify to the times when the Corporation of London held land by the common law of village rights before they had converted it into rent-bearing holdings.

We shall see more fully how these facts relating to citizen

[1] Introduction, pp. cx–cxiii.

tenements suggest an intrusion of a primitive village system if we turn to some remarkable evidence to be found in old citizen law. We have said that the tenement in the village was the basis of all rights in the village. This tenement was, therefore, an important symbol, and its destruction would be considered most fatal. Before the sanctions of law were clearly established, that is, before the establishment of a central sovereignty, the practice of destroying the village tenement was used as an engine of judicial procedure.

Now let us turn to London. The assize of Henry II. states "that the house of the individual who harbours a heretic *shall be carried out of the town and burnt.*"[1] There is the same principle underlying this and the above-mentioned law, and it is difficult to overlook the significance of such a law cropping up in the unwritten code of London municipal custom, where it must have entered from the barbaric law of Saxon conquerors. Examples occur of this custom in other places, accompanied by evidence that the framework of the old village houses was always put together by villagers in the forests whence they obtained their wood, and from thence carried into the town and fixed.[2]

This carrying of the framework to the site clearly explains the possibility of carrying the houses out of the city of London, and we must bear in mind the evidence given by the assize of Fitzalwyne, first Lord Mayor of London, that the houses in the city were all thatched ("Liber Albus," vol. i. p. 328), and the curious story told by Stow of his father's house having in one night been moved bodily some distance. From these scraps of information, pieced together from various sources, it is thus possible to discover one feature of barbaric law plainly written in the municipal life of London.

Another distinguishing feature of the early Teutonic community was the power of its assembly in the regulation and

[1] Section 21. See Palgrave's "English Commonwealth," vol. ii. p. clxxiii.
[2] See Dobson and Harland, "Preston Guild," p. 47; Ramsay's "Paston Letters," vol. i. p. 33; *Archæological Review*, vol. iv.

THE LONDON FOLKMOOT.   215

management of its lands. Such an assembly existed in some municipal boroughs in 1835 in a very distinct form; and the ancient powers of the London court of hustings are to be attributed to the same cause. In this court all kinds of real actions for the recovery of lands and tenements within the city and its liberties are cognizable; and in this language we can easily recognize a translation of that which would have described the archaic duties of the old village assembly, especially if we take into consideration the exceedingly curious powers which attend proceedings under this court. The recorder must pronounce judgment, and forty freeholders formed the inquest, chosen from twelve men and the aldermen from the ward where the tenements in question lie, and the same number from each of the three wards next to the said tenements.[1] Such a court as this was the result of no political legislation. It is the descendant of that archaic assembly which belonged to every village community.

But when we come to speak of the assembly of the citizens there is much closer analogy to the assembly of old Teutonic communities; and its decay and final wiping out from the institutions of the city mark the struggle between the community as the Saxon Londoners understood it and the community as the Roman Londoners sought to make it. Nothing is more curious than the history of the London folkmoot. We see it standing out, now and again, in all its original strength, attended by all the citizens in early Teutonic fashion; but we see towering behind it, overshadowing it too, a small compact body of aldermen, just such a body, in fact, as Mr. Coote tells us governed the Roman municipia, a high class of citizens—*optimates, meliores, primates, potentes*—who monopolized all municipal power and privilege to the absolute exclusion of the other class.[2] Though we see this struggle going on late down in history, though our only record of it is a post-Norman chronicler, it appears to me to be something far greater, historically speaking, than a

---
[1] See "Privilegia Londini," 1702, p. 162.
[2] "Romans of Britain," p. 368.

struggle for liberty against a mediæval tyrant king. If the actual struggle is against Henry III. and his faction, the contending parties are old foes, who have met and fought often before, and who fight on the historic ground chalked out by the place of meeting of an open-air folkmoot, and who use such archaic weapons as the "Yea, yea," and "Nay, nay," of Teutonic folk-speech. We know how late in modern times relics of archaic custom have survived; and when I consider these struggles of mediæval Londoners, and all that they reflect upon the past history of the city, it appears to me as if these citizens wielded weapons of stone and bronze, to tell us of the age from whence they are descended.

The folkmoot was held in the open air, upon a piece of ground at the east end of St. Paul's church, adjoining the cross.[1] Here, at all events, we stand upon undoubted Teutonic ground, conquered from the Roman by men who knew and loved the village institutions they sought to transplant into the city. But then there is no evidence that this assembly of the citizens ever wholly dominated the city, and was recognized as the supreme council; but it seems more than probable, since at times it took its part in those survivals of the old primary assemblies of the nation which met to elect their king.[2]

The fight between the popular assembly or folkmoot, where every citizen had a right to attend, and the smaller body, is well related in the "Chronicles of the Mayor and Sheriffs of London," 1188 to 1274. In 1249, upon the Abbot of Westminster and his advisers desiring to hold a conference with the mayor and aldermen, "the whole of the populace opposed it, and would not allow them, without the whole of the commons

[1] See "Liber Custumarum," pp. 338, 339, and my "Primitive Folkmoots," p. 158, where I have discussed the archaic importance of this.

[2] For the significance of the action of the London folkmoot in the election of Stephen, see Green's "History of the English People," vol. i. pp. 151, 152; Freeman's "Norman Conquest," vol. v. pp. 245, 305. That this connection of the London folkmoot was kept up is shown by the oath of fealty the citizens in assembly gave to Prince Edward, 1252. See "Chronicles of the Mayors and Sheriffs of London," p. 20.

being present, to treat at all of the matter" (p. 18). Again, in 1257, on the occasion of charges being made against certain aldermen, the king gave orders to the sheriffs to convene the folkmoot on the morrow at Saint Paul's Cross, upon which day all the aldermen and citizens came there. The proceedings are fully described, but the passage interesting to us is the following: "To which inquiry (no conference being first held among the discreet men of the city, as is usually the practice) answer was made by some of the populace, sons of divers mothers, many of them born without the city, and many of servile condition, with loud shouts of 'Nay, nay, nay'" (p. 38). In 1262 we have the following remarkable passage. "The mayor, Thomas FitzThomas, during the time of his mayoralty, had so pampered the city populace, that, styling themselves the 'commons of the city,' they had obtained the first voice in the city. For the mayor, in doing all that he had to do, acted and determined through them, and would say to them, 'Is it your will that so it shall be?' and then, if they answered 'Ya, ya,' so it was done. And on the other hand, the aldermen or chief citizens were little or not at all consulted on such matter" (p. 59). In 1265 the populace cried "Nay, nay," to the proposed election of William FitzRichard as sheriff, and demanded Thomas FitzThomas (p. 91). In 1266 "the low people arose, calling themselves the commons of the city" (p. 95). In 1271 the old dispute broke out again in the election of mayor, and the record of this is very instructive (pp. 154-156).

In these curious and instructive passages I cannot doubt that we have a record of the final chapters of the history of the Teutonic folkmoot in London. Its name, its place of meeting, its popular form, its formula of "Yea, yea," or "Nay, nay,"[1] all proclaim its primitive origin. But then under what circumstances do we see it with these evident signs of its historical origin? There are by its side "the discreet men of the city." We have never met with it, either before the date of these records we have quoted or afterwards, as the dominant

---

[1] Cf. Freeman's "Comparative Politics," sect. v.

power of the city, impressing its forms and ceremonies, its political system, its derivative forces, upon the municipal history of the city. It was never powerful; it was only fitful. And we may well ask why the Teutonic conqueror, who met in his folkmoot without let or hindrance, bowed in municipal government to another body, separate and distinct from it? The answer must be reserved until we have considered some other facts of London municipal custom.

Other subjects of municipal internal polity claim attention at this juncture before we turn our attention to London beyond the walls. At the election of chief magistrate in Teutonic communities many curious and significant customs were observed, chiefly in connection with the old religion. Among all primitive communities, when a village was first established, a stone was set up. To this stone the head man of the village made an offering once a year.[1] Of the many traces of this custom in England I will not speak here; but of its survival as a London municipal custom there exists some curious evidence accidentally preserved. Holinshed tells us that when Cade in 1450 forced his way into London he first of all proceeded to London Stone, and, having struck his sword upon it, said, "Now is Mortimer [*i.e.*, Cade] lord of this city." Pennant in 1793 was the first to note that this act was something more than meaningless nonsense,[2] but it was reserved for Mr. Coote to put it in its true place as a fragment of municipal folklore.[3] He points out that Holinshed attached a meaning to it, and that the crowd of Londoners who witnessed it must have attached a meaning to it. Well, what was that meaning? It is almost lost to us in London municipal custom. We find that London Stone entered into municipal legal procedure, as when the defendant in the lord mayor's court had to be summoned from that spot, and when proclamations, and other

---

[1] For examples, see "Indian Antiquary," vol. ii. p. 66; Biddulph's "Tribes of the Hindoo Koosh," pp. 105-107, 114; Forbes Leslie's "Early Races of Scotland," vol. ii. p. 497.

[2] "Some Account of London," p. 4.

[3] "London and Middlesex Archæological Society," vol. v. p. 282.

important business of the like nature, were transacted there;[1] but there is no direct clue to the action of Cade and its consequent association of London Stone with an archaic Teutonic custom. But if we turn to a parallel municipal custom elsewhere we shall find the clue we are in search of. On the mayor's day at Bovey Tracey the mayor used to ride round the stone cross and strike it with a stick.[2] This significant action proclaimed the authority of the mayor of Bovey, and it is not

LONDON STONE AS IT IS NOW PROTECTED.

difficult to translate this curious parallel into the explanation which comparative politics afford of the old municipal custom at London Stone. But it will be noted that, while at Bovey Tracey the custom obtains almost the force of a municipal law, in London it had sunk so low in its scale of importance as only to have been rescued by the record of the acts of a rebel.

[1] Brandon's "Customary Law of Foreign Attachment," p. 6; and "Lord Mayor's Court of the City of London," p. 14.
[2] Ormerod's "Archæology of Eastern Dartmoor," p. 11.

I have another remarkable custom to mention in connection with this stone-worship, if it may be so designated. In the *Totnes Times*, of 13th May, 1882, is an account of the customs adopted on Mayor's Monday at Bovey Tracey, which gives us the additional piece of information, unnoticed by Mr. Ormerod in the book above quoted, that young men were induced to kiss the magic stone, pledging allegiance in upholding ancient rights and privileges. In London there is a remarkable survival of such a custom, though it is not identified with London Stone. In Bagford's Letter to Hearne[1] there is related how the porters at Billingsgate "used civilly to intreat and desire every man that passed that way to salute a post that stood there in a vacant space. If he quietly submitted to kiss the same and paid down sixpence, then they gave him a name, and chose some one of the gang to be his godfather." Now, in these curious relics of old London life we have stumbled upon a set of facts altogether outside the municipal formularies of Roman London. That they are hidden among the popular customs, as distinct from municipal law, proclaims that they had been ousted from their official place by a power that we must recognize to be Roman, but that they exist at all shows that they owed their origin to a power which we must recognize as extremely archaic, and therefore brought in by the intruding Teutonic villagers.

In strict association with this subject is a piece of curious legal procedure, preserved for us in the "Chronicles of the Mayors and Sheriffs of London." In the charter of Henry III., granted in 1267, is the following clause, that, as to pleas of the Crown, the citizens "may deraign themselves according to the ancient custom of the said city; this, however, excepted, that upon the graves of the dead it shall not be lawful to make oath in the precise words as to what the dead persons themselves would have said if they had been living." This custom was common to the Teutons and Scandinavians in ancient times.[2]

---

[1] See Hearne's "Leland's Itinerary," vol. i. p. lxxiv.
[2] See Thorpe's "Ancient Laws and Institutes of England," pp. 59, 123.

In the present instance allusion is made, says Mr. Riley, to a privilege which had been allowed in London to a person when accused: to the effect that when one of his compurgators or jurors had died, whom he had selected to clear or exonerate him by making oath as to his belief of his innocence, it was allowable for the accused to say on oath, over the deceased person's grave, what the precise nature of his intended verdict would have been; such oath having the same virtue as that of the deceased in favour of the person so accused.[1]

The other subject of municipal internal polity which we must consider is that of punishment awarded for offences against the laws. Pennant has a very interesting note about Execution Dock, which in his time still remained at Wapping. The criminals, he says, are to this day executed on a temporary gallows, placed at low-water mark, but the custom of leaving the body to be overflowed by three tides has long since been omitted.[2] It appears to me that this curious practice bears upon the face of it the character of an archaic survival, and something which indicates a Teutonic origin. These things do not originate in the days of Charters and Acts of Parliament, and we see here an old custom passing away into oblivion. There can be no doubt, I think, that this represents the old punishment by drowning, an undoubted Teutonic and Scandinavian custom.[3] This old custom was extant in the Cinque Ports; and it is an important fact to notice that the transitional custom mentioned by Pennant is confirmed by a record of the actual practice. Kemble, in the first volume of his "Codex Diplomaticus," speaks of a woman who, being condemned to death for aiming at the life of a nobleman, was executed by drowning on London Bridge, in the middle of the tenth century. A singular prerogative, belonging to the castellan of Baynard's Castle, consisted in the fact that, if any traitor was taken within his soke or jurisdiction, it was his duty

---

[1] "Chronicles of London," p. 108.
[2] "Some Account of London," p. 324.
[3] See Hampson's "Origines Patriciae," pp. 104–105; Grimm's "Deutsche Rechtsaltherthümer," pp. 696–699.

to sentence him to death by drowning, in conformity wherewith the offender was bound to a pillar in the Thames, used for mooring vessels, at Woodwharf, near Baynard's Castle, and left there two floods and two ebbs of the tide.[1] We read also in the "Liber de Antiquis Legibus," that in the year 1266, while the Earl of Gloucester was treating for peace with Henry III., at Westminster, certain of his partizans pillaged many of the citizens of London, and slew one of their number; whereupon the Earl had four of the offenders seized, bound hand and foot, thrown into the Thames, and drowned. And such, the chronicler adds, was the judgment passed during all this period upon those who were condemned.[2] I should like to lay stress upon the importance of this piece of evidence, because it is an example, all too seldom found, of a modern custom meeting its true explanation and significance by a reference to ancient custom, and it thus illustrates the correctness of the principle I have followed in less certain cases.

There are other modes of punishment in London which take us back to the village life of our Teutonic ancestors. In the "Chronicles of the Mayors and Sheriffs of London" we read that the bakers, " whose bread did not weigh according to the assay of the city, not being placed in the pillory, as they used to be, but at the will of the Justiciar and Earl exalted in the tumbril, against the ancient usage of the city and all the realm " (p. 43). There were two pillories in London; one stood in Cheapside. In 1269 we read, in the above-named Chronicle (p. 127), it was out of repair.

A curious legal custom is mentioned by Aubrey as still obtaining in London during his day, he having observed one instance. If an unmarried man was capitally condemned, he was pardoned if a woman begged for his release upon condition that he married her.[3] This is old German law.

Now the particular fact upon which I wish to dwell in con-

---

[1] See Stow's " London " (edit. Thoms), p. 25.

[2] Riley's " Liber Custumarum," Introd. pp. lxxxiii, lxxxiv; "Chronicles of the Mayors and Sheriffs of London," p. 97.

[3] Aubrey's " Remaines of Gentilisme and Judaisme," p. 126.

nection with these various subjects is that they do not exist in any of the recognized collections of city law and custom. They have never been codified, never been able to lift themselves beyond the title of municipal usage. I have collected them from all sorts of places, and have had to piece them together in a kind of patchwork, with no chronological basis of connection between them. Archæologically they present us with a fair field of observation, because they belong to the era of archaic society; but before the tribunal of historical succession they have been found wanting. And, I think, if we look a little further we shall find that the Roman Londoner had an excellent piece of machinery wherewith to thrust in the background the barbaric usages of his conquerors. Roman law and Roman lawyers were all-powerful where commerce was concerned; and their recognition by the ignorant Teutons was, as we well know, among the first steps towards the formation of the Anglo-Saxon kingdom. Well, how do we find that Roman law and Roman lawyers were treated in London? Legal history contains within it some of the most archaic survivals of our complicated social system, and when its details are treated minutely it comes home to the student with considerable force. Now the order of the coif is the oldest established association of lawyers in our country; there is no law for its first institution, no charter from a sovereign, nothing to show from whence it sprang except its remarkable parallel to Roman customs. The assembling of the Roman Jurisperiti at early morn, *sub galli cantum*, and their peripatetic exercise up and down the Forum, in actual consultation, or ready to confer with the *consultores* or clients, is described by Horace and many other writers. Horace alludes to it in the following lines (Sat. I. i. 9):—

> "Agricolam laudat juris legumque peritus
> Sub galli cantum consultor ubi ostia pulsat;"

and again in the first epistle of his second book he explains more at large the custom, which is again mentioned by Cicero in his oration for Murena. But this practice applied to those lawyers whose years and honours had grown with their knowledge of the laws. In their younger days, on the public days of market or assembly, the masters of the art, says Gibbon, were seen walking in the Forum ready to impart the needful advice to the meanest of their fellow-citizens, from whose votes on a future occasion they might solicit a grateful return. Let us take a step further in the history of Roman lawyers. When they awaited their clients at home the youths of their own order and family were permitted to listen; and Gibbon goes on to point out the evident corollary from this, that some families, as for instance the Mucian, were long renowned for their hereditary knowledge of the civil law.

Now all these facts are in exact parallel to the early customs of the order of the coif. Serjeant Pulling points out the significance of the order as a family of lawyers, so to speak, who appear at the earliest dawn of English history, but originating from no special enactment from the government of the day, called into being by no charter or sanction of the sovereign. But the close parallel between the order of the coif as a family or corporation of lawyers and the Roman lawyers who developed into hereditary custodians of legal knowledge becomes even more remarkable when we consider their practices, and the theory of their duties. They assembled in the parvis of old St. Paul's Cathedral, each serjeant having been allotted a special pillar in the cathedral at his appointment, where they met their clients in legal consultation, hearing the facts of the case, and taking notes of the evidence, or pacing up and down. Parvis sometimes implies the church porch, but in the case of St. Paul's it comprehended the nave or the middle aisle of the old cathedral, or Paul's Walk. This is only the old Roman practice over again, and a practice which was clearly related in the nature of parent to child, not that of descendant from a common ancestor. Further than this is the parallel between the theory of their action. As the Roman lawyer was ready to give aid to the poorest citizen without pecuniary reward, so was the serjeant "truly to serve the King's people" without pecuniary reward.

It is before such an institution as this, formed of men learned in law far more extensive and philosophical than the barbarian codes could furnish, that Teutonic custom in London gradually declined into municipal usage of mediæval and later days. The law administered in this centre of Roman life was doubtless the *lex mercatoria* which contributed to the continued life in London, perhaps alone, of all the cities of Roman Britain.[1]

We have now reviewed some of the municipal customs of London, and they have shown to us, according to my interpretation of the facts, some features of the contest between Roman and Saxon. The men who occupied, in early days, the little hill-fort, and who built up around it a flourishing commercial port, stood the shock of isolation, and then the shock of conquest, without giving up everything to the newcomers. Fortunately for them, the new-comers did not understand, and did not appreciate, the commercial importance of the place, and did not comprehend the system of government necessary for such a place. They occupied the lower part of the ruined city while the Roman traders kept to their old bounds. This seems to me to be the state of affairs as revealed to us by a study of the institutions as far as we have gone. And we now have to go a step further, and ask, Did the Saxon conquerors and settlers of London, who gave to the Roman city her Teutonic folkmoot, her Teutonic modes of punishment, did they also bring with them their agricultural system? London decommercialized (if I may coin such a word) must have become London agriculturalized. The limits of the old walls did not bind the limits of the new citizenship. A Saxon citizen not only possessed tenements within, but he possessed his corn-lands, pastures, wood and forest, without

[1] That the *lex mercatoria* was formed by the merchants themselves is a curious point in legal history of much significance when dealing with the question of origins (see Maitland's "Select Pleas of Manorial Courts," p. 132), and in the courts of the merchants alone did they have advocates or professional lawyers (Maitland, p. 136). This fact is certainly remarkable in connection with the evidence set forth above.

the town boundaries. And he possessed them not by individual ownership, but as a member of the whole community. I am now speaking of times when London was supported by her agriculture, and not by her commerce. These agricultural lands without the boundary were held in common tenure, as we know the agricultural lands of other municipal towns were held down to within recent days. But we see here, just as we saw in matters relating to internal polity, that the influence of the Roman began to exert itself very early. Lands held in common were converted either into corporate property, let out to tenants paying rent, or were seized upon by citizens who had ceased to be members of an agricultural community, and had begun to see the advantage of individual ownership.

FitzStephen, so late as the reign of Henry II., was able to give an account sufficiently archaic to afford evidence of the general agricultural aspect of London citizenship. Everywhere, he says, without the houses of the suburbs, the citizens have gardens extensive and beautiful, and one joining to the other (*contigui*). Then he describes the arable lands of the citizens as bringing plentiful corn, and being like the rich fields of Asia. And then come the pastures. On the north side there are pasture fields, and pleasant meadows intersected by streams, the waters of which turn the wheels of mills with delightful sounds. Very near lies a large forest in which are wild beasts, bucks and does, wild boars, and bulls.[1] Now, such a description as this, coming from a Norman chronicler at a time when Roman and Teuton had both become Londoners, and when London was the capital of the nation, tells a great deal more than the meagre words of the Latin narrative. It must be noted that the citizens owned all these lands—garden grounds, arable lands, and pasture. The citizens then were agriculturists. The gardens were contiguous, and the pasture and forest were in common. This much we do know; and by analogy we know also that such a state of things shows a Teutonic settlement, shows a remark-

[1] "Liber Custumarum," vol. i. p. 4.

able parallel to the land system of other English municipal towns—Berwick, Nottingham, Malmesbury, and others.[1] The long series of parallel customs and remarkable archaic analogies, which, I think, proclaim English municipal institutions to have been founded upon a Teutonic basis, proclaims, too, that London municipal institutions possess a large share of the same original stock. The very name of Long Acre, preserved in modern street nomenclature, tells its tale of archaic land tenure. It was one of the long narrow strips of arable into which the lands of the citizen community were divided. Such strips, possessing exactly the same name, "Long Acre," exist in many parts of the country as portions of the village community, as it survives in England to this day, and we cannot disassociate the London "Long Acre" from the same set of facts. When once we can grasp the conception, and FitzStephen enables us to do so, that London was once agricultural London; that her citizens depended upon their garden ground, arable lands, and pastures for the means of existence ; and when we add to this that her folkmoot was the old Teutonic folkmoot, where one and all had a right of attendance; that her hustings court, possessing its ancient name, was the court which governed the tenures of citizen landholding; that parts of her criminal law belonged to the ancient code which was extant in the homes of Scandinavia and Germany—we may identify some portions of the early history of municipal London as belonging to Teutonic times. And correlatively I would urge that because we see signs of the imperfect development of this archaic system, signs of a something which exists always alongside of it and yet is not a part of it, we see the latent powers of Roman citizenship exerting themselves.

What, then, has become of the garden ground, arable lands, and pastures of London citizenship? Some of it became corporate property, and remains so to this day, the city still owning their conduit-mead estate in Marylebone, which was once citizen meadow land, lying by the conduit which supplied

[1] See *Archæologia*, vol. xlvi. pp. 403-422.

water to the city. But this last outlying relic of old citizen land does not tell us of the alienations which have taken place during these last eight hundred years. Just let us turn, for instance, to the "Liber Albus,"[1] and study that most instructive list of grants and agreements made by the city. "Concessio majoris et communitatis" is the formula. And the mayor and commonalty grant extra-mural property away with a free hand—"de domo vocata Bedlem extra Bysshopisgate, de domo extra Newgate, de quadam domo extra Crepulgate." And besides these there are such instructive documents as "Memorandum de quadam Placea terrae extra Crepulgate capta in manum civitatis."[2] I cannot conceive a more instructive piece of work than a map of the city property, restored from the archives and documents of the city, to show the possessions of the earliest times.

Some of the old citizen land remained citizen land, changing its uses as the circumstances of the time changed. Thus Finsbury Field[3] and Smithfield were used for games and sports, as open lands outside the city, long after their archaic significance as open lands had passed away.

Thus, then, it appears that we may translate these phenomena of the early municipal history of London as representing the intrusive influence of a primitive village organization upon the settled constitution of a Roman town, and the distinctions so clearly manifest between the two systems afford evidence that they could not commingle, and that even on admitted Roman territory Roman institutions could not enter within the bounds of the village system. There remains the second part of this proposition to consider—how far were the village communities round London influenced by the Roman constitution of the great city?

[1] Vol. i. p. 552.

[2] In the "Chronicles of the Mayors and Sheriffs of London" we read how Henry III. in 1265 came to London and took all the *foreign* lands of the citizens into his hands, foreign lands being those without the liberties of the city (see p. 83).

[3] See "Chronicles of the Mayors and Sheriffs of London," p. 174, for a relation of the possible loss of this to the citizens in 1173.

In the long series of charters, which a recently published work has made more generally accessible to readers, there is a charter [1] granted by Henry I. confirming to the city of London the county of Middlesex in fee-farm. Such a grant as this points to much more than a King's favour, even if we take into account Henry's peculiar position. There is evidence of ancient rights claimed by the citizens, "and the citizens of London may have their chases to hunt *as well and fully as their ancestors have had.*" Mr. Green places these ancient rights far back in the past. "Middlesex," he says, "possibly represents a district which depended on London in this earlier [*i.e.*, 500–577] as it certainly did in a later time; and the privileges of the chase which its citizens enjoyed throughout the Middle Ages in the woodland that covered the heights of Hampstead, and along the southern bank of the river as far as the Cray, may have been drawn from the rights of the Roman burghers." [2] No doubt, I think, the limits of the "territorium" of Roman London determined the limits of the wood and forest rights of Saxon and later London. No doubt the jurisdiction of the London sheriff over the county of Middlesex is a relic of Roman times, but, in spite of all, the walls of Roman London determined the limits of the city boundary.

---

[1] "Historical Charters and Constitutional Documents of the City of London," 1884.

[2] "The Making of England," pp. 106, 107. One or two instances of the usages of the citizens outside the city boundaries may perhaps be useful; they are taken from the "Chronicles of the Mayor of London." In 1232 the citizens of London mustered in arms at the Mile End and were arrayed in the London Chepe ("Chronicles of London," p. 7). "His Lordship the King requested them [the Corporation] to permit the Abbot of Westminster to enjoy the franchise which the King had granted him in Middlesex in exchange for other liberties which the citizens might of right demand. To which the citizens made answer that they could do nothing as to such matter without the consent of the whole community" (Ibid. p. 16). This subject was afterwards settled, it being decided that the Sheriffs of London may enter all vills and tenements which the Abbot holds in Middlesex, even unto the gate of his abbey (Ibid. p. 61). "Upon the King (1257) approaching Westminster the mayor and citizens went forth to salute him, *as the usage is*, as far as Kniwtebrigge" (Ibid. p. 34).

Unlike Lauder, Malmesbury, Buckingham, and other municipal towns, the boundaries of London did not extend beyond the wall, and become co-terminous with the burghal lands. The village communities exercised their powers here unaffected by the Romans of London, and thus we find the manors of Middlesex, Surrey, and Kent do not differ from those of other parts of the country, and old parishes like Fulham possess common lands to this day on tenures closely assimilating to those of the village community.[1] The intrusion of village institutions into London is not therefore accompanied by the overflow of Roman institutions into the villages around, and no better evidence could be adduced to prove how completely outside the village system the power of Roman influences was.

In this interesting group of survivals of the village community in Britain only some few analogies to the Indian village community have been pointed out, without entering into closer comparison or giving further examples. I think this course may be justified on the ground that constant reiteration of the many points of parallelism which present themselves would be wearisome and needless. The student has but to refer back for himself, and compare each English type with the Indian types described in the second chapter. But I have this to point out. It is almost certain that but for the discovery of the Indian communities we should never have been able to discover these remnants of archaic life in our own land. It is not the laborious study of historical documents, nor minute and patient research into fragments of early law, which has testified to the existence of the village community in the Western world; but it is the survival in custom and usage of primitive agricultural economy and of a *lex loci* which defies codification because of its diversity, and which has only not been crushed out of existence by the professional law because,

[1] *Cf.* the printed manor laws of Stepney and Wimbledon; Hales, "Domesday of St. Paul's," and the Isleworth Manor Rolls in the Fifth Report of the Historical MSS. Commission. Also Gomme's "Primitive Folkmoots," p. 157, for the open-air court held formerly in the Strand.

first, of its safe home in the unwritten common law of the land, and secondly, because it did not trench upon any of the recognized legal maxims which governed the advanced portion of the nation. How little that advanced portion has hitherto had to do with the great mass of the nation! If ever it is true that there is one law for the poor and another for the rich, it is true as an outcome of the development of law from custom, and it is not due to the initiative of the rich. The ruling classes of this country have governed themselves, and have sought to govern the whole nation, by uniform laws derived from philosophical sources, and defined and put into force by the king's courts; the peasant and the yeoman have constantly ignored the law of the king's courts, and have governed themselves, by their own preference, by maxims and rules obtaining in the manorial courts and in the old parish assemblies. Older than the law of the king's courts, the *lex loci* shows the marks of its primitive origin by its diversity and by its capacity for keeping up its special characteristics. Accordingly when we come to examine the constitution of the communities which are the natural home of this local law, we detect so much divergence from a common standard, and yet so many points of likeness, that we are justified in the argument that the unstable primitive communities must be the ancestor of the present local communities. At all events, I would submit that the variations in the types of survival which we have examined prove beyond doubt that we cannot absolutely solve the question of origins until we have settled what the normal type is like, and that therefore the true line of future inquiry is to gather together all examples of the village community which local survival has preserved.

CHAPTER IX.

FRAGMENTS OF THE VILLAGE COMMUNITY SURVIVING IN LOCAL CUSTOM.

The breaking up of the village communities under the advancing conditions which economical and political necessity have forced upon the nation, did not proceed at a uniform rate all over the country. The examples we have examined show some of the latest survivals of the old order of things. Elsewhere we come upon mere fragments, preserved from further destruction by various causes, sometimes by the minute form in which they have survived, sometimes by their unimportance, or we might say by their innocuous influence upon the prevailing system of the age. These fragments are well worth studying. We cannot do now much more than indicate their existence and their main characteristics, but a detailed examination of them would lead to much valuable information as to the condition of the country when it was passing slowly from primitive to civilized conditions, and as to the wide-spread influences which the primitive organization of society has exercised upon the development of the nation.

If we analyze and set down the most significant of the characteristics of the village communities in Britain, judged by the types we have already examined, we find them to fall under the following heads :—

1. Recognition of kinship.
2. The mixture of races.
3. The homestead as the source of rights in the village.

4. The open village assembly.
5. The periodical allotment of lands.
6. The existence within the village of a servile class.
7. Primitive agricultural economy.
8. The manorial element.

And we will examine some of the survivals in custom of these several characteristics of the village community.

1. A very considerable amount of controversy has arisen both in Germany and England upon the constitution of the Anglo-Saxon family, the best comment upon which, for our present purpose, has been made by an American writer, who, after reviewing the most important authorities, points out that "one fact is made evident by this controversy, that no system can ever be found which will be in all respects consistent with all the sources: the German laws of inheritance were not the results of legislation based on philosophic principles, but rather the slow outgrowth of custom adapting itself to special needs. It is useless to expect that uniformity of system and logical application of fundamental rules which characterize Roman law."[1] It will be seen that this observation made of the Anglo-Saxon family is true of the other branches of the Teutonic social organization in England the relics of which we have been examining. We do not know of the Anglo-Saxon family what we do of the Indian family, but that it occupied a corresponding position in the village system, we are more than justified in assuming from the relics of its organization, which are to be traced in law, custom, and usage.

We are not now concerned, however, with the Anglo-Saxon family in its ancient integrity: all we want is to point out its influence while the primitive village community was gradually breaking up. In the primitive system of the Punjab, as Mr. Tupper has pointed out, "*status* formed the whole, or nearly the whole, civil law; and kinship, which is a department of status, is a paramount influence in regulating property and obligations. As Sir Henry Davies

[1] "Anglo-Saxon Law," p. 132.

pointed out in his report on Gurdáspur, this system served in troublous times, and for several centuries, instead of title deeds."[1] In India a special class exists among some tribes for the purpose of keeping a knowledge of the facts of relationship, and it is noted that they can tell the genealogical descent of the family without missing a name. It is surely a relic of the same condition of the law that in all the chief divisions of Great Britain the same evidence is forthcoming. Among the Irish and the Scottish every chief had a poet whose duties included the recitation of the pedigree of his lord. Giraldus Cambrensis (c. xvii.) describes how even the common people of Wales kept their genealogies, and could not only readily recount the names of their grandfathers and great-grandfathers, but even refer back to the sixth and seventh generation. And there is at least very good evidence of the custom among the English villani, as Mr. Seebohm points out from the "Codex Diplomaticus"[2]; while local dialect has preserved the old kinship of the primitive clan in the word "kit" which, in Northamptonshire, is applied to denote collectively a number of families of the same name, among which a kind of ideal clanship still existed, never more discernible, says Sternberg, than in the broils and pugnacious manifestations which are continually occurring to disturb the harmony of the feast-day.[3] It is also significant to note the expression of a manorial tenant being "of the blood of" the manor, which is printed by Mr. Maitland, from the rolls of Kings Ripton, in 1296—de sanguine de Repton Regis.[4] I think this expression must carry with it a surviving belief in common descent and common blood kinship.

Many authorities, including Brentano, Sullivan, Herbert Spencer, and Sir Henry Maine, are agreed that the origin of gilds is due to the primitive family, and Sir Henry Maine has

[1] Tupper, "Punjab Customary Law," vol. ii. p. 84.
[2] Seebohm's "Village Community," p. 139. *Cf.* "Codex Diplomaticus," No. MCCCLIV.; Kemble's "Saxons in England," vol. i. p. 226.
[3] Sternberg's "Dialect of Northamptonshire," p. 59.
[4] "Select Pleas of Manorial Courts," p. 122.

stated the general conclusion in language which will bear quotation. "The ideas of kinship," he says, "and the phraseology proper to consanguinity, are extended to associations which we should now contemplate as exclusively founded on contract, such as partnerships and gilds. . . . It is most instructive to find the same words used to describe bodies of co-partners formed by contract, and bodies of co-heirs, or co-parceners, formed by common descent. As regards gilds, I certainly think that they have been too confidently attributed to a relatively modern origin, and that many of them, and much which is common to all of them, may be suspected to have grown out of the primitive brotherhoods of co-villagers and kinsmen—joint in food, worship, and estate."[1] It does not seem worth while to pursue this subject any further here, because of the generally accepted theory as set forth in easily accessible works; but I wish to emphasize its significance as bearing upon the continuance in England, to later times than is generally supposed, of the old ties of kinship in the village community, and therefore as supporting the theory of a survival of ancestral shares in the village lands by which I have ventured to explain certain phenomena which have been brought under notice in describing the customs of Aston, Malmesbury, Kells, and other places.

A fact which has not hitherto been noted, and which must be referred to the same basis of kinship, should, however, be more formally mentioned. To many of the Domesday manors are said to belong so many burgesses, just as in Russia at the present day members of the *mir* frequently go to the towns to work while retaining, and ultimately returning to claim, all the privileges of their ancestral villages. To give one example, we will note the case of the Wiltshire manors. In Wilton there were five burgesses of Nigrave, seven of Sarisberie, one of Stradford, two of Fifhide, one of Come, four of Diarneford, one of Scarentone, one of Meresdene, and one of Odestoke. In Cricklade there were six burgesses of Aldeborne, five of Ramesherie,

[1] Maine's "Early History of Institutions," p. 232; Gomme's "Literature of Local Institutions," section Gilds; Hearn's "Aryan Household," p. 241.

one of Badeberie, one of Piritone, six of Chiseldene, one of Ledentone, seven of Lediar, three of Clive, and three of Colecote. In Malmesbury there were one burgess of Langhelei, one of Sumreford, two of Werocheshalle, two of Come, one of Wodetone, one of Hunlavintone, one of Aldritone, one of Foxelege, and one of Segrie. In Calne there were three burgesses of Calestone, and one of Cainingham. Thus each of these Wiltshire boroughs included within their membership men living under the different laws of their parent manors,[1] and the continental picture, drawn by Bishop Agobardus, of men standing side by side in cities and large towns, each one of whom is governed by a different law, namely the law of the place where he comes from, is thus reproduced in England; law being incidental not to the locality, but to the person, flowing not from the sovereign of the country, but from the kinship which binds together all descendants of a common ancestor.[2]

No doubt when we are able to catch a glimpse at this phase of the old tribal law the increasing powers of towns were gradually trespassing upon the older village rights; so that when a community sent forth some of its members to settle down elsewhere, the newly formed communities thus invigorated from without would constantly absorb the laws and customs of their members. In this way special and peculiar customs would be spread, and when the sovereign law of united England began to take cognisance of them, and to allow their existence as a part of the law of the land, it classified them as *lex loci*.

2. In pointing out what evidence there appears to exist for the late survival of the intermixture of races, and hence of tribal laws and customs, in some parts of the British Isles long after the political advancement of the nation had permanently fixed the settling places of the bulk of the population, we must

---

[1] The formula in these cases is invariably as follows:—"huic manerio [Aldeborne] pertinent 6 burgenses in Crickelade"; "ad hoc manerium [Nigrave] pertinent 5 burgenses in Wiltune"; "in burgo Caune una domus pertinet huic manerio" [Cainingham].

[2] For examples as to how this acted in Gild History, see Ashley's "Economic History," p. 75.

rest our evidence almost entirely upon the relics of clan feuds which are known as so prominent a factor in early society.

An important passage from Cæsar has not been noted as it deserves to be. He says, "Factions exist not only in the states and in all the cantons and their divisions, but almost in each family, and that seems to have been instituted in ancient times with a view that no one of the common people should be in want of support against one more powerful."[1] Such a state of things could not be made to fit in with the generally accepted view of homogeneous tribes descended from a common ancestor, but it almost exactly explains the state of things which we see reproduced in our own land from the evidence that remains of the English conquest. Of course Cæsar's own supposition as to the origin of these intertribal conflicts must be passed over as the only possible idea that could have occurred to a Roman statesman ignorant of the first elements of tribal history; but in the light of Mr. McLennan's researches we may re-quote the passage with some degree of certainty that it reflects the tribal stage when each clan within the tribe was of different kinship and at enmity with the other clans.

Mr. Kemble was the first to note that " the Gentile names of Germany, Norway, Sweden, and Denmark" are reproduced upon our own shores. Thus he goes on to say Harlings and Waelsings and Billings are reproduced in several localities in England, and his well-known table showing the wide distribution of English clan names may easily be referred to as evidence.[2] In explaining this phenomenon of the English settlement, Mr. Kemble cannot account for its non-agreement with the generally received origin of tribes and clans being homogeneous descendants from a common ancestor, and he falls back upon the "restless movements of our progenitors," and the possibility of a leader being followed by " comrades glad to constitute themselves around him under an appellation long recognized as heroic," or of a leader "distinguished for skill, valour, and success imposing the name of his own race

[1] "De Bello Gall.," lib. vi., cap. xi.
[2] Kemble's " Saxons in England," vol. i. p. 59.

upon all who shared in his adventures." But against this explanation Mr. Lang has set some very powerful difficulties. First, that of accounting for the non-homogeneous character of local tribes; secondly, the difficulty of accounting for the union of elements confessedly so exclusive as the different families; thirdly, of understanding how the same family names were scattered through many local tribes.[1] Clearly if a successful leader, calling himself and his followers Harlings, or Waelsings, or Billings, had conquered territory enough to settle and found a home, he would not split up his band and scatter it in face of the perils they had to encounter as conquerors; and as clearly the only satisfactory explanation of this wide scattering of family names is that each tribe was composed of mixed kinships caused by the almost universal tribal practice of exogamy among the clans of each tribe.

The late survival of clanship in Scotland ought to give us some evidence of the same system of clan exogamy. Mr. Skene has once for all established that the organization which was known to the travellers of the seventeenth and eighteenth centuries, and which is known to all readers of Scott's novels, is historically a late development, based though it is upon kinship and not upon locality.[2] This important fact ought to enable us to get a glimpse of the older organization from which the later was developed; and we know sufficient of the name-system to show that originally each clan was composed, not as lately of all Campbells, or all Macintoshes, or all Rosses, but of intermixed names.[3] Thus in Burt's "Letters from the Highlands" (p. 17), first published in 1754, we are told that "the different surnames of the Highlanders in general are but few; in regard they are divided into large families, and hardly any strangers have intermarried with or settled among them; and with respect to particular tribes they commonly make that alliance among themselves who are all of

---

[1] Bolland and Lang's "Aristotle," introd. p. 99.

[2] Skene's "Celtic Scotland," vol. iii. p. 324.

[3] Mr. Skene has worked out the history of the clans in "Celtic Scotland," cf. vol. iii. p. 332.

one name, except some few who may have affected to annex themselves to the clan, and those for the most part assume the name." The significance of the latter portion of this paragraph is made perfectly clear by a statement in an account of the Highlanders, written in 1747, and communicated by Sir Walter Scott to Dr. Jamieson, the editor of Burt's "Letters," in 1818. This account sets forth that " it hath been for some time a custom through the Highlands, amongst those who pretend to be chiefs or leaders of clans, to *oblige* all the farmers or cottars that gett possessions in their grounds, to take their names. In a generation or two it is believed that they really are of that name, and this not only adds to the number of the clan and keeps it up, but superinduces the tye of kindred to the obligation and interest of the former."[1] Thus, although the Scottish clans present in their more popular aspect homogeneous groups all bearing the common patronymic, we see by this that formerly they must have conformed to the general tribal practice of clan exogamy, each local settlement therefore being made up of different kinships. A picture of Inverness before it had grown into a town, when the hovels and lanes might well have belonged to a village of an Indian hill tribe, tells us how these mixed kindreds kept up the blood feud of archaic times. " Those houses that were not sashed have two shutters that turn upon hinges for the lower half of the window. The people still continue these shutters as an old custom which was first occasioned by danger, for in their clan quarrels several had been shot from the opposite side of the way."[2] We have already seen that in Camden's time the windows of Lauder were sashed.

So far, then, as the clans of Scotland and so far as the local settlements founded by such clans are concerned, we have evidence of the ancient tribal phenomenon of intermixed kinships.

---

[1] Appendix to Burt's "Letters," p. 362. On the custom of giving nick-names in the Highlands, see Guthrie's "Old Scottish Customs," p. 133, and compare the anonymous book on "Scotch Surnames," Edinburgh, 1860, pp. 24 *et seq*.

[2] Burt's "Letters," p. 61.

Cæsar's language about the organization of the Gallic and German tribes into "cantons" and "tribes"[1] prepares us to find evidence of tribal kinships formed for the purpose of carrying on wars. Giraldus Cambrensis, speaking of the condition of things in Wales in the twelfth century, says, "The young men move about in troops and families, under the direction of chosen leaders: . . . they have free admittance into every house as if it were their own."[2]

In the passage above quoted from Burt as to the condition of Inverness a hundred years ago, we were introduced to an example of the late survival of clan feuds. I now wish to note in what manner these clan feuds have survived in England. If we only possessed early maps of all our towns it would be seen how the formation of the village was almost invariably based upon the aggregation of different clans. In one instance, that of Witney, in Oxfordshire, we meet with a most singular example of this, and the evidence of the construction of the town is enhanced by a very shrewd suggestion made by the local historian. I must quote this entire passage: "An old map of the country (engraved in Hamper's 'Life of Sir William Dugdale') represents Witney in former days as two separate towns, an upper and a lower; and Mr. Langford suggests that the yearly fights which take place on the 5th of November between the up-town and the down-town boys, may be a lingering relic of the former state of things."[3] Here not only do we have distinct evidence of the old clan divisions, but of the old clan antagonisms. It may be well, therefore, to use the remarkable instance which Witney affords as a type example which may serve the purpose of leading the way to other and perhaps less perfect types.

We will confine our attention to examples which show

[1] "Commentaries," lib. i. caps. 12, 37, 51; lib. iv. cap. 1; lib. vii. cap. 36.
[2] "Description of Wales," lib. i. cap. 10.
[3] Dr. Giles, "History of Witney," p. 21. I cannot discover the map here alluded to in any of the copies of Hamper's "Life of Dugdale" that I have been able to consult. Nor have I been able to find a trace of this interesting map elsewhere.

definite traces of clan divisions. At Scarborough on the morning of Shrove Tuesday hawkers parade the streets with party-coloured balls which are purchased by all ranks of the community. With these, and armed with sticks, men, women, and children repair to the sands below the old town and indiscriminately commence a contest. At Ludlow there was a grand "tug of war" between the inhabitants of Broad Street and Corve Street Wards with a rope three inches thick and thirty-six yards long, with a large knob at each end. The shops were shut at four o'clock, when the rope, which was bought by the Corporation, was given out of the Market Hall window by the Mayor. One man stood on another's shoulders, and the chimney-sweep's wife on his shoulders. These represented the Red Knob; three others, mounted in the same way, representing the Blue Knob. When they got the rope, if the struggle were carried down Mill Street, the Red Knob had won, and the knobs were dipped in the river Teme in token of victory; if the contest were carried through the Bull Ring, the Blue Knob won, and the dipping took place in the river Corve. After the rope was won it was taken back to the Market Hall and given out again, and if the same side won, the contest was ended; but if the opposite side conquered, then it was given out and pulled once more, and whichever side won remained the victors. The rope was sold, and the money got for it spent in beer, and then the fighting and quarrelling commenced. These disorderly scenes and the dangerous accidents resulting caused it to be discontinued in 1851.[1]

At Derby there was a football contest between the parishes of All Saints' and St. Peter's. The ball was thrown into the market-place from the Town Hall. The moment it was thrown the "war cries" of the rival parishes began, and the contest, nominally that of a football match, was in reality a fight between the two sections of the town: and the victors were announced by the joyful ringing of their parish bells.[2] At

[1] Burne's "Shropshire Folklore," p. 319; Brand's "Popular Antiquities," vol. i. p. 92.
[2] Dyer's "Popular Customs," p. 75.

Chester-le-Street the game is played between what are termed "Up-streeters" and "Down-streeters," one side endeavouring to get the ball to the top of the town, whilst their opponents try to keep it near the lower or north end. At one o'clock the ball is thrown out from near the old commercial hotel, the Queen's Head, in the centre of the town, and it has often been received by over three and four hundred people, so great is the interest taken in this ancient sport. At Asborne the struggle was between the up'ards and down'ards. At Dorking the divisions were between the east and west ends of the town, and there was first a perambulation of the streets by the football retinue composed of grotesquely dressed persons.[1] At Alnwick the divisions were the parishes of St. Michael's and St. Paul's. At Kirkwall the contest is on New Year's Day, and is between "up the gates" and "down the gates," the ball being thrown up at the Cross.

It is impossible, I think, to contemplate these fierce contests, to note their connection with official authorities and official boundaries, without coming to the conclusion that the struggles were after all not rope matches or football games so much as local struggles;[2] and when we observe further that locality now takes the place of clanship, the argument is forced home to us that we have in these modern games the surviving relics of the earliest conditions of village life and organization, when different clans settled down side by side, but always with the recollection of their tribal distinctions. And I may note here that such contests are well-ascertained features of tribal society. Mr. Morgan has noticed this fact, and puts forth an example from the Seneca Indians who play a ball game by phratries one against the other,[3] and the Greek phratries certainly developed the same characteristic. Again in the North-West Provinces of India

---

[1] Dyer's "Popular Customs," p. 87.

[2] Colonel Forbes Leslie notes that "The playing ball was not originally football, for no one was allowed to kick it" ("Early Races of Scotland," vol. i. p. 125).

[3] "Ancient Society," p. 94.

a very thick grass rope is pulled by the villagers among themselves. The party in whose quarter the rope is broken, or by whom the rope is pulled out of the hands of their antagonests, are the victors, and retain the rope for the year.[1] The quarters of an Indian village are clan quarters. In Wales we know the old tribal system lasted much longer than in England, and it is here also that tribal games, as we may perhaps call them, have lasted in their purest form. To Miss Burne, author of "Shropshire Folklore," I am indebted for the following graphic account of Welsh customs which was printed in the *Oswestry Observer* of March 2, 1887 : "In South Cardiganshire it seems that about eighty years ago the population, rich and poor, male and female, of opposing parishes, turned out on Christmas Day and indulged in the game of football with such vigour that it became little short of a serious fight. The parishioners of Cellan and Pencarreg were particularly bitter in their conflicts; men threw off their coats and waistcoats and women their gowns, and sometimes their petticoats. At Llanwenog, an extensive parish below Lampeter, the inhabitants for football purposes were divided into the Bros and the Blaenaus. My informant, a man over eighty, now an inmate of Lampeter Workhouse, gives the following particulars:—In North Wales the ball is called the Bêl Troed, and was made with a bladder covered with a Cwd Tarw. In South Wales it is called Bél Ddu, and was usually made by the shoemaker of the parish, who appeared on the ground on Christmas Day with the ball under his arm, and, said my informant, he took good care not to give it up until he got his money for making it. The Bros, it should be stated, occupied the high ground of the parish. They were nick-named 'Paddy Bros,' from a tradition that they were descendants from Irish people who settled on the hills in days long gone by. The Blaenaus occupied the lowlands, and, it may be presumed, were purebred Brythons. The more devout of the Bros and Blaenaus joined in the service at the parish church on Christmas morning. At any rate, the match did not begin until about

[1] Carnegy's "Kachahrî Technicalities," see *Folklore Record*, vol. v. p. 36.

midday, when the service was finished. Then the whole of the Bros and Blaenaus, rich and poor, male and female, assembled on the turnpike road which divided the highlands from the lowlands. The ball having been redeemed from the crydd, it was thrown high in the air by a strong man, and when it fell Bros and Blaenaus scrambled for its possession, and a quarter of an hour frequently elapsed before the ball was got out from among the struggling heap of human beings. Then if the Bros, by hook or by crook, could succeed in taking the ball up the mountain to their hamlet of Rhyddlan they won the day; while the Blaenaus were successful if they got the ball to their end of the parish at New Court. The whole parish was the field of operations, and sometimes it would be dark before either party scored a victory. In the meantime many kicks would be given and taken, so that on the following day some of the competitors would be unable to walk, and sometimes a kick on the shins would lead the two men concerned to abandon the game until they had decided which was the better pugilist. There do not appear to have been any rules for the regulation of the game; and the art of football playing in the olden time seems to have been to reach the goal. When once the goal was reached, the victory was celebrated by loud hurrahs and the firing of guns, and was not disturbed until the following Christmas Day. Victory on Christmas Day, added the old man, was so highly esteemed by the whole country-side, that a Bro or Blaenau would as soon lose a cow from his cowhouse, as the football from his portion of the parish."

The traditions of race are here most marked, and it is an important addition to former observations to see that the distinction of race is also a distinction between hill folk and valley folk. From this we may turn to a still earlier form of tribal games where the element of clan feuds is more decidedly preserved. In the first volume of the "Archæologia Scotica," published by the Society of Antiquaries of Scotland in 1792, there is a very good description of the manner in which the Lammas festival used to be celebrated in Midlothian about the middle of the eighteenth century. This account is all the more valuable because it is in all probability unique. From this paper it appears that all the herds within a certain district towards the beginning of summer associated themselves into bands, sometimes to the number of a hundred and more. Each of these communities agreed to build a tower in some conspicuous place near the centre of their district. This tower was usually built of sods, though sometimes of stones. It was for the most part square, about 4 feet in diameter at the bottom, and tapering to a point at the top, which was seldom above 7 feet or 8 feet from the ground. In building it a hole was left in the centre for admitting a flagstaff, on which were displayed their colours on the great day of the festival. This tower was usually begun to be built about a month before Lammas, being seldom entirely completed till a few days before. From the moment the foundation of the tower was laid it became an object of care and attention to the whole community, for it was reckoned a disgrace to suffer it to be defaced. As the honour that was acquired by the demolition of a tower, if effected by those belonging to another, was in proportion to the disgrace of suffering it to be demolished, each party endeavoured to circumvent the other as much as possible. To give the alarm of the approach of an attacking party every person was armed with a tooting-horn. As the great day of Lammas approached each community chose one from among themselves for their captain. They marched forth early in the morning on Lammas Day dressed in their best apparel, each armed with a stout cudgel, and, repairing to their tower, there displayed their colours in triumph. If news was brought that a hostile party approached, the horns sounded to arms. Seldom did they admit the approach of the enemy, but usually went forth to meet them. When the two parties met they mutually desired each other to lower their colours in sign of subjection, and if there appeared to be a great disproportion in the strength of the parties, the weaker usually submitted to this ceremony without much difficulty. But if they were nearly equal in strength none of them would yield, and it ended in blows, and sometimes in bloodshed. When they had remained at their tower till about midday, if no opponent appeared, or if they themselves had no intention of making an attack, they then took down their colours and marched with horns sounding towards the most considerable village in their district, when the lasses and all the people came out to meet them and partake of their diversions. Boundaries were immediately appointed and a proclamation made that all who intended to compete in this race should appear. A bonnet ornamented with ribbons was displayed upon a pole as the prize of the victor. The prize of the second race was a pair of garters, and the third a knife. When two parties met, and one yielded to the other, they marched together for some time in two separate bodies, the subjected body behind the other; and then they parted good friends, each party performing their races at their own appointed place.

We now turn to other evidence for the like facts of early life. The mode of settlement in some of our great towns exhibits clear traces of tribal divisions. At Nottingham, until so recently as 1715, the market-place was divided lengthwise by an ancient wall breast-high, supposed to have been erected to provide separate market-places for the irreconcilable Saxons and Normans. This wall was taken down about this date, and the market-place for the first time was paved.[1] This division is most probably much older than the Norman era, as at Nottingham we have that remarkable instance of a difference between the two parts of the town in the modes of descent of property, one part following the rule of primogeniture, the other that of junior right or borough English,[2] and junior right is at all events older than political history. Some manors are also thus divided in their methods of treating descent of property. Thus at Eling, in Hampshire, "the custom of the manor is that in the south part of the manor

---

[1] *Antiquary*, 1887, vol. xv. p. 90.

[2] "Yearbook 1 Edward III.," 12a; Robinson, "Gavelkind," p. 386; "Records of the Borough of Nottingham," vol. i. p. 173. The Danish element at Nottingham is much stronger than the Norman, see W. H. Stevenson's "Early History of Nottingham" (a pamphlet), p. 14.

the youngest son of an intestate is the heir, and in the north part the eldest son."[1] Outside Shrewsbury, beyond the Severn, and at the foot of the Welsh Bridge, there is a suburb called Frankwell, written in the oldest documents in which it is mentioned "Frauncheville," which has always been reputed a *free town*, beyond the jurisdiction of the burgesses of Shrewsbury, and of the merchant companies who had the monopoly of trade within the town. By Acts passed in the reigns of Henry IV. and Henry VI., no Welshman might hold lands within an English "merchant town," or become a burgess of it, or even buy and sell within it; and even when these Acts fell into abeyance the race enmity between English and Welsh would make the Shrewsbury trading companies very chary of admitting any Welshman to their fellowship. Hence the "free town" without the walls became the resort of such Welshmen as embarked in trade with England. Within the memory of aged, but still living, persons it was inhabited almost wholly by a Welsh population, and Welsh, not English, was the language which visitors heard spoken as they passed through the streets. The Municipal Reform Act of 1835, by abolishing the exclusive rights of the trading companies, was the cause of the amalgamation of the two races, for the Welsh character of Frankwell has now almost, if not quite, disappeared. The name of "D. Lloyd ap Roger, 1623," on an old house, and the still-remembered site of St. Cadogan's Chapel (pulled down before the civil wars), are relics of the old state of things, and the privileges of the "free town" are not yet forgotten. Any supposed slight to Frankwell still arouses the old watchword, "Frankwell, maintain your rights!" which so late as 1821, when the population was still Welsh, was used to incite resistance to a newly-passed street Act, under which the Corporation proposed to cleanse the streets of the suburb as well as of the borough itself.[2]

The question as to the early history of the Boley Hill at

[1] Easton's "Statements Relative to Pauperism of Kirriemuir, Forfarshire," 1825, p. 176. A similar division occurs at Cheshunt, Herts. See *Notes and Queries*, 7th Ser. ix. 206.

[2] Miss C. S. Burne, in the *Athenæum*, August 7, 1886.

Rochester affords another illustration of the long survival of race divisions in local settlements, and it is worth while, I think, tracing out this interesting point, because it may serve to show how much may be accomplished by a close examination of local history.

Mr. Clark has taught us the relationship between Norman castle and early earthworks, and he has thus described those at Rochester. They "are on a large scale," and "seem to have been composed of an oblong space included within a ditch which commenced near the bridge foot, and was carried eastwards for about 130 yards, when it turned to the south and ran for about 270 yards, roughly, parallel to the river, towards which it was again returned. This oblong area was sub-divided into two unequal parts, the southern being the smaller, by a cross ditch, and the latter part was occupied by a large flat-topped conical mound known as Boley Hill. The northern part contains the castle. . . . The area thus included is about 7¼ acres. The mound is of large size, though reduced by modern operations. It is in part natural, in part formed by the adjacent ditches."[1] I gather from this that the earthwork, as a whole, may be said to have preceded both Boley Hill and the Castle as they are presented to us now, and that it formed the original British settlement before Roman or Saxon had put their stamp upon it. Rochester has not an entrenched area surrounding an inner earthwork such as Wareham and York have; but it has, like Wareham and York, not only the castle mound, but what Mr. Clark designates as purely English work, another mound dominating the river. Thus when we consider this latter mound, the Boley Hill, as a part of the earthworks, there does not seem much to distinguish it from other well-known characteristics of English defensive positions. It was, together with the castle mound, thrown up by the English occupiers of the British Oppidum, when they in their turn had to face the foe in the shape of Danish and Norwegian Vikings. Subsequently, when the Normans took possession of the stronghold, they built the castle, as in all other cases, on one

[1] "Mediæval Military Architecture," vol. ii. p. 406.

of the English mounds, and the other mound, the Boley Hill, remained untouched by any works of masonry.

Almost all that is known of this district is collected by Hasted (vol. iv. pp. 161, 163-164), from whom, for my immediate purpose, I will quote the following passages. The hill was "in all likelihood thrown up by the Danes in the year 855, at the time they besieged this city, a circumstance mentioned by most of our ancient historians. . . . By King Edward IV.'s charter to the citizens of Rochester he granted to them a view of frank pledge and also to hold a court of pie powder in a certain place called the Boley within the bounds of the city. This is a separate leet from that held in the Guildhall, and the inhabitants of this small district are bound to appear before the recorder as steward of the court of the mayor and citizens, which is annually held on the Monday after St. Michael, who then appoints an officer, called the Baron of the Bully, for the year ensuing by presenting him with staff of office. The court is holden under an elm tree at the east end of the hill. The householders of this spot are generally appointed to the above office in succession."

The first thing to note about this account is the charter of Edward IV. This document must not be supposed to have originated the court leet that met on Boley Hill. As a matter of fact, the charter of Henry VI. is the first to mention the court leet, while the charter of Edward IV. adds the information about its meeting-place being the Boley Hill. One cannot, therefore, resist the conclusion that this additional clause in the charter of Edward IV. is one of those delightful accidents in record history which help the student so materially in gathering up the fragments of an unrecorded past. Mr. Thomson was, I believe, one of the first to point out that the charters of the Norman sovereigns did little more than cover with official or regal authority privileges which already existed ; Mr. Peacock has urged the same view; and I myself have more than once brought forward proof of what is now admitted as a feature of charter-sanctions. If it were not for an apparently accidental clause in the charter of Edward IV. which is not given in the previous charter of Henry VI., we should not be able to carry back the documentary evidence of the Boley Hill beyond the eighteenth century; but contrariwise because of this reference in the charter of Edward IV. we must not stop at that date and say that the gay, pleasure-loving monarch in London knew and cared sufficiently for Rochester and its local history to make such a grant, the real fact being that the men of Rochester obtained at this time legal sanction to an institution that had existed for ages before.

What we then have to consider is a most singular jurisdiction, of unknown date and origin, within the municipal jurisdiction of Rochester city. Now this special jurisdiction appertains to a particular district. It is most important to note that the locality itself can have had very little to do with forming the special jurisdiction belonging to it, but that this must have been derived from the community which settled down upon the locality. The "inhabitants of the district," in the language of the modern historian, are the descendants of a community who at one time or other settled in Rochester and stamped its influence upon the city's history. And it is from this little Boley Hill community that are derived the customs and privileges now appertaining to the district.

What was this little community which has stamped itself so indelibly upon the municipal history of Rochester? We see it now in its degenerate stage. There is nothing in it necessary to the modern government of the city; it is too unimportant to be antagonistic to the municipal authority; but still it has lived on side by side with the progress of Rochester through all the struggles which mark the mediæval history of English towns, and it has thus shown a vitality which stamps it as a phenomenon of some significance.

Let us first notice the meeting-place—in the open air under a tree. That this is the survival of an archaic custom, and therefore descended from an archaic community, is, I think, proved by the mass of evidence adduced in my "Primitive Folkmoots." Next, there is the democratic constitution of this little community—all the inhabitants of the district, just as in the Russian "Mir" and in the "Things" of the Danish districts of Orkney and Shetland.

Through the kindness of Mr. T. H. Baker, I have received the following account from Miss Katherine Gunning, who remembered the ceremony of electing a new "Baron of the Boley":—"The Mayor and some members of the Corporation, with the householders living at Boley Hill, walked round the old elm tree, *and a form of words was said.* The '*coming in*' Baron sent his servants with supplies of cake and wine, which were consumed on the spot. The staff of office was a shabby black wooden pole, resembling a warming-pan handle in shape and size. It had blue and red and faded gold letters on it. When my father was the Baron, the staff always hung in our hall at the Friary. The old elm tree stood nearly opposite Mr. Simmons' gateway. It was cut down and carried away at the time Mr. Styles, the Quaker, built his school-house close to it. He said that the tree shaded his house, and to the great regret of all the other Boley Hill householders the elm tree was destroyed." It cannot fail to be observed that the ceremonial at the tree is singularly archaic in its nature.

Thus far we have noted the shreds of information left to us about the community itself. Of its independence of the city authorities there is important evidence by a writer in *Notes and Queries* (3rd S. xi. 124), who says that the mayor, attended by the officers of the corporation, always proceeded to the elm tree, where the courts were held, for the purpose of reading royal proclamations, &c.—a proceeding which clearly shows that the reading of proclamations at the Guildhall of the city did not carry any authority within the precincts of the Boley Hill community.

Now comes the final and perhaps most important question, Of what race and origin was this Boley Hill community at Rochester? All tradition points to the Boley Hill as connected with the Danes. It is highly improbable that the hill itself was actually thrown up during the attack on the city in 855; but it is not improbable that a community of this race settled there during the prevalence of Danish rule in England a century and a half later. We know how greatly the Danes influenced the local history of our land, even if we cannot yet fully trace their influence upon national history; and in London there is a somewhat curious analogy to what I am trying to prove at Rochester. Just near the portion of the Strand where stands St. Clement Danes Church, a little eminence admittedly occupied by a Danish colony, there was once a court held in the open air near a large stone. Here, then, we have a Danish colony surrounded by other races impressing its peculiar customs on the history of London; and similarly I would suggest that the facts and traditions connected with the Boley Hill community at Rochester, with its independence and its open-air democratic assembly, point to the time when the Danes occupied the city in sufficient strength to obtain a special, though not a dominant, power in its government. As time went on and the later municipal organization became more complete, the Boley Hill community sank into insignificance until it reappears in history as the charter-sanctioned court of view of frankpledge for a special district, the inhabitants of which, for local or traditional reasons, kept up their old privileges.

In Ireland we meet with the extreme form of these race distinctions continued down to within political times, and almost for political reasons. But they tell exactly the same story. "In many of the ancient corporate towns and boroughs in Ireland, certain quarters are known under the appellation of *Irish Town*, and were occupied by the so-called 'mere Irish,' in contradistinction to the more favoured inhabitants of a different caste. In walled towns the quarters very commonly stood outside."[1]

It is impossible, as it seems to me, to neglect the lessons to be derived from evidence like this. Alike from the feuds and the settlement of clans we find proof of their difference in race. Much that is still obscure in our early history may be explained if we turn to these hitherto neglected facts of local history.

[1] "Statistical Survey of Roscommon," p. 196.

Somewhere from among these facts, for instance, will be found the key to that position which the lord appears to occupy everywhere in English history, and certain features of which must be noted a little later on. If the pure genealogic clan settled down amidst alien races whom they had reduced to servitude, there would easily arise a strong body of antagonistic forces, the clashing of which would naturally tend to produce enhanced power to the *primus inter pares*. Beyond the boundary of kinship there were the non-kindred, and Dr. Hearn has already noted some signs which tell of the influence of dependents, among which he puts, first, the strengthening of the lords against their own clans; secondly, the forcing their way, not indeed over the close barriers of the genealogic tribe, but into the new political association in which those tribes were absorbed. The language used is too advanced for the period and the races to which I would point for the origin of the growth of the lord's power, but it serves to show that already something has been done towards solving the question.

3. The possession of a homestead was the source of all other rights.[1] We have noted how this early law operates in the barbarous communities outside the Aryan race, and how strongly it appears in the surviving types of the village community in England. We have also noted how, at London, the negative side of this law is represented by the custom of destroying the village tenement as a punishment for crime. This custom was widely prevalent in French municipal law, and it appears to be one of the minutiæ of a large subject which may afford considerable information if it is investigated. In the meantime it may be useful to note some of the English examples, which are introduced by the law of King Ine (lxviii.). "If a gesithcund man be driven off, it must be from the botl [homestead], not from the setene."

"The punishment of Petit Jurors attainted of giving a verdict contrary to evidence, wittingly, is severe and terrible; they are condemned to lose the franchise or freedom of the law; that

[1] Grimm, "Deutsche Rechtsalterthümer," p. 539; Hearn, "Aryan Household," p. 212.

is, become infamous and of no credit, uncapable of being a witness or of a jury; their houses, lands, and goods shall be seized into the king's hands, their houses pulled down, their meadows ploughed up, their trees rooted up, all their lands laid waste, and their bodies imprisoned." [1]

At Folkestone, if either the mayor or any of the jurats refused to assume their respective offices upon being elected, "the commons were to go and beat down their principal messuage." [2] On the occasion of the election of bailiff at Hastings it was a law that "if the said bailiff be absent, or will not accept the charge, all the commoners shall go and beat down his chief tenement." [3] The same law obtained in all the Cinque Ports. At Preston it is somewhat modified. A debtor for the king's farm is liable to have the door of his burgage tenement taken away, which he cannot replace until he has paid his debt. [4]

Of course the chief interest of these old customs is their extreme independence of anything like a central system of law. Maine has already drawn our attention to a very well-marked feature of early legal codes, namely, the absence of any notice of a penalty to be inflicted upon breakers of the laws, and he goes on to point out that in the most primitive codes the penalty or sanction, as the technical phrase is, is to be inflicted in another state of existence. It appears that before English law had passed into its final stages, where the sovereign power stood by its side to enforce its commands, it must have passed through a stage when destruction of the delinquent's property represents the sanction—practically that is outlawry. All communities who can at once place its malefactors outside its bounds have little need of an elaborate criminal jurisprudence, and we have seen at Malmesbury that excommunication or outlawry was the means adopted there.

---

[1] Chamberlayne, "State of England" (1687), vol. i. p. 47.

[2] "Report of the Record Commission," 1837, p. 453.

[3] "Sussex Archæological Collections," vol. xii. p. 197. *Cf.* Mr. Round's admirable paper in *Archæological Review*, vol. iv. p. 366.

[4] Dobson and Harland, "Preston Guild," p. 75.

But an outlaw from one village community was in the territory of another village community, and from what is known of the history of "broken men" and their influence upon the formation of society we may suggest that a wide field of inquiry is yet open for an investigation of the operations of outlawry.[1] I must presently recur to this subject, and will therefore give one example of this primitive system of punishment. "When two Kháns or maliks chance to fall out, or have any dispute, the people expel both parties from the place. The two disputants are then termed sharrúni, or the driven out, or expelled, from the Pushto verb *sharral*, to drive away, &c.; and in this state they are compelled to seek shelter in other villages, and are obliged to live on the charity of those who will take them in; for they lose all civil rights on such occasions, and have no claim to wife, or children, dwelling, cattle, horses, or anything whatsoever. Some continue in this helpless state until they can come to an accommodation or reconciliation, which often does not take place for years. In Upper Sumát they are even more severe than this; for there they expel the families also, and confiscate the property of the disputants altogether. Yet these people seem to be always at feud."[2]

We are taken back by this evidence and by the direct evidence of such examples as Lauder, Whitsome, Malmesbury, and others to a totally different state of things to that upon which Mr. Seebohm has laid so much stress. From the evidence of the Welsh laws he argues that the acre strips of the English open-field system were allotted in respect of the oxen contributed to the village plough teams. Whatever the evidence of the Welsh laws on this point may prove, it cannot prove that a system of co-operative ploughing is the foundation of the English village community, in face of the evidence

[1] *Cf.* what Skene has to say of the Fuidhir class of tenants ("Celtic Scotland," vol. iii. pp. 173–323); and Seebohm ("Village Community," 191). Hearn ("Aryan Household," p. 132) notes the Irish formula of expulsion and its significant place in Aryan society.
[2] *Journal of the Asiatic Society of Bengal*, 1862, p. 272.

brought forward in this and preceding chapters that the possession of a homestead in the village was the basis of allotment in the village lands. This evidence is far from being exhausted in the examples already quoted. For instance, at Kilmaurs "the land of the barony was divided into five-pound lands consisting of 240 acres, each such five-pound land being disponed to forty different persons in feu-farm and free burgage, and to be held in equal proportions by them, their heirs and successors. The mode of holding this was by run-rig. The number of the portioners is now (1795) less than when the charter was granted, several of the fortieth parts having been sold and laid together by one purchaser, and it is probable that they will all in time become one property. *No man can be elected a magistrate unless he be also a portioner, and none but those who are portioners can vote in such elections.*[1] It appears to me that in this as in other details we may see the contrast between the tribal and the village communities; but I see nothing to indicate that the tribal system of co-operative ploughing became the actual parent of the village system. It may well be that the tribal communities, arrested in their progress towards village communities in the manner we have already explained, would easily and readily develop into communities of cultivators bound together by an economical tie of co-operative labour after the kinship tie had ceased to be paramount or operative. But in the case of village communities, originating from the break-up of the tribe as it settled down among the already-formed villages of Southern and Western Britain, it is easy to discern that the homestead might become the most fixed point of cohesion; and that this was actually the case the examples brought forward seem to me to be conclusive evidence. We may once more refer back, in face of this evidence, to the Aston and Rothwell village communities, which so plainly revealed the late survival of the primitive unity of the hide. To the hide was attached the domus, and the domus was the fountain of all village rights, a fact of early English history

---

[1] Sinclair, "Statistical Account of Scotland," vol. ix. pp. 368, 370; Fullarton, "Agriculture of Ayrshire," p. 23.

revealed most plainly by the Domesday survey, and reappearing in later surveys, as in the already quoted case of Thorp, surveyed in 1222.[1]

4. In the open village assembly which we have noted at Aston, at Newton, at Whitsome, and above all in London, there seems to me to be ample evidence of the descent of the village community from primitive elements. I have discussed this subject at some length in my book on "Primitive Folkmoots," and whatever need there may be for a revision of some passages in this little work, it has a certain value in showing the cumulative evidence in favour of a primitive origin of the village assembly in Britain. I have suggested that in custom and usage must be sought the true history of the divergent types of the village community to be met with, and I now suggest that in the long-continued idea of the peculiar sanctity of assemblies held in the open air must be sought one of the causes for the survival of custom and usage in sufficient force to affect the history of the local institutions of the land.

The Hindu sacred law declares that cases decided inside a house are *ipso facto* null and void, a conception of the evil surroundings derived from the close confinement of buildings which reappears in early English ideas when Beda recorded the meeting between Augustine and Ethelbert of Kent as taking place in the open air, "for he had taken the precaution that they should not come to him in any house, lest, *according to an ancient superstition*, they practised any magical arts upon him, and so got the better of him."[2] The same idea of magic being associated with roofed buildings appears with reference to the judgments of the Brehons in Ireland and of the Deemsters in the Isle of Man,[3] and it cannot be doubted that it kept alive the custom of holding the local assemblies of shire, hundred, and manor in the open air until comparatively recent times. What seems to me important is that an assembly meeting in this primitive fashion, performing both legislative and judicial

[1] Seebohm, "English Village Community," p. 53.
[2] Beda, lib. i. cap. 25.
[3] Train, "History of the Isle of Man," vol. i. p. 269.

functions, must indicate to us a community of primitive origin. Turning back to that Birlie court at Whitsome, in Berwickshire, already described, where the Birliemen sit on the raised mound in the village, and the villagers receive from them their decisions on matters in dispute, we can see that it is exactly the same system as Campion describes in Ireland in 1571—"The Breighoon sitteth downe on a banke, the Lords and Gentlemen at variance round about him, and then they proceede;"[1] and as Ritson describes of the English manor courts generally, which "formerly used to be held in the open air upon a fair green on the side of a hill or under a large tree."[2]

Now, the history of the manor courts has scarcely yet been approached. When it is taken up by competent authority the primitive methods of meeting must form a very important chapter in the inquiry. In the meantime it may be asserted that from the materials already in hand Sir Henry Maine's general conclusion as to their origin is practically correct. "Under the name of manorial courts," he says, "three courts are usually included which legal theory keeps apart—the court leet, the court baron, and the customary court of the manor. There cannot be reasonable doubt of the legitimate descent of all three from the assembly of the township. Besides the wide criminal and civil jurisdiction which belonged to them, and which, though it has been partly abolished, has chiefly lost its importance through insensible decay, they long continued in the exercise of administrative or regulative powers which are scarcely distinguishable from legislation."[3] We may read their acts of legislation in the curious little volumes occasionally published for the use of the tenants and in the codes of Birlaw laws which are sometimes to be met with, and some examples of which I have printed in my "Primitive Folkmoots." Other

---

[1] "Historie of Ireland," p. 26. [2] Ritson, "Court Leets," p. ix.
[3] Maine, "Village Communities," p. 139. Mr. Maitland ("Select Pleas of Manorial Courts," p. xvi) says there is no evidence that the three courts were separately named in the thirteenth century. "It would seem that to a definite classification of courts the legal theory of the time had not attained" (p. xvii.). *Cf.* p. lxiv., on the customary court.

features of their constitution and their practice illustrate their primitive organization. Every free tenant was bound to attend, and a penalty was imposed upon every one who was absent;[1] the court had the right of admitting a new tenant; it had to judge in matters of dispute or in matters of offence against the community; and it had the duty of determining the bye-laws for the regulation of the common husbandry. The right of attendance, the fine for non-attendance, the judicial functions, the power of admitting new tenants, the duty of regulating agricultural matters, are all features which are not peculiar to the English manorial courts, but are general characteristics of the assembly of village communities. "Even in the last extremity of decline," says Sir Henry Maine, "the manorial courts have not wholly ceased to be regarded as the tie which connects the common interests of a definite group of persons engaged in the cultivation of the soil."[2]

Between these features of the manorial courts and the constitution of some municipal assemblies there is but a thin wall of partition. At Berwick-on-Tweed, at an annual meeting of the burgesses called the "meadow guild," the meadow lands are distributed as they become vacant by the death or non-residence of the last occupiers among the senior resident burgesses and widows of burgesses, and the conditions of husbandry are prescribed.[3] At Lauder, Malmesbury, and other places it is the town council who perform the duties generally attributed to manor courts, and there are many instances, as at Tottenham and Hornsey in Middlesex, and at Yardley or Ardley in Hertfordshire, where agricultural rights and duties reside in the modern vestry or township assembly. The merely nominal presence of the lord in this organization is not accidental, as the Domesday example of Alverstoke well illustrates. This entry shows that the manor was held by the forty-eight villeins, and I will draw attention to the fact

---

[1] "Year Book of Edward I.," p. xxi., Middlesex Iter.
[2] "Village Communities," p. 140; Maitland, "Select Pleas of Manorial Courts," p. xl.
[3] "Municipal Corporation Commission," vol. iii. p. 1443.

that this body of forty-eight is a multiple of sixteen, which has already been identified at Aston as an ancient organization.[1] A similar community existed at Millbrook and other places in Hampshire.

"Several manors in Hampshire," says Mr. T. W. Shore, "have peculiar customs, which appear to have come down from a remote time, before the manorial system had taken the place of the village community. The most remarkable instance is that of Ibthorpe, which is now a hamlet in the parish of Hurstbourn Tarrant, and is about six miles north of Andover. The people of Ibthorpe are lords of their own manor, and to this day exercise their manorial rights, in respect of which they have exclusive common rights on the seventy acres of common-land at Pillheath, including a right to everything that grows on this common, with liberty to take it away for their use in Ibthorpe, but not for sale. They have also a right of pasturage in common with the Hurstbourn people on Hurstbourn Common. On the south of Hurstbourn Tarrant is a hill of considerable height above the village, now covered with wood, stretching away towards Andover, and called Doles Wood. From the circumstance that this part of Hurstbourn was subject to common pasturage to within recent time, it is probable that the ancient pasturage acres or Doles which were held in community, and which can be traced in Wessex as early as the seventh century, as Mr. Seebohm has pointed out, were situated here. The wood itself, which now forms a beautiful hanger, is probably modern; but it was until recent times subject to the common pasturage, which the Hurstbourn commoners latterly maintained by annually driving a cow through Doles House, situated upon it."[2]

It appears to me from this evidence, and from what Mr. Maitland has advanced relative to a similar communitas of villeins at Brightwalltham in Berkshire,[3] that the identification

[1] The seal of the men of Alverstoke is figured in the Winchester volume of the *Archæological Journal*.

[2] *Antiquary*, 1888, vol. xvii. p. 52; *cf.* Seebohm's "Village Community," p. 70.

[3] "Select Pleas of Manorial Courts," p. 163.

of manor courts with the old township assemblies, and hence
with the assembly of the primitive village community, cannot
be reasonably denied, and future investigation must certainly
be extended beyond the area of manorial courts if it is to be
of scientific value. But at present I am anxious to dwell upon
the exceedingly rude characteristics of these manorial assemblies, and the absolute identification of them with village
assemblies in countries where the primitive community has
not been transformed into manors. In Switzerland all the
commoners assemble every year in April to receive reports of
accounts and to regulate current affairs. In Germany the
inhabitants assembled to deliberate on all that concerned the
cultivation, and to determine the order and time of the various
agricultural operations. In Holland the partners in the work
met once a year, on St. Peter's Day, in a general assembly, or
holting. They appeared in arms; and no one could absent
himself, under pain of a fine. This assembly directed all the
details as to the enjoyment of the common property; appointed
the works to be executed; imposed pecuniary penalties for the
violation of rules, and nominated the officers charged with the
executive power. The mound where the *holting* met (*Malen-
pol*) is still visible in Heldermalenveld, and at Spoolderberg,
near Zwolle.[1] Neither of these are manorial courts, and yet
they perform identical duties, and meet in the same primitive
fashion, as the manorial courts of England. As we get nearer
the east, we get more absolute identification with the primitive
assembly of the village community. Among the South Sla-
vonians every male of the brotherhood has a voice in its
government. The assembly of kinsmen meets every day as
a rule, generally in the evening when the work is over, under a
tree in the neighbourhood of the common dwelling. All the
affairs of the community are there discussed, and every man may
theoretically mingle in the deliberations.[2] In Russia, where, Sir
Henry Maine reminds us, the village communities were seen to
be identical with the Indian village communities, only if anything

---

[1] Laveleye's "Primitive Property," pp. 94, 111, 283.
[2] Maine's "Early Law and Custom," p. 245.

in a more archaic condition than the eastern cultivating group, the assembly of the mir, or commune, met under the village tree, and determined all matters relating to agricultural and other village affairs, and one feature of this assembly which appears to be essential, namely, that all decisions must be unanimous,[1] reappears in the constitution of the English jury —that assembly of men's peers which can certainly trace its genealogy back to the village community. Turning finally to India, we find that the mandu is the open public place in every village where business is transacted and public games carried on;[2] and in the panchayet, an assembly which Indian scholars have not yet clearly defined,[3] there exists the rudiments of all that we have been considering about these rude survivals of English manor courts.

It is difficult to see how any investigation into the history of the village community in Britain can be considered satisfactory unless it has taken into due account all that the rude constitution of these open-air assemblies means in such an inquiry. They add much towards tracing out the original status of the villein tenants. If, as we have already noted above, the villeins, as *adscripti glebæ*, were *de facto* landowners up to the time when Glanville introduced his legal conceptions of ownership, filched from the highly philosophical law of the Justinian codes, and distinctly alien to English common law; if these landowners had a right of attendance in the assembly of their commune, and the right of vote and speech there; if this assembly was noted for and preserved by its strict adherence to traditional forms and ceremonies derived from primitive times yet to be traced in Aryan history—the tenants of manors were originally no serfs under a lord, but co-equal partners in a social group to which the lord himself belonged. " Let the

---

[1] Laveleye, " Primitive Property," p. 14; Wallace's " Russia," vol. i. pp. 194-196.

[2] Gover, " Folk Songs of Southern India," p. 108.

[3] Elliot, " Races of North-West Provinces of India," vol. i. p. 279; Tupper, " Punjab Customary Law," vol. ii. p. 111; Hearn, " Aryan Household," p. 129, point out some of the lines of parallel development.

lawyers say what they will," says a distinguished legal scholar, "the manorial jurisdiction is a true jurisdiction, an administration of the custom of the manor; it is no mere exhibition of the will of a lord who is owner of the villan tenements and owner of the villans."[1] This is what the evidence of the thirteenth century has to tell us. Going back by the aid of unbroken traditional observance of a once sacred custom, to meet *sub dio*, under the light of heaven, is it not an admissible conclusion to set forth that if the English settlers brought with them to their new home in Britain the free open-air assembly, they brought with them the free community in tribal form ready to settle down with alien serfs under it?

The exact contribution which the history of the village assembly may ultimately supply towards the elucidation of the history of the village community in Britain cannot now be stated, because it is a subject by itself, and one of some considerable magnitude. But following up a subject touched upon in the last section of this chapter, namely, the original absence of, and subsequent rude substitute for, the sanction necessary to the carrying out of English village law, we may point out one phase in the history of the village assembly which may be accepted as of some considerable importance. The council of village elders, says Sir Henry Maine, "does not command anything; it merely declares what has always been . . . in the almost inconceivable case of disobedience to the award of the village council the sole punishment, or the sole certain punishment, would be universal disapprobation."[2] How was the step from this condition of things to that of enforcing outlawry and the destruction of the village holding arrived at? The answer seems to be that just as the sovereign kingly power supplied the state with the necessary force to compel obedience to the state law throughout the Western world,[3] so it supplied to the lord of each manor, the elected or the most able, sufficient power to

---

[1] Maitland, "Select Pleas of Manorial Courts," p. lx.
[2] "Village Communities," p. 68.
[3] *Cf.* Maine, "Early Law and Custom," cap. vi.; "Essays in Anglo-Saxon Law," pp. 262–305.

bring about obedience to village law. At first this power was simply, no doubt, the power of an arbitrator in a dispute, the parties to which had agreed to refer it to the lord, and traces of which very primitive phase of local law are to be found in the history of Hundred Courts.[1] But such a power once assumed would soon grow. Norden, in 1607, wrote, "Is not every manor a little commonwealth, whereof the tenants are the members, the land the bulke, and the lord the head?"[2] The analogy is true to a greater extent than has been recognized. The sanctions of village law grew in the hands of chiefs who were originally only *primi inter pares*. Fines, amercements, duties, and obligations, nominally due to the lord under the manorial system, actually appertaining to him in their ultimate destination, were primarily dealt with in the manorial courts—the assembly of the villagers.[3] Thus it is through the medium of the assembly that the position of the lord constantly improved — that duties to the community became duties to the lord. When the lord of Aston and Cote began his fight with the village assembly, the Court of Sixteens, he was two or three centuries behind time. They could appeal to the King's Law Courts against the lord, and they had no need of his services for the enforcement of their own commands. Very often in manorial laws there is a clause forbidding tenants to appeal for justice to any courts outside the manor courts. We can understand this prohibition if we take it back to the times when the lord was building up his position as the sovereign power within the little community which put into operation the commands of the assembly; and it serves as a key to an obscure point in manorial history whereby it seems possible that the connection between manor court and village assembly—between manor and village community — may yet be plainly shown. Writers who have ignored the assistance which the history of the village com-

[1] "Essays in Anglo-Saxon Law," p. 53.
[2] "Surveyor's Dialogue," p. 28.
[3] Mr. Maitland gives us some evidence of the importance of the assembly to the lord, "Select Pleas of Manorial Courts," p. lvii.

munity affords upon the early periods of historical institutions have missed points which appear to me to be made perfectly clear. On the origin of manor courts and their jurisdiction in law, Mr. Kemble, Bishop Stubbs, and Dr. Konrad Maurer agree that they are to be found much earlier than can be traced back by documentary evidence. But Mr. Adams, a very able American writer, prefers to consider them of later origin, though he hits upon an explanation which might almost be accepted by his opponents. He says, " The peasant cultivator would be inclined to accept, or even to invite, the decision of his lord rather than incur the risks of a public suit without his lord's support, or the possibility of drawing upon himself the extremity of his lord's disfavour. It was therefore natural that the lord should have developed for his own use a certain system of law in mediating between his own people in their disagreements with each other or with the public. It was natural, too, that this system should be based upon the ordinary Hundred law—the only code known to England. Yet all this did not create a jurisdiction in the eye of the law . . . [though] the great landed proprietors appear to have been actively supported by the Crown."[1] Going back once more to the Birlie court, at Whitsome, with "its cheap and sapient decisions," to the Irish Brehon sitting on the bank deciding disputes, to the Deemster of the Isle of Man always compelled to stop and hear suits, we may picture to ourselves the growth of the lord's power as arbitrator overtaking the powers of the village assembly, "which did not command anything," and building up a system of village law based upon a much older code than that of the Hundred courts. When we pass away from documentary evidence, therefore, we must proceed to the assembly of the village community for the earlier evidence, and there we see the history of English lordship following the history of English kingship, and developing its power and position as the chief executive authority of the assembly.[2]

[1] "Essays in Anglo-Saxon Law," pp. 27–28.
[2] How independent of the sovereign the local jurisdictions of manorial lords were may be seen by reference to Maitland's "Select Pleas of Manorial Courts," pp. xxiii–xxiv.

5. We have spoken of there being proof that the tenants of English manors were descended from co-equal partners in a social group. One of the proofs of this point rests upon a most interesting characteristic of the village community, namely, the periodical redistribution of the arable lands. We have had examples of this, but the subject is one of some considerable importance, and is worth paying more attention to. Enumerating some of the features in correspondence between the Teutonic and Indian village communities, Sir Henry Maine says: "The evidence appears to me to establish that the arable mark of the Teutonic village community was occasionally shifted from one part of the general village domain to another. It seems also to show that the original distribution of the arable area was always into exactly equal portions corresponding to the number of free families in the township. Nor can it be seriously doubted upon the evidence that the proprietary equality of the families composing the group was at first still further secured by a periodical redistribution of the several assignments. The point is one of some importance." [1] Mr. Tupper, investigating this subject in India, brings sufficient proof to support his suggestion, that it is a distinct relic of the tribal community before it had split up into villages. The land, he says, being originally held by the whole community on shares, possession was readjusted when necessity arose.[2] We have noted these redistributions in the tribal communities of the west upon the introduction of a new tribesman, and the relics still remaining of periodical redistribution of village lands suggests not only the prevalence of collective ownership, but of ownership by the tribe.

In England there are examples of the distribution by annual allotment of arable lands and of meadow lands, the latter well known by the name of lot meads. It appears to me from the evidence that this process of allotting meadow land is derived from the older process of allotting arable lands to the members of the village community. In the remarkable

[1] "Village Communities," p. 81; Hearn, "Aryan Household," p. 226.
[2] "Punjab Customary Law," vol. iii. p. 138.

example of Newton-upon-Ayr, in Scotland, we have seen by what kind of process this crude method of land tenure was gradually abolished, and it is a process which constantly comes before the land settlement officers in India. Referring back to the Indian examples of the village community given in the second chapter, where the methods adopted for the yearly distribution of land are set forth in detail, there will, I think, be little difficulty in identifying the English examples as the western descendants from a common original. And it is important to note that we identify the process of allotting arable land with the possession of a homestead in the village, so that the necessary connection between homestead and land is again brought to the front.

That the land-marks of the modern English villagers may be identified with the ancient homestead or clan-marks receives illustration from the strongly surviving Scandinavian custom. Mr. Du Chaillu, in his "Land of the Midnight Sun," says: "Each farmer seemed to have a mark of his own; the agricultural implements and other articles being stamped differently. This old custom is called Bo-märken, and each family has inherited its distinguishing mark from its ancestors. Each parish has its own Bo-märke." [1]

Every one has his own mark branded on the ears of all his reindeer, and no other person has a right to have the same, as this is lawful proof of ownership. According to custom, no one can make a new mark, but must buy that of an extinct herd; if these are scarce, the price paid to the families that own them is often high; the name of the purchaser and each mark have to be recorded in court like those of any other owner and property.[2]

This system of house-marks prevails in North Germany, and Professor Michelsen, in his treatise *Die Hausemarke*, traces them to a prehistoric period. Mr. Williams thus summarises the evidence in a valuable paper in *Archæologia*.[3] In southern Ditmarsh a stone slab of the sepulchral chamber in one of the hunengräbe or gigantic tumuli of the stone period has been

[1] Vol. i. p. 314.   [2] Vol. ii. p. 168.   [3] Vol. xxvii. pp. 383–384.

found, rudely engraved with a mark of a type which is still popular. Weapons of stone and metal are also thus found marked. Marks have been found on Urgräber in the south of Sweden and the north of Europe. They were in common use in Norway, Sweden, Iceland, and Denmark in the twelfth and thirteenth centuries, and the Icelandic Gragas in particular contain numerous minute regulations as to the adoption and the use of marks for sheep, house-cattle, eider-ducks, harpoons, &c. They are also mentioned in the Old Norse and Swedish Rights. In Iceland marks were not to be taken arbitrarily, but the owner's intention was to be announced before five neighbours, and also at the spring *Thing*. In Ditmarsh and Denmark the owner's mark was cut in stone over the principal door of the house; it designated not only his land and cattle, but his stall in the church, and his grave when he was no more. In Holstein the beams of the cottages of the bondservants were incised with the marks of their masters. A pastor writing from Angeln says: "The hides had their marks, which served instead of the names of their owners." In the island of Föhr, the mark cut on a wooden ticket is always sold with the house, and it is cut in stone over the door; and the same custom is still in use in Schleswig and Holstein.

From these important facts it may be concluded that the ancient house-mark included the land-mark, cattle-mark, implement-mark, and grave-mark appertaining to each house, and that house, land, cattle, and grave, thus linked together under a common mark, were the descendants of the once undivided possessions of the clan.

I will now proceed to note such survivals as occur in England, taking first the arable allotments, and secondly the meadow allotments.

In the parishes of Congresbury and Puxton (Somersetshire) are two large pieces of common land, called East and West Dolemoors (from the Saxon *dal*, which signifies a share or portion), which are divided into single acres, each bearing a peculiar and different mark cut in the turf—such as a horn, four oxen and a mare, two oxen and a mare, a pole-axe, cross, dung-fork, oven, duck's nest, hand-reel, and hare's tail. On the Saturday before old Midsummer several proprietors of estates in the parishes of Congresbury, Puxton, and Week St. Lawrence, or their tenants, assemble on the commons. A number of apples are previously prepared, marked in the same manner with the before-mentioned acres, which are distributed by a young lad to each of the commoners from a bag or hat. At the close of the distribution each person repairs to his allotment, as his apple directs him, and takes possession for the ensuing year. An adjournment then takes place to the house of the overseer of Dolemoors (an officer annually elected from the tenants), when four acres, reserved for the purpose of paying expenses, are let by inch of candle.

Bridges, in his "History of Northamptonshire," (vol. i. p. 219) tells us: "Within the Liberty of Warkworth is Ashe Meadow, divided amongst the neighbouring parishes, and famed for the following customs observed in the mowing of it. The meadow is divided into fifteen portions, answering to fifteen lots, which are pieces of wood cut off from an arrow, and marked according to the landmarks in the field. To each lot are allowed eight mowers, amounting to 120 in the whole. On the Saturday seven nights before Midsummer Day, these portions are laid out by six persons, of whom two are chosen from Warkworth, two from Overthorp, one from Grimsbury, and one from Nethercote. These are called field-men, and have an entertainment provided for them upon the day of laying out the meadow at the appointment of the lord of the manor. As soon as the meadow is measured, the man who provides the feast, attended by the Hayward of Warkworth, brings into the field three gallons of ale. After this the meadow is run, as they term it, or trod, to distinguish the lots; and when this is over the hayward brings into the field a rump of beef, six penny loaves, and three gallons of ale, and is allowed a certain portion of hay in return, though not of equal value with his provision. This hayward and the master of the feast have the name of crocus-men. In running the field each man has a boy allowed to assist him. On Monday morning lots are drawn, consisting some of eight swaths, and others of four. Of these the first and last carry the garlands. The two first lots are of four swaths, and whilst these are mowing the mowers go double, and as soon as these are finished the following orders are read aloud:—'Oyez, oyez, oyez, I charge you under God, and in his Majesty's name, that you keep the king's peace in the lord of the manor's behalf, according to the orders and customs of this meadow. No man or men shall go before the two garlands; if you do you shall pay your penny, or deliver your scythe at the first demand, and this so often as you shall transgress. No man or men shall mow above eight swaths over their lots, before they lay down their scythes and go to breakfast. No man or men shall mow any further than Monks holm Brook, but leave their scythes there and go to dinner, according to the custom and manner of this manor. God save the King.'"

Mr. Rose has described as follows the method of allotting the meadow lands at Haddenham, in Bucks. "The method of deciding the ownership, after the meadow was plotted out, was by drawing lots. This was done by cutting up a common dock-weed into the required number of pieces to represent the lots, a well-understood sign being carved on each piece, representing crows' feet, hog-troughs, and so on; these were placed in a hat and shaken up. Before this could be done, however, notice must be given by one of the men calling out at the top of his voice, 'Harko,' and using some sort of rigmarole, calling people to witness that the lots were drawn fairly and without favour. Long Crendon men working at Notley Abbey (just opposite Anxey) used to be highly amused with this custom, and the word 'harko' was echoed back with remarkable power, not only then but for weeks afterwards. The hat being shaken up, and one of the boys standing by, looking on with the greatest interest, is pitched upon as a disinterested person to draw the lots; and each owner had to 'sup up' with the lot that fell to him."

In the parish of Southease, in Sussex, on July 10th, those tenants who possessed rights met on the ground and drew lots for the hides, commencing at the south end. The mode of drawing lots was as follows:—Fourteen pieces of stick, five or six inches in length, were severally notched or marked with a knife, with certain characters named as follows:—

1. One score.   6. Six score.   11. C.
2. Two score.   7. Seven score. 12. C.
3. Three score. 8. The Doter.   13. D.
4. Four score. 9. Dunghook.   14. The Drinker.
5. Five score. 10. Cross.

These hides were not each mown wholly by one tenant, but in various proportions; for instance, No. 8 was in six parts, No. 9 in six parts, No. 10 in three, and so on. The tenants having met, the following was the mode of proceeding:—These marked pieces of stick were put into the pocket of one of the party and drawn at random by those who had rights. As soon as the first stick was drawn it was stuck into the ground on the south side of the first hide, and the turf was cut with a mark similar to that on the stick; and so on till all the sticks were drawn and the several pieces marked.[1]

6. The existence within the village of a servile class is proved by many well-known authorities who group whole sections of the early population of England into unfree classes, one of the results of which has been the creation of the now famous formula of the village community in serfdom under a lord. One instructive feature of these unfree classes has been lost by ignoring the question of race admixture upon which we have dwelt throughout these researches. Another and almost equally important feature has only incidentally been touched upon, but that it is to be met with as one of the scattered fragments of the primitive system is significant because of its direct parallel to Indian facts. Dr. Hearn puts this important fact most elaborately before us. He says: "We find, in the archaic community, vestiges of an elaborate organization of inferior offices. Every Indian village contains a number of hereditary trades, which seem to be the relics of such a system. It is noteworthy that there are some trades in

[1] "Sussex Archæological Colllections," vol. iv. pp. 305-308.

these villages which are not hereditary. The exceptions include those which belong to commerce rather than to trade —that is, which involve a supply of goods from distant markets. These employments, although lucrative and respectable, do not appear to be regarded as customary offices, or to confer any status in the community. Such, for example, is the business of the grain dealer. In early Greece the δημιουργοι seem to be the analogues of these Hindo officials. Homer mentions the herald, the prophet, and the bard, the carpenter, the fisherman, and the leech, all of whom, although we cannot trace their exact position, appear to have exercised some kind of public function. Among the Keltic clans similar classes are known to have existed."[1] Now, at Aston, and in a minor degree at Malmesbury, we have already noticed that some of the villagers were set apart as village servants, paid for out of village lands, and regarded as a necessary part of the village system. Everywhere in India these servants belong to a low caste non-Aryan race, and everywhere they help to make the Indian village community self supporting and independent of each other. The servants thus belonging to the village system have of course gradually dwindled down under the influence of economical progress in England. In Scotland, however, we have found them occupying villages by themselves in serfdom under the tribal community. The means of identifying these relics of old village economy in England, are not so telling as in the Scottish examples, but they are by no means insignificant. Sir Henry Maine puts it in this way: "It is the assignment of a definite lot in the cultivated area to particular trades which allows us to suspect that the early Teutonic groups were similarly self-sufficing. There are several English parishes in which certain pieces of land in the common field have from time immemorial been known by the name of a particular trade; and there is often a popular belief that nobody, not following the trade, can legally be owner of the lot associated with it. And it is possible that we have here a key to the plentifulness and persistence of certain names of trades as

[1] "Aryan Household," p. 130.

surnames among us."[1] It may be advisable to show that this quotation is based upon actual facts, although the labour of collecting examples from existing field names is too great to compensate for the results. But some few examples will serve to show not only that such evidence exists, but that the sources from which it is to be derived are very scattered.

Field allotments for village servants form a valuable portion of our early municipal history. The aldermen of Nottingham were paid by an allotment of the seventh part of a meadow to each, called an alderman's part. The chamberlain, mace-bearer, and mayor's common serjeant had likewise an allotment. The alderman was chief man of the borough of Malmesbury, and he was paid by a piece of land called the alderman's kitchen. The field grieve of Berwick-upon-Tweed had an allowance of money in lieu of a meadow. The portreeve, haywards, and other officers of Aberavon had a field of enclosed hay-land divided amongst them. The hayward of Godmanchester received an annual sum of money in lieu of land. The bailiffs of Northampton were allowed the rent of a piece of ground called the bailiff's hook, and the bailiff of Axbridge possessed a piece of ground called the bailiff's wall. The mayor of Queenborowe had, too, a right of depasturing a certain number of sheep, cows, and horses all the year. The pinder of Doncaster had a small piece of land in Doncaster field called the pinder's balk; and we have some examples of this system fallen into disuse in the name of bellman's acre, at Newport, which is still extant, though the office is obsolete.

We will now turn to corresponding evidence in manorial tenements. These seem to carry us at once to many of the surrounding circumstances of early village life. I collect a few of my first instances of trade-allotments in the village lands from a Paper contributed to the *Law Magazine and Review*, on the "Rights, Disabilities, and Usages of the Ancient English Peasantry." For his services the smith at Chalgrave had an acre of meadow called Sundacre. At Ashbury the "berebrat,"

[1] "Village Communities," p. 126; "Early History of Institutions," p. 173.

the old Saxon designation of the garnier or keeper of the granary, held a yardland almost freely for his services. The hayward at the same place had an acre of the lord's corn in autumn, always in a certain part of the field. The Saxon laws of Landright ordain that the sheaves granted to the hayward in harvest should be assigned to him out of the part of the field adjoining the pastures, and that any strip of land conceded to him should likewise be next to the pastures, that the hayward's own corn might be the first to be trodden by prowling cattle. At Darent, near Rochester, the beadle held five acres as beadle, shepherd, and hayward. At Ickham, in the same county, the beadle's office was hereditary, and he held five acres and a cottage. The office of reeve was hereditary at Clapham in Yorkshire, and he held an oxgang of land and eight acres. In many places he had a small meadow called ref-ham or ref-mede, and in the same way the meadow allowed to the beadle was called beadel-mead. The reeve of Winterborne had two cartloads of hay out of the lord's meadow called ref-ham.[1] At Bleadon Manor there is an allotment called revelond, occupied *ex officio* by the reve.[2] The owner of Colchester Castle had a right to appoint the steward and bailiff of the hundred and to demise to the latter an acre of land called the bailiff's acre.[3] The custumal of the manor of Isleworth states that every tenant of half a virgate shall be bedell, and then be quit of all rent and customs except tallage, and shall have the meadow called bedelmead.[4]

And thus we pass on to less distinctive evidence than these manorial holdings. In a schedule of the names and areas of the furlongs into which the open arable fields in the parish of Whitechurch, near Stratford-on-Avon, had been divided prior to their enclosure we find two names of fields, barber's furlong, and blacksmith's furlong, which illustrate our subject.[5] In

[1] *Law Magazine and Review*, vol. xiii. pp. 205–216.
[2] "Archæological Institute, Salisbury Meeting," p. 199.
[3] "Commissioners' Reports on Common Law," vol. iv. p. 101.
[4] "Historical Manuscripts Commission," vol. vi. p. 233.
[5] *Notes and Queries*, Fifth Series, vol. viii. p. 192.

Scotton (Lincolnshire), we have Pinder's Piece; in Barrow, Pinder's Thing. Then there are Constable's Lands, Constable's Meadow, Smythie Thing, Smith Land, Piper's Acre, Piper's Close, Borsholder Hill, Notheard's Mead, Reeve's Meadow, and other names, not perhaps now needful to specify in detail, which show that the old system of having village officers and paying them by grants of lands are fully represented in the fields of English manors, by which evidence alone can be interpreted the phenomena mentioned by Mr. Seebohm, from the Boldon Book.[1]

In Scotland we find the Smith's Croft, the Arrow-maker's, the Bow-maker's, the Waulker's, the Cook's, the Baker's, the Piper's, the Fiddler's, &c. In one parish there are Belnagown, the town of the Smiths, Teanafile, the residence of the fiddler, and Cruitach, the field of the harp, or harper's field. All the above names and more from the same origin are to be found near ancient seats.[2]

In Ireland the same evidence meets us. In Tullarvan cantred, Kilkenny, there is a townland of the physician, of the huntsman, of the tailor, and, in short, of every necessary dependent; the hawker had his portion allotted in another portion of the cantred, but the swineherd was nearer the castle.[3]

7. The primitive agricultural economy is not fully described when it has been ascertained that villagers till their lands upon the open-field system. There are the implements of tillage. It is singular that in discussing the various phases in which primitive systems of agriculture have survived in Britain, so little attention should have been given to at least one available source of information, namely, the implements by which agriculture has been carried on. The proposition presents itself in this way. The methods of cultivation, the common rights of landholders in arable, meadow, and pasture, the position of the servile class, the relics of the old house religion, as set

---

[1] "English Village Community," p. 70.
[2] Sinclair's "Statistical Account of Scotland," vol. vii. p. 259.
[3] "Statistical Account of Ireland," p. 652.

forth in the previous pages, have all tended towards the conclusion that the village community, to which these elements all belong, was derived from the primitive races who have occupied and settled in this island; and that the influences of the Roman civilization upon this section of our institutions was not very deep. Who then supplied us with our agricultural implements? Did the village communities continue using their own; did they borrow the Roman implements? Very considerable stress has been laid upon the position which the plough holds in the history of agricultural economy. What was this plough—was it the Roman aratrum, and did the Anglo-Saxons borrow it, and with it borrow also the bulk of the usages which belonged to it in the Roman system? It will be seen that the questions to be asked upon approaching this question are by no means few or unimportant. They have been pushed into the background by some more weighty questions perhaps; but they cannot always be ignored, and though it is not intended on this occasion to do more that just signify some of the important conclusions to be derived from a study of the old agricultural implements of this country, and their methods of use, there is much room for a more extended research.

Mr. Seebohm has a somewhat remarkable passage towards the close of his book on the use of the plough-team of eight oxen, which occupies so important a place in his researches. He says, "The presence of the team of eight oxen in Wales and Scotland, as well as in England, and the mention of teams of six and eight oxen mentioned in the Vedas as used by Aryan husbandmen in the East, centuries earlier, makes it possible, if not probable, that the Romans in this instance, as in so many others, adopted and adapted to their purpose a practice which they found already at work, connected perhaps with a heavier soil and a clumsier plough than they were used to south of the Alps."[1] It does not seem clear that the conclusion here arrived at is sufficient for the facts. The question as to whether the Romans adopted the eight-oxen plough team

[1] "English Village Community," p. 388.

into their system cannot depend upon the wide prevalence of such a team in Aryan countries. The conclusion from such evidence is rather that the plough team, as an essential in primitive agriculture, lies altogether outside the sphere of Roman influences one way or the other, and that in this as in other evidence we have proof of the primitive origin of the village community in England. But the argument may be pushed further home than this. The Roman instruments of husbandry are well known, and in countries where Roman influence was most felt they are actually in use at the present day, without much difference in their structure. Thus the wheel plough, with its earth-boards, handle, crossbar, and coulter, capable of accurate description from the writings of classical authors, and figured on a piece of engraved jasper of Roman workmanship, is, in all essential particulars, the same as that used about Mantua and Venice.

Speaking of reaping corn, Pliny says, "There are different modes of reaping. In the vast plains of Gaul very large wooden machines, armed with teeth on their edges, and mounted on two wheels, are forced through the standing corn by an animal propelling them from behind; thus, as the ears are cut off, they fall into the machines." And Palladius, in his "De re Rustica," says, "The more level parts of Gaul use the following expeditious method for reaping, and dispensing with the labour of men, with a single ox complete the whole extent of the harvest. For this purpose a vehicle is made, carried upon two low wheels. Its surface is square and bordered by planks, which, sloping outwards, make the inside wider at top than bottom. On the fore part of the carriage the planks are not so high as at the sides, and here are planted in a row numerous small teeth, set at distances according to the size of the wheat ears, and all curving upwards. From the rear of the aforesaid vehicle a couple of small poles are arranged just like the poles used in carrying litters (sedan-poles), into which the ox is fastened, his head towards the carriage, by means of a yoke and straps. He must, however, be a quiet beast, so as not to go beyond the direction of his driver (the pace required).

278   SURVIVALS IN LOCAL CUSTOM.

When the latter begins to drive the machine through the standing corn, all the ears that are seized by the teeth are carried in a heap into the vehicle, the straw being torn off and left standing; the ox-driver following behind, regulating the elevation or depression of the machine occasionally, and thus in a few goings forward and returnings, in the short space of a few hours the whole harvest is carried (or completed). This plan is suitable for plains and level ground, and where the straw is not considered a thing of importance."

REAPING MACHINE USED IN ROMAN GAUL.

These instruments have been used in late times, and an example is figured in the third volume of the "Memoires de l'institute Royal" of France (plate iv.), which is here reproduced.

When we turn to the implements used by the village communities of Britain, it is remarkable what a very different picture we have to draw. It is a picture which confirms the view taken throughout these pages, namely, that in Britain we have evidence of the oldest forms of agricultural settlement, commencing far back in the past before the Aryan conquest, that is, to times prior to the use of the plough. Let me note how important this is to us.

Reverting to the examples of terrace cultivation, it seems perfectly obvious that the plough could not have been used on these high narrow hill ridges,[1] and it so happens that not only can we point to terrace cultivation as examples of agriculture before the use of the plough, but we can point to the instrument which took the place of the plough.

Dr. E. B. Tylor has traced out the development of the plough from the earliest stages of agricultural implements. For the purpose of preparing the ground ready for use, two implements are in use among primitive people—namely, the digging-stick and the hoe, and both of these have been developed in Britain in rather a remarkable degree.

The digging-stick is, of course, the ancestor of the spade. It was first long in use simply in the form of a digging-stick. The Tahitians have agricultural implements of hard wood,

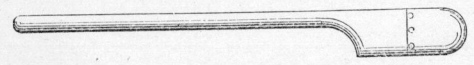

THE HIGHLAND SPADE.

about 5 feet long, with sharp edges and pointed, which they use as spades or hoes.[2] The only instrument used by the Maori New Zealanders for tillage was a long narrow stake, sharpened to an edge at one end, with a short piece fastened transversely at a little distance above it for the convenience of pressing it down with the foot.[3] The Fijians use digging-sticks made of the young mangrove tree. They are about the size of an ordinary hay-fork, and the lower end is tapered off on one side after the shape of a quill tooth-pick. In digging this flattened side is kept downwards.[4] Comparing these with the Highland spade, we shall find that the development is very slight. This rude instrument is a strong stick about 6 feet in length; the shaft is round, and bended a little for the sake of purchase. The head or lower part is about 14 inches long,

---

[1] See "Wilts Archæological Society," vol. xii. p. 190 ; vol. xvii. p. 296.
[2] Lubbock's "Prehistoric Times," p. 373.   [3] Ibid., p. 365.
[4] Williams' "Fiji and the Fijians," vol. i. p. 63.

and 4 to 6 broad. This is furnished with a plate of iron that covers the fore part about 6 or 8 inches up, but behind it does not reach above 2 or 3. The notch in which the foot is placed in time of delving is on the right side, and is commonly very narrow.[1] A still further development is to be met with in which the spade or digging action has been applied to ploughing purposes. This is in the caschrom, which is a crooked piece of wood, the lower end of which is about 2½ feet in length, somewhat thick, pretty straight, and armed at the end with iron, made thin and square, to cut the earth. The upper end of this instrument is called the shaft, and the lower is termed the head. The shaft above the crook is 6 feet long, and tapering towards the end, which is slender. Just below

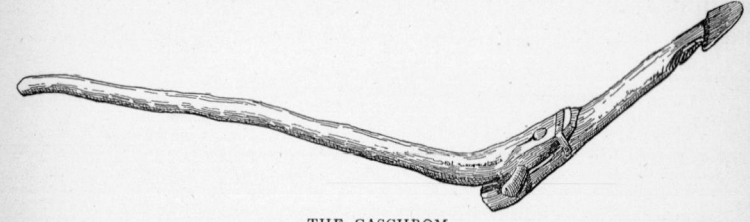

THE CASCHROM.

the crook or angle, which is an obtuse one, there must be a hole wherein a strong peg must be fixed for the workman's right foot, in order to push the instrument into the earth. While standing upon his left foot and holding the shaft firm with both his hands, he with his right foot drives the head far enough into the earth with one bend of his body; he then raises the clod by the iron headed part of his instrument, making use of the heel or hindpart of the head as a fulcrum; in so doing turns it over always to the left hand, and then proceeds to push for another clod in the same manner. With some disadvantages, it is of all instruments the fittest for turning up ground in a rocky country, where a plough can do little or nothing, either from a multitude of rocks, or from the earth being so marshy that cattle cannot pass over it without sinking.

[1] Ure's "Agriculture of Dumbarton," p. 39.

It is asserted that one man can turn over more ground with it in a day than four can do with a common spade.[1]

This adherence to the use of implements which originate in the earliest stages of agricultural progress, before the introduction of the plough, is a very important illustration of the adherence to old methods of cultivation which have been previously examined. Not only do we get the archæological remains of old cultivation sites on the terrace-cut hill-sides from the south to the north of Britain; but we get the primitive implements which were used where no plough could have been used. I am anxious to dwell upon the significance of these two parallel streams of survival. They each help us to form some notion of how complete the survival of archaic life in Britain has been, and how recent the filtration of highly developed society to all parts of the nation has been. The survival of primitive agricultural implements implies the survival of primitive agricultural usages. We have noted how far these are reflected in the social group which the cultivating communities assume—co-operation between the members of each group being the economical feature corresponding to the blood kinship between the members of each group. Co-operative ploughing is a well marked feature of the village community. Co-operative digging is as well marked among peoples who have not reached the stage of complete development, which marks the history of the Aryan communities. Thus in the village communities in Fiji, when preparing a piece of ground for yams, a number of men are employed, divided into groups of three or four. Each man being furnished with a digging-stick, they drive them into the ground so as to enclose a circle of about 2 feet in diameter. When by repeated strokes the sticks reach the depth of 18 inches, they are used as levers, and the mass of soil between them is thus loosened and raised.[2] The same practice is adopted by the Basutos with their hoe-

---

[1] "Statistical Account of Scotland," vol. vi. p. 288; Mitchell's "Past in the Present," p. 95; Robertson's "Agriculture of Inverness," p. 102; "Proceedings of the Society of Antiquaries of Scotland," vol. iii. p. 463.

[2] Williams, "Fiji and Fijians," vol. i. p. 63.

like implement, and Casalis, in his account of the practice, has inserted a spirited sketch, showing a long line of natives simultaneously lifting their implements to strike into the earth.[1] But then this was exactly the practice of Scottish Highlanders. Highland spades, says Ure, are found to be of great utility in cultivating small pieces of ground on the declivities of hills, to which the plough cannot have access. It is the common practice for eight or ten men and women to assemble with their spades for the purpose of digging a piece of ground; and it is amazing with what speed they accomplish their work. They begin at the lower extremity of the ground, and form themselves into a row at a convenient distance from one another; they cut with their spades a line in the ground, 9 or 10 inches deep, and then, with one united effort, throw over at once a furrow or piece of ground about 18 or 20 feet in length, and 8 or 10 inches in breadth.[2] Such close analogies in customs, as well as in the implements used, imply much more than can conveniently be stated. Backwardness in culture and in inventive capacity are among the least important points to be considered. What is far more important is to reckon the length of time, to be numbered by centuries, during which these outlying populations of our island, and of Europe, have continued the practices of their fathers. The grip of Roman civilization, the grip of Anglo-Saxon kingship, the grip of feudalism, was not strong enough to lift the peasantry out of barbarism, and the nation went on developing for centuries without much, if any, aid from the peasantry.

Let us now turn to the plough. Dr. Tylor conclusively proves that it was "a hoe dragged through the ground to form a continuous furrow."[3] The earliest transitional forms from the hoe to the plough seem to have survived longest in Sweden,[4] but the next stage is undoubtedly represented by the old Scottish one-stilt plough. In Orkney, in the year 1808, "The plough [had] only one stilt with neither rest nor

[1] Casalis' "Basutos," p. 163.
[2] Ure's "Agriculture of Dumbarton," p. 40.
[3] *Journal of the Anthropological Institute*, vol. x. p. 77. [4] Ibid.

mould-board, and its other parts [were] joined in such a form that it had not a single quality to recommend it but its simplicity."[1] This was used last century throughout Scotland and in some parts of England. Comparing it with the rude instrument in use in some of the outlying parts of India, there can be no doubt of its vast antiquity. The Indian plough is described as "consisting of a simple crooked stick with a handle fastened to it, the lower part being of conical shape, with a handle fastened to it. To its point is affixed a bar of iron, about a foot in length and an inch and a half in thickness, sharpened at the end, which serves merely to scratch the ground, but does not turn up the soil."[2] That the Scottish plough could do no more is stated over and over again by the old writers on agriculture in the last century, and it is proved by the singular and barbarous practice of drawing it by attaching it to a horse's tail. I have not come across any mention of this cruel custom outside the British Isles, in Scotland and in Ireland, but it signifies once more what rude barbarism has survived amidst our civilization.[3]

Now this is a very different implement to the plough with its team of eight oxen, but we can show the means by which the one developed from the other. In the same district of India where it has just been noted the primitive hoe-plough was used, the plough is drawn by a pair of bullocks, in a yoke, which are guided by the ploughman himself with a goad. These bullocks however "only work for a part of the day, as two or three pairs of tilling cattle are assigned to each plough. When it is necessary to plough the ground to a considerable depth, several

---

[1] Barry's "History of Orkney," p. 353; cf. Mitchell, "Past in Present," p. 95.

[2] Carmichael's "Manual of the District of Vizagapatam," p. 150; cf. *Journal of the Asiatic Society of Bengal*, vol. xiii. p. 265.

[3] In Scotland I can note the following references to this practice; Smith's "Agriculture of Argyle," p. 65; "Proceedings of the Society of Antiquaries of Scotland," vol. v. p. 201. In Ireland the following: *Ulster Journal of Archæology*, vol. vi. pp. 212-221, 363; "Statistical Survey of Roscommon," p. 654; *Gentleman's Magazine*, 1855, vol. ii. pp. 136-140; Lithgow's "Travels," 1619, p. 411.

ploughs follow one another. For each crop the ground is prepared by being ploughed up a certain number of times."[1] This is very instructive information. In the first place, it sets forth the intermediate stages of co-operative ploughing before the establishment of the heavy plough with a team of eight oxen; it also enables us to identify this as the earliest Anglo-Saxon practice. In the Harley Psalter, a manuscript of the eleventh century, is a drawing, in colour, of a man ploughing with a very crude wheel-less plough drawn by two oxen, directed simply by the goad, with no head gear or driver, and this may be compared with the rock drawing at Tegneby, in Bohuslän in Sweden.[2] This is not the only early drawing showing the

ANGLO-SAXON TWO-OXEN PLOUGH TEAM.
(*From the Harleian MS.*)

two-oxen plough among the Anglo-Saxons, and one instance is here figured. It disproves the strict uniformity of Anglo-Saxon agricultural practices, and once more turns us back from a more advanced type to a backward type—from an eight-oxen plough team, with all its accompaniment of rights and privileges in the common field, to the two-oxen plough team, with its significant rudeness of structure and use, and its more than probable use prescribed after the manner of its Indian prototype. There is certainly no room to argue for a uniformity of practice with such evidence before us, and it confirms the evidence elsewhere given that we must turn back upon more primitive institutions and more primitive communities for some of the lost facts in the English evidence.

[1] Carmichael, *loc. cit.*
[2] Du Chaillu's "Land of the Midnight Sun," vol. i. p. 351.

AGRICULTURAL IMPLEMENTS. 285

I now turn to the reaping implements and customs. In the Harleian MS., No. 603, are some outline drawings of agricultural operations throughout the year, and Mr. Wright reproduced a few in one of his miscellaneous publications. Describing this picture, "the activity of the reapers," says Mr. Wright, "is well represented. The corn appears at this period not to have been sheaved in the field, but to have been carried directly away. The warrior with his spear and horn appears to be guardian of the field, whose duty it was to watch against sudden attacks on the harvest in those unsettled times."[1] But incidentally we are also introduced in this interesting illustration to the balks and the long narrow strips indicative of the open-field system, and we may add this to the many proofs that exist of the existence of the village community among the Anglo-Saxons. Two facts will be noticed about the reaping. The sickle is simply a hand implement, and it is used to cut off the tops of the grain, leaving the straw standing.[2]

ANGLO-SAXON REAPING.
(*From the Harleian MS.*)

In this illustration a wheeled cart is figured, and the wheels

[1] "Archæological Album," p. 64.

[2] *Cf.* Boyd Dawkins' "Early Man in Britain," p. 360; Elton, "Origins of English History," pp. 32-33.

are spoked. Noting that Dr. Tylor has traced out the various stages of development in the wheeled cart,[1] it is significant that the introduction of wheeled carts is so recent in many parts of Britain. Sir Arthur Mitchell has touched upon this topic, and has figured three examples of the kind of sledge-cart used in the Highlands;[2] but the evidence is far more extensive than would at first thought be imagined. General Pitt-Rivers has drawn attention to evidence of the use of the sledge-cart in the Rushmore excavations. Mr. Lucas, in his "Studies in Nidderdale" (pp. 214-215), observes that wheeled conveyances are of very recent introduction in the upper part of the dale, and he gives an account of the first pair of wheels seen. They were all of one piece, and quite solid, being cut out of a single piece of wood, and before this the vehicle used for the conveyance of the dead was a kind of litter drawn by two horses, one before and one behind. In Ross-shire the farmers collected their manure into dunghills, and spread it on their fields by means of a kind of cart called *kellachies*. They consist of small solid wheels on which a frame is placed, and in an opening a conical coarse wicker basket is set wherein the dung is carried.[3] In Dumbarton sledges were used to a considerable extent,[4] and the same was the case all over Stirlingshire.[5] In Caithness there were no carts made use of. The farmers carried their manure to the land and their corn from it in creels upon the backs of horses,[6] and in Galloway the same kind of contrivance was used, persons being employed on each side with forks to keep the basket in a proper poise.[7] In the districts of Culdaff, Ireland, it is observed, "very few of the inhabitants possess wheeled cars or carts, the substitute for them being slide cars. A pair of shafts, connected by a few cross bars,

---

[1] *Journal of the Anthropological Institute*, vol. x. pp. 79-81.

[2] "Past in the Present," p. 97.

[3] Sinclair's "Statistical Account of Scotland," vol. iii. p. 11; Donaldson's "Agriculture of Elgin," p. 22.

[4] Ure's "Agriculture of Dumbarton," p. 43.

[5] Belsche's "Agriculture of Stirling," p. 41.

[6] Marshall's "Agriculture of the Highlands," p. 204.

[7] Webster's "Agriculture of Galloway," p. 12.

constitute this vehicle, which is dragged along the ground by a horse, to the great injury of the public roads." Other districts of Ireland are similarly situated.[1]

Turning back now to that picture of domestic economy which was noted in a previous chapter, we find that it does not stand alone. The more we penetrate into the details of English agricultural economy, the more we find that it presents the inquirer with evidence of its primitive origin. And when at last a manufacturing industry arises, we can see it in its very earliest stages. Mr. Ashley points out from the records of gild history some of the most salient features, but even these do not take us so far back as we can get among the peasantry of Aberdeenshire in the last century. The knitting of stockings was the principal manufacture of this district. It was carried on by almost all the women, and by many boys and old men. "A woman," says the local historian, "can work at her stocking while feeding her cows in the baulks or patches of grass between the ridges, which are not uncommon in this district."[2]

8. There remains one word to be said about the manorial element of the English village community. In the types which have been used for the purpose of the present study the manorial element does not find a prominent place. I think too much has been made of the manorial element in England, and I think its origin has been antedated. That it has absorbed much of the primitive institutions in England is undoubted; that it did not originate those institutions, and did not stamp them with any of their primary features, seems to be the proper conclusion from the evidence we have now examined. I am, however, aware that this evidence does not stand alone, and that it has to compete with Mr. Seebohm's dictum that "there were manors everywhere." In the meantime much has been done by independent workers to enable us to understand more about the position of the manor. Mr. Maitland has discussed one important subject in this connection, and has made the acute suggestion that there may have

---

[1] Mason's "Statistical Account of Ireland," vol. ii. p. 165; vol. iii. p. 8.
[2] Sinclair's "Statistical Account of Scotland," vol. ii. p. 539.

been a time when township and hundred were identical, and he refers to some interesting evidence "which seems to show that the vill of ancient times was often a much larger tract of land than the vill of modern times; that the area belonging to an agricultural community was not unfrequently as large as the area of some of our hundreds."[1] Of course there are limitations to this suggestion, which Mr. Maitland has taken care to note, but I allude to it now in order to point out one other problem which it helps to solve.

We have, on the one hand, the non-manorial type of Lauder, with its extensive area of nearly thirty thousand acres, and, on the other hand, the village type of Aston, held under a superior manor, whose lands were intermixed with the contiguous manor of Shifford. The Lauder type helps us to understand Mr. Maitland's suggestion without much trouble, and I think the Aston type will help in the same direction. We know that manors having their lands intermixed is not an uncommon feature of manorial land rights. If we may go back to the hundreds of Southern England as the representatives of the village community, it is clear that the manor must have been carved out of the older village community as land came to be held under feudal tenures. This process might well have brought about the imprint of ownership by a lord at the same time as it transferred the only known system of agricultural economy then obtaining, namely, that developed under the older village community. The intermixture of manorial lands, therefore, would be the natural outcome of an original intermixed tribal ownership in the hundred, and thus manors must have been a late derivative institution from the village community, and not a primary institution from which the village community evolved. This is borne out by an extremely suggestive parallel between the intermixture of lands belonging to different manors and the intermixture of parish lands within one township. A case is given in the evidence before the Enclosure Commission of 1844. Donisthorpe is situated in three parishes, each parish being scattered about in the open

[1] *Archæological Review*, vol. iv. p. 235.

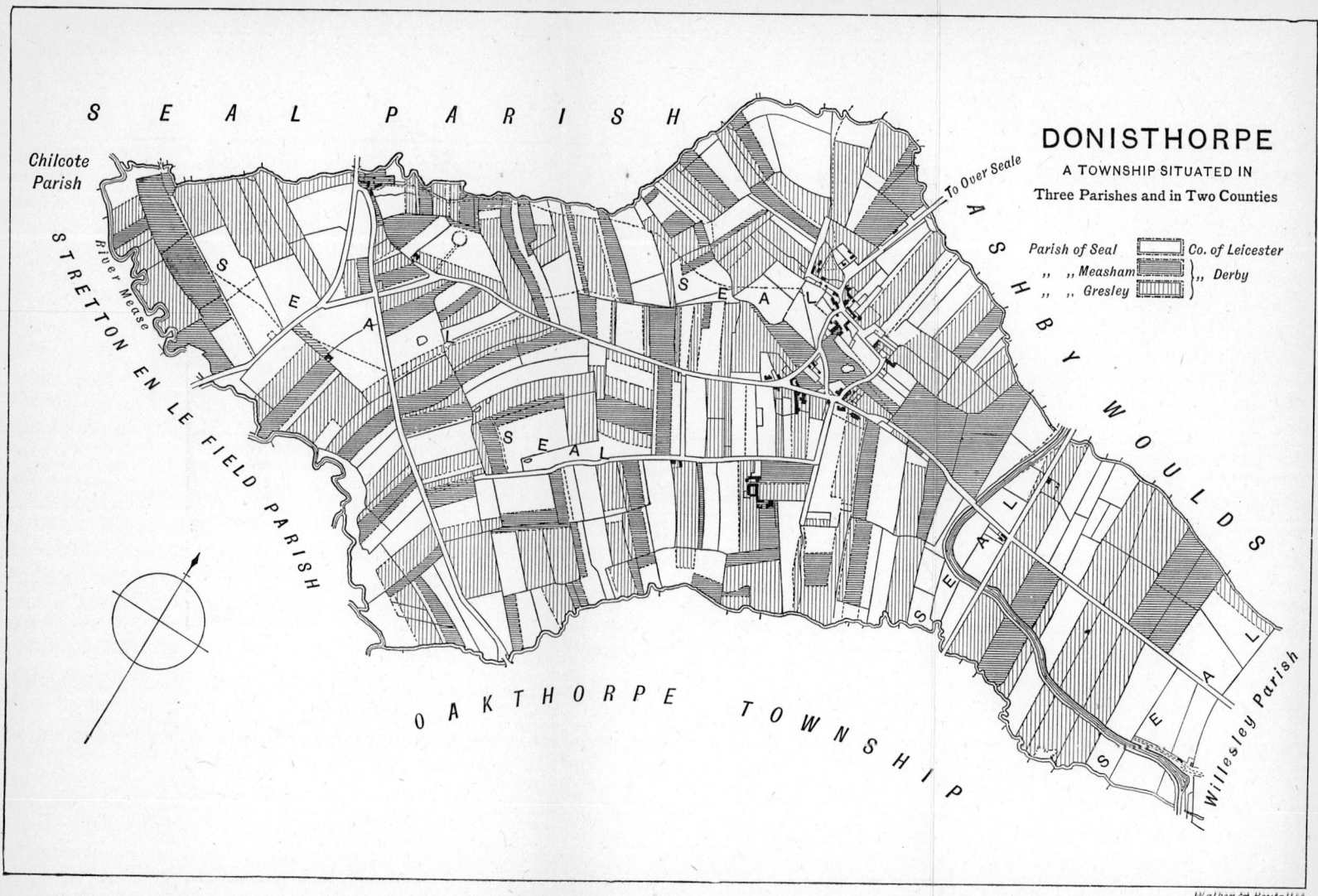

THE MANOR.

fields of the township, as illustrated in the accompanying map. Now we know that parishes are the outcome, to a large extent, of ecclesiastical requirements and of the operation of the poor law. If, therefore, such a late institution as the parish stands in relation to the township in much the same position as the manor stands in relation to its parent institution, whatever that may prove to be, it is an admissible conjecture that the manor like the parish is a late derivative institution, and not an early primary institution. To the evidence of non-manorial types of the village community which has been adduced we may add the additional evidence as to the possibly late origin of manors; and, on the whole, it appears to me that the conclusion is irresistible that the village community in England owes its form and growth, its agricultural economy, its homestead rights and privileges, to primitive institutions and not to the manor.

The fragmentary survivals of the village community have now been examined with a view of showing that they all have a place in determining the history of that institution in Britain. This is a portion of the subject which needs careful handling, and a considerable amount of reconstruction is needed before these fragments can be fitted into their several positions. But the fact of their fragmentary condition goes far to suggest that they are more primitive, and carry us further back into the past, than more perfect examples. They have not been able to resist the march of political progress. Those who know by repeated evidence all over the world how extremely slowly man changes his customs and practices will not be disposed to question the place I have attempted to give to some apparently trivial facts in village life. These are more likely to be descended from older facts than to have originated in the current events of political life, with which the peasant portion of the population have had so little to do. It only remains now for the student to get all of them together, and then to redraw the picture of the past which they present.

CHAPTER X.

SUMMARY AND CONCLUSION.

I HAVE ventured in these pages to apply the methods of anthropological research to the investigation of the origin and development of the village community in Britain.

The usages and beliefs of the races inhabiting Britain have been used by anthropologists for proof of several phases in the early history of man. Mr. McLennan notably has deduced from the language of Cæsar evidence as to a distinct type of polyandry, which he classifies by the name British, and distinguishes from other types, the Nair type and the later types. Mr. Tylor and Sir John Lubbock have used the evidence of superstition and custom in their researches into the primitive history of man. Mr. Lang has drawn upon Scottish myth in discussing his important theories on early ritual and religion. Thus it appears that survivals in British usages and beliefs are fully recognized as standing in some definite relationship to the usages and beliefs of early mankind. But the complement to this state of things in anthropological evidence has never been quite recognized—British institutions have not been investigated thoroughly on the lines of anthropological research. To satisfy ourselves that this method would rightly apply to the village community, it was necessary, first of all, to understand that this institution was primitive, and not historical, in origin—due, that is, to the earliest instincts of our race, not to the political thought of a governing class, or to the commercial necessities of a trading class, in historical times.

We started off by showing that the village community was

not a modern institution, but that it must have begun far back in the history of the human race, and probably has been a phase of social existence through which all peoples who have progressed onwards from savagery to civilization must have passed. We examined some savage types of the village community, and we noted that its existence in the civilized countries of Europe must be due to survival.

We then referred to the well-known parallels which existed between the village community in India and in England, and we suggested that, in view of these parallels, facts now ascertainable of the former would no doubt explain the lost facts of the latter. But here intervened a new problem. It was proved that the village communities of India were not Aryan in origin, but were formed by a pre-Aryan race, who, having been conquered by the tribal Aryans, had thus had superimposed upon them the Aryan overlordship, with its fixed notions of sacredness in kinship and in domestic worship. In India these Aryans and non-Aryans exist side by side, the contributions of each to the building up of the Indian form of the village community being still stamped with the impress of race. And we argued that this impress of race, now lost in the uprise of British nationality, might be recovered by studying the analogy of institutions.

But in Britain there was the Roman conquest to account for. In the rearrangement of the evidence as to the village community in Britain, it was plainly necessary to understand what was the Roman contribution to the history of the village community, especially in view of the fact that English historians have at various times brought so much evidence to prove that English institutions are derived from Roman institutions. We then worked out the contrast between the Romans and the conquered Celts and the later-coming Teutons. On the one hand, there is the Roman imperial system extending over nationalities and races, knit together by vast political power; on the other hand, there are the tribal Celts and Teutons knit together by their faith to kin and chief. Under Carausius it might have been possible to have begun the history of the

British Empire. But this foretaste of what could be done with the splendid machinery of an island navy and an island army was due to Roman genius, not to British, and after the withdrawal of the Roman legions it was not a national or imperial army that met the invading Teutons, but clans and tribes, who fought with clans and tribes. How little Roman institutions affected the great mass of the Celts of Britain is clearly seen by this pregnant fact. Rome was outside the village system altogether. In her own home in Latium she had passed away from this phase to that of imperialism and nationality, and she could not again be compressed within the narrow boundaries of the village system. But the case was far different with the new conquerors of Celtic Britain. They were organized on the tribal system, and so Teuton and Celt stood upon a common level. The result of the English conquest was that the Celts had to give way in their villages. Room had to be made for the new incomers inside the village system, and tribal and clan society again became the type of civilization in Britain, never better illustrated than by the keen insight of Kingsley, who pictures Hereward as passionately resisting the notion that Harold's defeat at Hastings meant the conquest of Britain—it was merely the defeat of the local West Saxon army. This contrast between the Roman and Teutonic conquest brought us to two conclusions: That Rome left the village communities of Celtic Britain like England would leave the village communities of India, untouched in their inner life, but crystallized in form by the pressure from without; that the Teutons affected the inner life, and did not affect the outer shell.

This conclusion as to the non-interference of Roman influence on the village communities of Britain left us clear ground to inquire whether there were any traces of the pre-Aryan influences, and in the hill cultivation and settlement, parallel to so much that is known of the hill cultivation and settlement in India, we discovered the first clue to this pre-Aryan element. Also in the rude and fantastic, sometimes savage, customs of English villages we traced out strong parallels to similar customs in Indian villages, where they were observed distinctly and solely as the rights and privileges of the non-Aryan outcast tribes, which were doubtless wrung from their Aryan overlords through the ever-present fears arising out of the powers of an antagonistic race who were in communion with the gods of nature. And we concluded that these customs of India and England, parallel in their present form, must have been also parallel in origin.

With this equipment we turned to the evidences of the village communities in Britain as they have survived in historic observation. The old hearth religion and the tribal houses founded thereon were discovered in the usages and beliefs and in the undestroyed primitive structures of rural Britain. That this religion and its relics, as preserved in folklore, must be considered as part and parcel of the village community, was insisted upon by the evidence which folklore is so prominently bringing before us now, and the intimate connection thus brought out explained clearly that economical features were not the sole survivals from the village communities of Britain.

Passing on to the surviving types we first examined the tribal form of the village community, and it appeared that the well-known description of Tacitus was true in all essentials of the survivals in the last century. The community in its tribal form was the prominent feature; the village of serfs was the subordinate feature. Groups of kindred occupying their several homesteads and the lands around; small villages of serfs occupying cottage homes massed together and using the lands around them in intermixed or run-rig occupation. And from this evidence it was suggested that Mr. Seebohm's famous formula defining the English institution as a manor with a village community in serfdom under it, must be rewritten as a tribal community with a village in serfdom under it. Then some transitional types were examined, showing the development from the tribal community to the village community. Finally, the villages of the more thickly-populated parts of Britain were examined, and it appeared not only that the ordinary manorial type was insufficient to account for types that did not assimilate to the manorial type, but that municipal institutions yielded up evidence as to their origin in the village community. The case of London was then examined, and it appeared by the curious and interesting distribution of municipal law with unrecognized custom that the primitive village system was not absolute here, as it was in the villages of rural Britain. This was to be explained, however, by evidence in full support of the position which has been asserted for Roman influences. In London there are distinct traces of the continuity of Roman institutions. The presence of village institutions must therefore be due to an intrusion from the surrounding settlements—an intrusion, which is even more significant of the relative position of Roman organization to village institutions than the general evidence derivable from other sources previously examined.

This concluded the examination of the surviving types of the village community in Britain. No one of these types, taken singly, can be said to illustrate all the points in its history. The development has been irregular in the various localities where they have survived, and the true method of treating the subject is to collect together as many varieties of type as can be got, and to draw from their differences as much as from their identities the necessary evidence. Only a portion of this work has been attempted in these pages, but it may be hoped that it is a representative portion.

Finally, we examined some of the fragments of village community which survive in unconnected form. This was important because it indicates the variety of degrees in which survivals must necessarily appear. If all examples of the village community assumed a more or less identical form, the probability of them having originated in some well-known political or national event would be enormous. If manors only were the source from which all evidence was to be derived, if Hitchin were the normal type to which all others assimilated, it would be difficult to get away from the argument that it arose from a fusion with the Roman villa. But that Hitchin does not, in the first place, represent anything like a normal type of the English village community, and, in the second place, that scattered here and there among the local institutions of the country are innumerable fragments of the village community now separated and distinct from any definite examples, we have proof that the survivals of this primitive institution have met with the fate and experience which we know survivals in myth and belief have met.

The limits of the present work will be apparent to most scholars. The task has been a difficult and complex one, and it is easy to see that it requires much more research and study before the final word is said. On some points I have done little more than indicate the direction of future research if the view I take is admitted as a tenable one. There has been no opportunity of examining the village community as it survives in the Russian mir, and parallels to which exist in many of the most curious features of English manorial history. There has been no opportunity of turning to the details of the German system which Von Maurer and others have investigated and set before us. Close up to the boundaries of Italian cities there exist forms of old tribal communities, and in France the village system is even yet in vigorous existence. But the special object of the present inquiry was to establish, if possible, that the pre-Celtic inhabitants of this island, surviving, as Dr. Beddoe has proved, in the physical peculiarities of many localities in the British Isles, must have lent their aid in the fashioning of British institutions. The tenacity of custom, the potent force of tradition, the indestructibility of superstitious practices, have been brought to bear upon the evidence of comparative institutions. Much of this evidence is argumentative; much of it is not to be brought within the bounds of explanation except by frequent repetition of argument and elaboration of detailed proof; some of it is capable of other explanation than that I have sought to give it. Still, on the whole, it seems to me that we must give up the theory of a Roman origin for what has hitherto seemed to be adequately explained by that theory. The Celtic tribal communities have been examined, and much of their common characteristics are known to be present in the later village communities, but the tribal communities of all Aryan stocks are proved to have possessed the germ of the villages of serfs resting under their headship. If this be admitted there is no logical, as there certainly is no scientific, reason, why we should not carry back our research even to those far-off times when an Iberic people began to sow the cereals and to practise some of the domestic arts which we do to this day.

THE END.

INDEX.

"Acre," the term, 193
Allotment of lands, 266-271
Anglo-Saxon commerce, 52
Anglo-Saxon London, 54
Aryan elements in village community, 20
Aryan lordship, development of, 111
Ashley's "Economic History," quoted, 160
Assembly (the) of the village, 257-265
Aston and Cote, 158

Baring-Gould, quoted, 117
Basutos, village community among, 12
Beddoe (Dr.), quoted, 103
Bede, quoted, 128
Boate, "Ireland's Natural History," quoted, 88
Boley Hill, Rochester, 247
Bovey Tracey, Mayor's Monday at, 220
Boyd Dawkins (Prof.), quoted, 2, 70, 101, 285

Chippenham village community, 173; British element in, 185; Danes in, 187
Chirnside village community, 207
Clan feuds, 237-245

Coif, Order of the, 224
Commerce, Anglo-Saxon, 52
Coorgs, 97
Corn in Anglo-Saxon times, 53
Craik's "History of Commerce," quoted, 53
Crawford village community, 205

Derby, clan divisions at, 241
Dravidian villages, 26
Drowning, execution by, 221
Druids, non-Aryan, 104, 111
Dyaks, village community among, 10

Earle (Prof.), quoted, 57
Elgin, village community at, 170
Elton (C. J.), quoted, 2, 103, 129, 285

Fiji, village community in, 9, 55
Fraser (J. G.), quoted, 113

Gatacre Hall, 44
Greaves Ash, 92
Green's "History," quoted, 48, 50
Greenwell (Canon), quoted, 94
Guest (Dr.), quoted, 48, 52

Hall (Hubert), quoted, 121
Harris community, 134
Harrison's "Description of England," quoted, 64

Hearn (Dr.), quoted, 71, 106, 129, 253
Hearth cult, primitive, 129
Heisgeir community, 143
Hewett (Mr.), quoted, 23
Highland communities, 138
Hill farming, 85
Hill forts and terrace cultivation, 91
Hill tribes of India, 21; of Britain, 75
Holme, Milne (Dr.), quoted, 88
Homestead, 116–131; sacredness of, 116; the lord's, 117; the villager's, 121; the source of all rights, 253–257
Humbledon Hill, 91

Iberic elements in Britain, 101
Implements, agricultural, 275–287
Indian village communities, 20–41
Inverness, primitive conditions at, 239
Irish tribal communities, 141

Jackson's "History of Chippenham," quoted, 85, 87, 174

Kachahrî, 55
Kells community, 151
Kemble (Mr.), quoted, 186
Khonds, 22
Kinship, 233–236
Kolis of Maha Kanta, 25

Lang (Mr.), quoted, 238
Lauder community, 148
London, origin of, 49; its unique history, 208; Roman, 211; village life in, 212; agriculture in, 226
London Stone, 218
Lord, manorial, 263–265
Lubbock (Sir J.), quoted, 6, 102
Lyall (J. B.), quoted, 62

McLennan (Mr.), quoted 4, 8
Maine (Sir H.), quoted, 1, 4, 58, 129, 148
Maitland (Mr.), quoted, 47, 54 288
Malmesbury village community, 187
Manors, 287–289
Manu, 30
Marshall, "Rural Economy," quoted, 81
Mitchell (Sir Arthur), quoted, 125
Mock mayors, 107
Morgan (L.), quoted, 6, 8

Nasse, "Agricultural Community," quoted, 180
Newton-upon-Ayr village community, 200
No Man's land, 115
Non-Aryan survivals in Britain, 69–115

Offices, village, 271–275
Origin (primitive) of village community, 1–19

Pathan tribes of Peshawur, 35
Prestwick village community, 205

Race-elements of the village community, 20–41, 236–253
Rhyming formula at Malmesbury, 191
Rhys (Prof.), quoted, 104
Rogers (Thorold), quoted, 44
Roman influences, 43–63
Roman London, 49
Rothwell village community, 171

Savage type of village community, 9–15
Sayce (Prof.), quoted, 17
Scarborough, clan divisions at, 241
Scrope (Poulett), quoted, 81, 83, 87

Seebohm (Mr.), quoted, 1, 42, 52, 55, 61, 83, 85, 114, 139, 175, 196, 255
Serfdom, English, 55, 271–275
Shealings in Scotland, 125
Smith (Adam), quoted, 132

Terrace cultivation in England, 75; in Wales, 77; in Scotland, 78; in Ireland, 80; origin of, 81; its agricultural origin, 83; ancient practice of, 87; construction of, 89; summary of evidence, 95; in China, 96; in India, 97
Topley (Mr.), quoted, 74
Traditional usages, 17–18
Transitional types in Britain, 147–156
Tribal communities in Britain, 132–146
Tribal games, 243
Tylor (Dr.), quoted, 6

Village, the primitive English, 45
Village community, origin of, 15; Aryan and non-Aryan elements, 20; parallels between India and Britain, 31; persistence of, in England, 56; in Wales, 61; in the Punjab, 62; transitional type, 147; final type, 157; at Aston and Cote, 158; at Elgin, 170; at Rothwell, 171; at Chippenham, 173; at Malmesbury, 187; at Newton-upon-Ayr, 200; at Prestwick, 205; at Crawford, 205; at Whitsome, 206; at Chirnside, 207; in London, 212; importance of the Indian examples, 230; survivals of, in local custom, 232; in recognition of kinship, 233; in mixture of races, 236; in homestead as source of all rights, 253

Wansdyke, 100
Wapping, Execution Dock at, 221
Welsh tribal communities, 143, 196
Whitsome village community, 206
Wiltshire, Teutonic settlement of, 73

UNWIN BROTHERS,
THE GRESHAM PRESS,
CHILWORTH AND LONDON.

NEW BOOKS

IMPORTED BY

CHARLES SCRIBNER'S SONS,

NEW YORK CITY.

GREAT WRITERS.

A NEW SERIES OF CRITICAL BIOGRAPHIES OF FAMOUS WRITERS OF EUROPE AND AMERICA.

LIBRARY EDITION.

Printed on large paper of extra quality, in handsome binding, Demy 8vo, price $1.00 each.

ALPHABETICAL LIST.

PRESS NOTICES.

Life of Jane Austen. By Goldwin Smith.

"Mr. Goldwin Smith has added another to the not inconsiderable roll of eminent men who have found their delight in Jane Austen. Certainly a fascinating book."—*Spectator.*

Life of Balzac. By Frederick Wedmore.

"A finished study, a concentrated summary, a succinct analysis of Balzac's successes and failures, and the causes of these successes and failures, and of the scope of his genius."—*Scottish Leader.*

Life of Charlotte Brontë. By A. Birrell.

"Those who know much of Charlotte Brontë will learn more, and those who know nothing about her will find all that is best worth learning in Mr. Birrell's pleasant book."—*St. James's Gazette.*

Life of Browning. By William Sharp.

"This little volume is a model of excellent English, and in every respec it seems to us what a biography should be."—*Public Opinion.*

New York: CHARLES SCRIBNER'S SONS.

Life of Bunyan. By Canon Venables.

"A most intelligent, appreciative, and valuable memoir."—*Scotsman*.

Life of Burns. By Professor Blackie.

"The editor certainly made a hit when he persuaded Blackie to write about Burns."—*Pall Mall Gazette*.

Life of Byron. By Hon. Roden Noel.

"He [Mr. Noel] has at any rate given to the world the most credible and comprehensible portrait of the poet ever drawn with pen and ink."—*Manchester Examiner*.

Life of Thomas Carlyle. By R. Garnett, LL.D.

"This is an admirable book. Nothing could be more felicitous and fairer than the way in which he takes us through Carlyle's life and works."—*Pall Mall Gazette*.

Life of Cervantes. By H. E. Watts.

"Let us rather say that no volume of this series, nor, so far as we can recollect, of any of the other numerous similar series, presents the facts of the subject in a more workmanlike style, or with more exhaustive knowledge."—*Manchester Guardian*.

Life of Coleridge. By Hall Caine.

"Brief and vigorous, written throughout with spirit and great literary skill."—*Scotsman*.

Life of Congreve. By Edmund Gosse.

"Mr. Gosse has written an admirable and most interesting biography of a man of letters who is of particular interest to other men of letters."—*The Academy*.

Life of Crabbe. By T. E. Kebbel.

"No English poet since Shakespeare has observed certain aspects of nature and of human life more closely; and in the qualities of manliness and of sincerity he is surpassed by none. . . . Mr. Kebbel's monograph is worthy of the subject."—*Athenæum*.

Life of Darwin. By G. T. Bettany.

"Mr. G. T. Bettany's *Life of Darwin* is a sound and conscientious work."—*Saturday Review*.

Life of Dickens. By Frank T. Marzials.

"Notwithstanding the mass of matter that has been printed relating to Dickens and his works, . . . we should, until we came across this volume, have been at a loss to recommend any popular life of England's most popular novelist as being really satisfactory. The difficulty is removed by Mr. Marzials' little book."—*Athenæum*.

Life of George Eliot. By Oscar Browning.

"We are thankful for this interesting addition to our knowledge of the great novelist."—*Literary World*.

New York: CHARLES SCRIBNER'S SONS.

Life of Emerson. By Richard Garnett, LL.D.

"As to the larger section of the public, to whom the series of Great Writers is addressed, no record of Emerson's life and work could be more desirable, both in breadth of treatment and lucidity of style, than Dr. Garnett's."—*Saturday Review.*

Life of Goethe. By James Sime.

"Mr. James Sime's competence as a biographer of Goethe, both in respect of knowledge of his special subject, and of German literature generally, is beyond question."—*Manchester Guardian.*

Life of Goldsmith. By Austin Dobson.

"The story of his literary and social life in London, with all its humorous and pathetic vicissitudes, is here retold as none could tell it better."—*Daily News.*

Life of Nathaniel Hawthorne. By Moncure Conway.

"Easy and conversational as the tone is throughout, no important fact is omitted, no useless fact is recalled."—*Speaker.*

Life of Heine. By William Sharp.

"This is an admirable monograph, . . . more fully written up to the level of recent knowledge and criticism of its theme than any other English work."—*Scotsman.*

Life of Victor Hugo. By Frank T. Marzials.

"Mr. Marzials' volume presents to us, in a more handy form than any English, or even French, handbook gives, the summary of what, up to the moment in which we write, is known or conjectured about the life of the great poet."—*Saturday Review.*

Life of Hunt. By Cosmo Monkhouse.

"Mr. Monkhouse has brought together and skilfully set in order much widely scattered material."—*Athenæum.*

Life of Samuel Johnson. By Colonel F. Grant.

"Colonel Grant has performed his task with diligence, sound judgment, good taste, and accuracy."—*Illustrated London News.*

Life of Keats. By W. M. Rossetti.

"Valuable for the ample information which it contains."—*Cambridge Independent.*

Life of Lessing. By T. W. Rolleston.

"A picture of Lessing which is vivid and truthful, and has enough of detail for all ordinary purposes." *Nation* (New York).

New York: CHARLES SCRIBNER'S SONS.

Life of Longfellow. By Prof. Eric S. Robertson.

"A most readable little book."—*Liverpool Mercury.*

Life of Marryat. By David Hannay.

"What Mr. Hannay had to do—give a craftsman-like account of a great craftsman who has been almost incomprehensibly undervalued—could hardly have been done better than in this little volume."—*Manchester Guardian.*

Life of Mill. By W. L. Courtney.

"A most sympathetic and discriminating memoir."—*Glasgow Herald.*

Life of Milton. By Richard Garnett, LL.D.

"Within equal compass the life-story of the great poet of Puritanism has never been more charmingly or adequately told."—*Scottish Leader.*

Life of Renan. By Francis Espinasse.

"Sufficiently full in details to give us a living picture of the great scholar, . . . and never tiresome or dull."—*Westminster Review.*

Life of Dante Gabriel Rossetti. By J. Knight.

"Mr. Knight's picture of the great poet and painter is the fullest and best yet presented to the public."—*The Graphic.*

Life of Schiller. By Henry W. Nevinson.

"This is a well-written little volume, which presents the leading facts of the poet's life in a neatly rounded picture."—*Scotsman.*

"Mr. Nevinson has added much to the charm of his book by his spirited translations, which give excellently both the ring and sense of the original."—*Manchester Guardian.*

Life of Arthur Schopenhauer. By William Wallace.

"The series of Great Writers has hardly had a contribution of more marked and peculiar excellence than the book which the Whyte Professor of Moral Philosophy at Oxford has written for it on the attractive and still (in England) little-known subject of Schopenhauer."—*Manchester Guardian.*

Life of Scott. By Professor Yonge.

"For readers and lovers of the poems and novels of Sir Walter Scott this is a most enjoyable book."—*Aberdeen Free Press.*

Life of Shelley. By William Sharp.

"The criticisms . . . entitle this capital monograph to be ranked with the best biographies of Shelley."—*Westminster Review.*

New York: CHARLES SCRIBNER'S SONS.

Life of Sheridan. By Lloyd Sanders.

"To say that Mr. Lloyd Sanders, in this volume, has produced the best existing memoir of Sheridan is really to award much fainter praise than the book deserves."—*Manchester Guardian*.

"Rapid and workmanlike in style, the author has evidently a good practical knowledge of the stage of Sheridan's day."—*Saturday Review*.

Life of Adam Smith. By R. B. Haldane, M.P.

"Written with a perspicuity seldom exemplified when dealing with economic science."—*Scotsman*.

"Mr. Haldane's handling of his subject impresses us as that of a man who well understands his theme, and who knows how to elucidate it."—*Scottish Leader*.

"A beginner in political economy might easily do worse than take Mr. Haldane's book as his first text-book."—*Graphic*.

Life of Smollett. By David Hannay.

"A capital record of a writer who still remains one of the great masters of the English novel."—*Saturday Review*.

"Mr. Hannay is excellently equipped for writing the life of Smollett. As a specialist on the history of the eighteenth century navy, he is at a great advantage in handling works so full of the sea and sailors as Smollett's three principal novels. Moreover, he has a complete acquaintance with the Spanish romancers, from whom Smollett drew so much of his inspiration. His criticism is generally acute and discriminating; and his narrative is well arranged, compact, and accurate."—*St. James's Gazette*.

Life of Thackeray. By Herman Merivale and Frank T. Marzials.

"The book, with its excellent bibliography, is one which neither the student nor the general reader can well afford to miss."—*Pall Mall Gazette*.

"The last book published by Messrs. Merivale and Marzials is full of very real and true things."—Mrs. ANNE THACKERAY RITCHIE on "Thackeray and his Biographers," in *Illustrated London News*

Life of Thoreau. By H. S. Salt.

"Mr. Salt's volume ought to do much towards widening the knowledge and appreciation in England of one of the most original men ever produced by the United States."—*Illustrated London News*.

Life of Voltaire. By Francis Espinasse.

"Up to date, accurate, impartial, and bright without any trace of affectation."—*Academy*.

Life of Whittier. By W. J. Linton.

"Mr. Linton is a sympathetic and yet judicious critic of Whittier."—*World*.

Complete Bibliography to each volume, by J. P. ANDERSON, British Museum, London.

New York: CHARLES SCRIBNER'S SONS.

"*An excellent series.*"—TELEGRAPH.

"*Excellently translated, beautifully bound, and elegantly printed.*"—LIVERPOOL MERCURY.

"*Notable for the high standard of taste and excellent judgment that characterise their editing, as well as for the brilliancy of the literature that they contain.*"—BOSTON GAZETTE, U.S.A.

Library of Humour.

Cloth Elegant, Large 12mo, Price $1.25 per vol.

VOLUMES ALREADY ISSUED.

The Humour of France. Translated, with an Introduction and Notes, by ELIZABETH LEE. With numerous Illustrations by PAUL FRÉNZENY.

The Humour of Germany. Translated, with an Introduction and Notes, by HANS MÜLLER-CASENOV. With numerous Illustrations by C. E. BROCK.

The Humour of Italy. Translated, with an Introduction and Notes, by A. WERNER. With 50 Illustrations and a Frontispiece by ARTURO FIELDI.

The Humour of America. Selected, with a copious Biographical Index of American Humorists, by JAMES BARR.

The Humour of Holland. Translated, with an Introduction and Notes, by A. WERNER. With numerous Illustrations by DUDLEY HARDY.

The Humour of Ireland. Selected by D. J. O'DONOGHUE. With numerous Illustrations by OLIVER PAQUE.

The Humour of Spain. Translated, with an Introduction and Notes, by SUSETTE M. TAYLOR. With numerous Illustrations by H. R. MILLAR.

The Humour of Russia. Translated, with Notes, by E. L. BOOLE, and an Introduction by STEPNIAK. With 50 Illustrations by PAUL FRÉNZENY.

New York: CHARLES SCRIBNER'S SONS.

In One Volume. Crown 8vo, Cloth, Richly Gilt. Price $1.25.

Musicians' Wit, Humour, and Anecdote:

BEING

ON DITS OF COMPOSERS, SINGERS, AND INSTRUMENTALISTS OF ALL TIMES.
By FREDERICK J. CROWEST,

Author of "The Great Tone Poets," "The Story of British Music"; Editor of "The Master Musicians" Series, etc., etc.

Profusely Illustrated with Quaint Drawings by J. P. DONNE.

WHAT ENGLISH REVIEWERS SAY:—

"It is one of those delightful medleys of anecdote of all times, seasons, and persons, in every page of which there is a new specimen of humour, strange adventure, and quaint saying."—T. P. O'CONNOR in *T. P.'s Weekly*.

"A remarkable collection of good stories which must have taken years of perseverance to get together."—*Morning Leader*.

"A book which should prove acceptable to two large sections of the public—those who are interested in musicians and those who have an adequate sense of the comic."—*Globe*.

THE USEFUL RED SERIES.

Red Cloth, Pocket Size, Price 50 Cents.

NEW IDEAS ON BRIDGE. By ARCHIBALD DUNN, JUN.

INDIGESTION: Its Prevention and Cure. By F. HERBERT ALDERSON, M.B.

ON CHOOSING A PIANO. By ALGERNON ROSE.

CONSUMPTION: Its Nature, Causes, Prevention, and Cure. By Dr. SICARD DE PLAUZOLES.

BUSINESS SUCCESS. By G. G. MILLAR.

PETROLEUM. By SYDNEY H. NORTH.

✶ INFANT FEEDING. By a PHYSICIAN.

THE LUNGS IN HEALTH AND DISEASE. By DR. PAUL NIEMEYER.

HOW TO PRESERVE THE TEETH. By a DENTAL SURGEON.

MOTHER AND CHILD. By L. M. MARRIOTT.

New York: CHARLES SCRIBNER'S SONS.

The Music Story Series.

A SERIES OF LITERARY-MUSICAL MONOGRAPHS.

Edited by FREDERICK J. CROWEST,

Author of "The Great Tone Poets," "Musicians' Wit and Humour," etc.

Illustrated with Photogravure and Collotype Portraits, Half-tone and Line Pictures, Facsimiles, etc.

Square Crown 8vo, Cloth, $1.25 net.

VOLUMES NOW READY.

THE STORY OF ORATORIO. By ANNIE W. PATTERSON, B.A., Mus. Doc.

THE STORY OF NOTATION. By C. F. ABDY WILLIAMS, M.A., Mus. Bac.

THE STORY OF THE ORGAN. By C. F. ABDY WILLIAMS, M.A.

THE STORY OF CHAMBER MUSIC. By N. KILBURN, Mus. Bac. (Cantab.).

THE STORY OF THE VIOLIN. By PAUL STOEVING, Professor of the Violin, Guildhall School of Music, London.

THE STORY OF THE HARP. By WILLIAM H. GRATTAN FLOOD, Mus. Doc.

THE STORY OF ORGAN MUSIC. By C. F. ABDY WILLIAMS, M.A., Mus. Bac.

THE STORY OF ENGLISH MUSIC (1604-1904): being the Worshipful Company of Musicians' Lectures.

THE STORY OF MINSTRELSY. By EDMONDSTOUNE DUNCAN.

THE STORY OF MUSICAL FORM. By CLARENCE LUCAS.

THE STORY OF OPERA. By E. MARKHAM LEE, Mus. Doc.

LATEST ADDITIONS.

THE STORY OF THE CAROL. By EDMONDSTOUNE DUNCAN.

THE STORY OF THE BAGPIPE. By WILLIAM H. GRATTAN FLOOD, Mus. Doc.

New York: CHARLES SCRIBNER'S SONS.

The Makers of British Art.

A Series of Illustrated Monographs

Edited by

James A. Manson.

Illustrated with Photogravure Portraits; Half-tone and Line Reproductions of the Best Pictures.

Square Crown 8vo, Cloth, $1.25 net.

LANDSEER, SIR EDWIN. By the EDITOR.
"This little volume may rank as the most complete account of Landseer that the world is likely to possess."—*Times*.

REYNOLDS, SIR JOSHUA. By ELSA D'ESTERRE-KEELING.
"An admirable little volume . . . Miss Keeling writes very justly and sympathetically."—*Daily Telegraph*.
"Useful as a handy work of reference."—*Athenæum*.

TURNER, J. W. M. By ROBERT CHIGNELL, Author of "The Life and Paintings of Vicat Cole, R.A."
"This book is thoroughly competent, and at the same time it is in the best sense popular in style and treatment."—*Literary World*.

ROMNEY, GEORGE. By Sir HERBERT MAXWELL, BART., F.R.S.
"Sir Herbert Maxwell's brightly written and accurate monograph will not disappoint even exacting students, while its charming reproductions are certain to render it an attractive gift-book."—*Standard*.
"It is a pleasure to read such a biography as this, so well considered, and written with such insight and literary skill."—*Daily News*.

WILKIE, SIR DAVID. By Professor BAYNE.
CONSTABLE, JOHN. By the EARL OF PLYMOUTH.
RAEBURN, SIR HENRY. By EDWARD PINNINGTON.
GAINSBOROUGH, THOMAS. By A. E. FLETCHER.
HOGARTH, WILLIAM. By Prof. G. BALDWIN BROWN.
MOORE, HENRY. By FRANK J. MACLEAN.
LEIGHTON, LORD. By EDGCUMBE STALEY.
MORLAND, GEORGE. By D. H. WILSON, M.A., LL.M.
WILSON, RICHARD. By BEAUMONT FLETCHER.
✽ **MILLAIS,** SIR JOHN EVERETT. By J. EADIE REID.

New York: CHARLES SCRIBNER'S SONS.

The Contemporary Science Series.

Edited by Havelock Ellis.

12mo.   Cloth.   Price $1.50 per Volume.

I. THE EVOLUTION OF SEX. By Prof. PATRICK GEDDES and J. A. THOMSON. With 90 Illustrations. Second Edition.

"The authors have brought to the task—as indeed their names guarantee—a wealth of knowledge, a lucid and attractive method of treatment, and a rich vein of picturesque language."—*Nature.*

II. ELECTRICITY IN MODERN LIFE. By G. W. DE TUNZELMANN. With 88 Illustrations.

"A clearly written and connected sketch of what is known about electricity and magnetism, the more prominent modern applications, and the principles on which they are based."—*Saturday Review.*

III. THE ORIGIN OF THE ARYANS. By Dr. ISAAC TAYLOR. Illustrated. Second Edition.

"Canon Taylor is probably the most encyclopædic all-round scholar now living. His new volume on the *Origin of the Aryans* is a first-rate example of the excellent account to which he can turn his exceptionally wide and varied information. . . . Masterly and exhaustive."—*Pall Mall Gazette.*

IV. PHYSIOGNOMY AND EXPRESSION. By P. MANTEGAZZA. Illustrated.

"Brings this highly interesting subject even with the latest researches. . . . Professor Mantegazza is a writer full of life and spirit, and the natural attractiveness of his subject is not destroyed by his scientific handling of it."—*Literary World* (Boston).

V. EVOLUTION AND DISEASE. By J. B. SUTTON, F.R.C.S. With 135 Illustrations.

"The book is as interesting as a novel, without sacrifice of accuracy or system, and is calculated to give an appreciation of the fundamentals of pathology to the lay reader, while forming a useful collection of illustrations of disease for medical reference."—*Journal of Mental Science.*

VI. THE VILLAGE COMMUNITY. By G. L. GOMME. Illustrated.

"His book will probably remain for some time the best work of reference for facts bearing on those traces of the village community which have not been effaced by conquest, encroachment, and the heavy hand of Roman law."—*Scottish Leader.*

VII. THE CRIMINAL. By HAVELOCK ELLIS. Illustrated. Fourth Edition, Revised and Enlarged.

"The sociologist, the philosopher, the philanthropist, the novelist—all, indeed, for whom the study of human nature has any attraction—will find Mr. Ellis full of interest and suggestiveness."—*Academy.*

✱ TO-DAY'S ADDITIONS:—
THE CRIMINAL. By HAVELOCK ELLIS. Fourth Edition, Revised and Enlarged.
THE JEWS: A Study of Race and Environment. By Dr. MAURICE FISHBERG.

New York: CHARLES SCRIBNER'S SONS.

VIII. SANITY AND INSANITY. By Dr. CHARLES MERCIER. Illustrated.

"Taken as a whole, it is the brightest book on the physical side of mental science published in our time."—*Pall Mall Gazette.*

IX. HYPNOTISM. By Dr. ALBERT MOLL. New and Enlarged Edition.

"Marks a step of some importance in the study of some difficult physiological and psychological problems which have not yet received much attention in the scientific world of England."—*Nature.*

X. MANUAL TRAINING. By Dr. C. M. WOODWARD, Director of the Manual Training School, St. Louis. Illustrated.

"There is no greater authority on the subject than Professor Woodward."—*Manchester Guardian.*

XI. THE SCIENCE OF FAIRY TALES. By E. SIDNEY HARTLAND.

"Mr. Hartland's book will win the sympathy of all earnest students, both by the knowledge it displays, and by a thorough love and appreciation of his subject, which is evident throughout."—*Spectator.*

XII. PRIMITIVE FOLK. By ELIE RECLUS.

"An attractive and useful introduction to the study of some aspects of ethnography."—*Nature.*

XIII. THE EVOLUTION OF MARRIAGE. By Professor LETOURNEAU.

"Among the distinguished French students of sociology, Professor Letourneau has long stood in the first rank. He approaches the great study of man free from bias and shy of generalisations. To collect, scrutinise, and appraise facts is his chief business. In the volume before us he shows these qualities in an admirable degree."—*Science.*

XIV. BACTERIA AND THEIR PRODUCTS. By Dr. G. SIMS WOODHEAD. Illustrated. Second Edition.

"An excellent summary of the present state of knowledge of the subject."—*Lancet.*

XV. EDUCATION AND HEREDITY. By J. M. GUYAU.

"It is at once a treatise on sociology, ethics, and pedagogics. It is doubtful whether, among all the ardent evolutionists who have had their say on the moral and the educational question, any one has carried forward the new doctrine so boldly to its extreme logical consequence."—Professor SULLY in *Mind.*

XVI. THE MAN OF GENIUS. By Prof. LOMBROSO. Illustrated.

"By far the most comprehensive and fascinating collection of facts and generalisations concerning genius which has yet been brought together."—*Journal of Mental Science.*

New York : CHARLES SCRIBNER'S SONS.

XVII. THE HISTORY OF THE EUROPEAN FAUNA.
By R. F. SCHARFF, B.Sc., Ph.D., F.Z.S. Illustrated.

XVIII. PROPERTY: ITS ORIGIN AND DEVELOPMENT.
By CH. LETOURNEAU, General Secretary to the Anthropological Society, Paris, and Professor in the School of Anthropology, Paris.

"M. Letourneau has read a great deal, and he seems to us to have selected and interpreted his facts with considerable judgment and learning."—*Westminster Review*.

XIX. VOLCANOES, PAST AND PRESENT. By Prof. EDWARD HULL, LL.D., F.R.S.

"A very readable account of the phenomena of volcanoes and earthquakes."—*Nature*.

XX. PUBLIC HEALTH. By Dr. J. F. J. SYKES. With numerous Illustrations.

"Not by any means a mere compilation or a dry record of details and statistics, but it takes up essential points in evolution, environment, prophylaxis, and sanitation bearing upon the preservation of public health."—*Lancet*.

XXI. MODERN METEOROLOGY. AN ACCOUNT OF THE GROWTH AND PRESENT CONDITION OF SOME BRANCHES OF METEOROLOGICAL SCIENCE. By FRANK WALDO, Ph.D., Member of the German and Austrian Meteorological Societies, etc.; late Junior Professor, Signal Service, U.S.A. With 112 Illustrations.

"The present volume is the best on the subject for general use that we have seen."—*Daily Telegraph* (London).

XXII. THE GERM-PLASM: A THEORY OF HEREDITY.
By AUGUST WEISMANN, Professor in the University of Freiburg-in-Breisgau. With 24 Illustrations. $2.50.

"There has been no work published since Darwin's own books which has so thoroughly handled the matter treated by him, or has done so much to place in order and clearness the immense complexity of the factors of heredity, or, lastly, has brought to light so many new facts and considerations bearing on the subject."—*British Medical Journal*.

XXIII. INDUSTRIES OF ANIMALS. By E. F. HOUSSAY. With numerous Illustrations.

"His accuracy is undoubted, yet his facts out-marvel all romance. These facts are here made use of as materials wherewith to form the mighty fabric of evolution."—*Manchester Guardian*.

New York: CHARLES SCRIBNER'S SONS.

XXIV. MAN AND WOMAN. By HAVELOCK ELLIS. Illustrated. Fourth and Revised Edition.

"Mr. Havelock Ellis belongs, in some measure, to the continental school of anthropologists; but while equally methodical in the collection of facts, he is far more cautious in the invention of theories, and he has the further distinction of being not only able to think, but able to write. His book is a sane and impartial consideration, from a psychological and anthropological point of view, of a subject which is certainly of primary interest."—*Athenæum*.

XXV. THE EVOLUTION OF MODERN CAPITALISM. By JOHN A. HOBSON, M.A. (New and Revised Edition.)

"Every page affords evidence of wide and minute study, a weighing of facts as conscientious as it is acute, a keen sense of the importance of certain points as to which economists of all schools have hitherto been confused and careless, and an impartiality generally so great as to give no indication of his [Mr. Hobson's] personal sympathies."—*Pall Mall Gazette*.

XXVI. APPARITIONS AND THOUGHT - TRANSFERENCE. By FRANK PODMORE, M.A.

"A very sober and interesting little book. . . . That thought-transference is a real thing, though not perhaps a very common thing, he certainly shows."—*Spectator*.

XXVII. AN INTRODUCTION TO COMPARATIVE PSYCHOLOGY. By Professor C. LLOYD MORGAN. With Diagrams.

"A strong and complete exposition of Psychology, as it takes shape in a mind previously informed with biological science. . . . Well written, extremely entertaining, and intrinsically valuable."—*Saturday Review*.

XXVIII. THE ORIGINS OF INVENTION: A STUDY OF INDUSTRY AMONG PRIMITIVE PEOPLES. By OTIS T. MASON, Curator of the Department of Ethnology in the United States National Museum.

"A valuable history of the development of the inventive faculty."—*Nature*.

XXIX. THE GROWTH OF THE BRAIN: A STUDY OF THE NERVOUS SYSTEM IN RELATION TO EDUCATION. By HENRY HERBERT DONALDSON, Professor of Neurology in the University of Chicago.

"We can say with confidence that Professor Donaldson has executed his work with much care, judgment, and discrimination."—*The Lancet*.

XXX. EVOLUTION IN ART: AS ILLUSTRATED BY THE LIFE-HISTORIES OF DESIGNS. By Professor ALFRED C. HADDON. With 130 Illustrations.

"It is impossible to speak too highly of this most unassuming and invaluable book."—*Journal of Anthropological Institute*.

New York: CHARLES SCRIBNER'S SONS.

XXXI. **THE PSYCHOLOGY OF THE EMOTIONS.** By TH. RIBOT, Professor at the College of France, Editor of the *Revue Philosophique*.

"Professor Ribot's treatment is careful, modern, and adequate."—*Academy*.

XXXII. **HALLUCINATIONS AND ILLUSIONS:** A STUDY OF THE FALLACIES OF PERCEPTION. By EDMUND PARISH.

"This remarkable little volume."—*Daily News*.

XXXIII. **THE NEW PSYCHOLOGY.** By E. W. SCRIPTURE, Ph.D. (Leipzig). With 124 Illustrations.

XXXIV. **SLEEP:** ITS PHYSIOLOGY, PATHOLOGY, HYGIENE, AND PSYCHOLOGY. BY MARIE DE MANACEÏNE (St. Petersburg). Illustrated.

XXXV. **THE NATURAL HISTORY OF DIGESTION.** By A. LOCKHART GILLESPIE, M.D., F.R.C.P. ED., F.R.S. ED. With a large number of Illustrations and Diagrams.

"Dr. Gillespie's work is one that has been greatly needed. No comprehensive collation of this kind exists in recent English Literature."—*American Journal of the Medical Sciences*.

XXXVI. **DEGENERACY:** ITS CAUSES, SIGNS, AND RESULTS. By Professor EUGENE S. TALBOT, M.D., Chicago. With Illustrations.

"The author is bold, original, and suggestive, and his work is a contribution of real and indeed great value, more so on the whole than anything that has yet appeared in this country."—*American Journal of Psychology*.

XXXVII. **THE RACES OF MAN:** A SKETCH OF ETHNOGRAPHY AND ANTHROPOLOGY. By J. DENIKER. With 178 Illustrations.

"Dr. Deniker has achieved a success which is well-nigh phenomenal."—*British Medical Journal*.

XXXVIII. **THE PSYCHOLOGY OF RELIGION.** AN EMPIRICAL STUDY OF THE GROWTH OF RELIGIOUS CONSCIOUSNESS. By EDWIN DILLER STARBUCK Ph.D., Assistant Professor of Education, Leland Stanford Junior University.

"No one interested in the study of religious life and experience can afford to neglect this volume."—*Morning Herald*.

XXXIX. **THE CHILD:** A STUDY IN THE EVOLUTION OF MAN. By Dr. ALEXANDER FRANCIS CHAMBERLAIN, M.A., Ph.D., Lecturer on Anthropology in Clark University, Worcester (Mass.). With Illustrations.

"The work contains much curious information, and should be studied by those who have to do with children."—*Sheffield Daily Telegraph*.

New York: CHARLES SCRIBNER'S SONS.

XL. THE MEDITERRANEAN RACE. By Professor SERGI. With over 100 Illustrations.

"M. Sergi has given us a lucid and complete exposition of his views on a subject of supreme interest."—*Irish Times*.

XLI. THE STUDY OF RELIGION. By MORRIS JASTROW, Jun., Ph.D., Professor in the University of Pennsylvania.

"This work presents a careful survey of the subject, and forms an admirable introduction to any particular branch of it."—*Methodist Times*.

XLII. HISTORY OF GEOLOGY AND PALÆONTOLOGY TO THE END OF THE NINETEENTH CENTURY. By KARL VON ZITTEL.

"It is a very masterly treatise, written with a wide grasp of recent discoveries."—*Publishers' Circular*.

XLIII. THE MAKING OF CITIZENS: A STUDY IN COMPARATIVE EDUCATION. By R. E. HUGHES, M.A. (Oxon.), B.Sc. (Lond.).

"Mr. Hughes gives a lucid account of the exact position of Education in England, Germany, France, and the United States. The statistics present a clear and attractive picture of the manner in which one of the greatest questions now at issue is being solved both at home and abroad."—*Standard*.

XLIV. MORALS: A TREATISE ON THE PSYCHO-SOCIOLOGICAL BASES OF ETHICS. By PROFESSOR G. L. DUPRAT. Translated by W. J. GREENSTREET, M.A., F.R.A.S.

"The present work is representative of the modern departure in the treatment of the theory of morals. The author brings a wide knowledge to bear on his subject."—*Education*.

XLV. A STUDY OF RECENT EARTHQUAKES. By CHARLES DAVISON, D.SC., F.G.S. With Illustrations.

"Dr. Davison has done his work well."—*Westminster Gazette*.

XLVI. MODERN ORGANIC CHEMISTRY. By DR. C. A. KEANE, D.SC., PH.D., F.I.C. With Diagrams.

"This volume provides an instructive and suggestive survey of the great range of knowledge covered by modern organic chemistry."—*Scotsman*.

TO-DAY'S ADDITIONS:—

THE CRIMINAL. By HAVELOCK ELLIS. Fourth Edition, Revised and Enlarged.

XLVII. THE JEWS: A STUDY OF RACE AND ENVIRONMENT. By Dr. MAURICE FISHBERG.

"It shows abounding evidence in its pages that it is intended to show, immense industry, consummate pains, vast literary and statistical resources. It contains, to be sure, much information of great value, and it sets forth many facts absorbing in their interest for any who desire to study the Jewish people."—*Jewish Chronicle*.

New York: CHARLES SCRIBNER'S SONS.

IBSEN'S DRAMAS.

Edited by WILLIAM ARCHER.

THREE PLAYS TO THE VOLUME.

12mo, CLOTH, PRICE $1.25 PER VOLUME.

"We seem at last to be shown men and women as they are; and at first it is more than we can endure. . . . All Ibsen's characters speak and act as if they were hypnotised, and under their creator's imperious demand to reveal themselves. There never was such a mirror held up to nature before: it is too terrible. . . . Yet we must return to Ibsen, with his remorseless surgery, his remorseless electric-light, until we, too, have grown strong and learned to face the naked—if necessary, the flayed and bleeding—reality."—SPEAKER (London).

※ THIS IS THE BEST AND CHEAPEST EDITION OF IBSEN, THERE BEING 3 PLAYS TO EACH VOLUME.

VOL. I. "A DOLL'S HOUSE," "THE LEAGUE OF YOUTH," and "THE PILLARS OF SOCIETY." With Portrait of the Author, and Biographical Introduction by WILLIAM ARCHER.

VOL. II. "GHOSTS," "AN ENEMY OF THE PEOPLE," and "THE WILD DUCK." With an Introductory Note.

VOL. III. "LADY INGER OF ÖSTRÅT," "THE VIKINGS AT HELGELAND," "THE PRETENDERS." With an Introductory Note.

VOL. IV. "EMPEROR AND GALILEAN." With an Introductory Note by WILLIAM ARCHER.

VOL. V. "ROSMERSHOLM," "THE LADY FROM THE SEA," "HEDDA GABLER." Translated by WILLIAM ARCHER. With an Introductory Note.

VOL. VI. "PEER GYNT: A DRAMATIC POEM." Authorised Translation by WILLIAM and CHARLES ARCHER.

The sequence of the plays *in each volume* is chronological; the complete set of volumes comprising the dramas thus presents them in chronological order.

"The art of prose translation does not perhaps enjoy a very high literary status in England, but we have no hesitation in numbering the present version of Ibsen, so far as it has gone (Vols. I. and II.), among the very best achievements, in that kind, of our generation."—*Academy*.

"We have seldom, if ever, met with a translation so absolutely idiomatic."—*Glasgow Herald*.

New York: CHARLES SCRIBNER'S SONS.

Rev p 41 x Lafargue "Property"